Project Management with AI

for
dummies®
A Wiley Brand

T0357609

Project Management with AI

By Daniel Stanton, MBA, PMP
Author of *Supply Chain Management For Dummies*

A Wiley Brand

Project Management with AI For Dummies®

Published by: **John Wiley & Sons, Inc.**, 111 River Street, Hoboken, NJ 07030-5774, www.wiley.com

For general information on our other products and services, please contact our Customer Care Department within the U.S. at 877-762-2974, outside the U.S. at 317-572-3993, or fax 317-572-4002. For technical support, please visit https://hub.wiley.com/community/support/dummies.

Wiley publishes in a variety of print and electronic formats and by print-on-demand. Some material included with standard print versions of this book may not be included in e-books or in print-on-demand. If this book refers to media that is not included in the version you purchased, you may download this material at http://booksupport.wiley.com. For more information about Wiley products, visit www.wiley.com.

Library of Congress Control Number: 2025934277

ISBN 978-1-394-32084-4 (pbk); ISBN 978-1-394-32086-8 (ebk); ISBN 978-1-394-32085-1 (ebk)

SKY10100407_031725

Contents at a Glance

Table of Contents

Introduction

In today's fast-paced, data-driven world, project managers face ever-increasing challenges to deliver successful projects on time and within budget. Fortunately, artificial intelligence (AI) is transforming how people manage projects, providing new tools and insights to improve decision-making, optimize resources, and automate repetitive tasks. *Project Management with AI For Dummies* is your guide to harnessing the power of AI to become a more efficient, effective, and data-driven project manager. Whether you're new to AI or a seasoned user looking to incorporate the latest technologies, this book equips you with practical knowledge and actionable tips to stay ahead in the evolving world of project management.

About This Book

Why do you need *Project Management with AI For Dummies*? While many books and resources touch on project management *or* AI, few combine both into a comprehensive guide that's easy to follow and full of practical advice. This book demystifies AI and shows you exactly how to apply it to everyday project management tasks — from planning and scheduling to risk management and performance reporting. You'll find step-by-step guidance on selecting the right AI tools, automating workflows, and enhancing collaboration within your team.

I organized this book to help you access information easily. Each chapter is designed so you can jump right in, whether you want to start at the beginning or skip to specific topics that interest you the most. The clear explanations, tips, and real-world examples will help you immediately put AI to use in your projects.

Foolish Assumptions

I've made a few assumptions about you, the reader:

>> You're familiar with basic project management principles, whether you are a project manager by trade or manage projects as part of your role.

>> You've heard about AI but may be unsure of how it applies to project management.

>> You're looking for practical ways to integrate AI into your project management workflows, regardless of your level of technical expertise.

>> You may be working with agile, waterfall, or hybrid methodologies, and you're curious about how AI can support them.

Whether you're a beginner exploring AI for the first time or an experienced manager wanting to sharpen your AI skills, this book has something for everyone.

Icons Used in This Book

The Tip icon marks tips (duh!) and shortcuts that you can use to make project management with AI easier.

Remember icons mark the information that's especially important to know. To siphon off the most important information in each chapter, just skim through these icons.

The Technical Stuff icon marks information of a highly technical nature that you can normally skip over.

The Warning icon tells you to watch out! It marks important information that may save you headaches.

Beyond the Book

For more information, resources, and tools related to *Project Management with AI For Dummies*, check out the online Cheat Sheet. It provides synopses of tasks you can do with AI and tools appropriate for those jobs. Whether you need a fast refresher on AI concepts or best practices for integrating AI into your projects, this Cheat Sheet offers practical guidance to keep you on track. Visit www.dummies.com and search for **Project Management with AI For Dummies** to access this valuable information.

Where to Go from Here

I designed this book so you can jump in wherever it makes the most sense for you. If you're completely new to AI, start with Part 1, where you'll get a clear understanding of the basics of AI and its impact on project management. If you're already familiar with AI but want to learn about specific tools or workflows, feel free to skip to Part 2 or Part 3. If you're focused on AI ethics and security, then you can flip to Part 4. For quick tips or best practices, check out Part 5 at the end of the book.

No matter where you start, you'll come away with practical tools, insights, and strategies to make AI an essential part of your project management toolkit.

1

Getting Started with AI and Project Management

Understand what artificial intelligence (AI) is and how it differs from traditional automation.

Examine the evolution of project management, from manual processes to AI-powered decision-making.

Uncover key concepts of AI like machine learning (ML), natural language processing (NLP), and large language models (LLMs).

Find out how AI enhances project management methodologies such as agile, waterfall, and hybrid.

Understand the measurable benefits AI brings to project management, including time savings, cost reduction, and better risk management.

Chapter **1**

What Is AI?

A rtificial intelligence, or AI, is transforming nearly every industry, including project management. From streamlining workflows to predicting outcomes, AI has the potential to make project managers more effective and efficient. But before I dive into how AI can benefit your projects, I want to help you understand what AI is, the key concepts that underpin it, and how it differs from automation. In this chapter, I break down the basics of AI, introduce you to the core concepts, and clarify the distinction between AI and automation.

Setting Your Expectations for This Book

I designed this book to guide you through the process of understanding and implementing AI in your work, from the basics to more advanced applications. Part 1 lays the foundation by explaining why AI is important in project management and how it's transforming the field:

» Chapter 1 explores the overall importance of AI in modern project management.

» Chapter 2 covers AI's impact on project efficiency and decision-making.

>> Chapter 3 provides an overview of how using AI in project management provides measurable benefits like time savings, cost reduction, and risk mitigation, which can be tracked through key performance indicators (KPIs) and baseline metrics.

Part 2 focuses on the practical steps of adopting AI tools and technologies:

>> Chapter 4 offers guidance on what to look for in AI software and helps you choose the right AI tools for your specific projects.

>> Chapter 5 delves into how AI can automate tasks and workflows to streamline processes to save time.

>> Chapter 6 emphasizes the role of AI in making data-driven decisions, enabling project managers to leverage insights from vast datasets.

>> Chapter 7 explains how AI tools can enhance team collaboration, ensuring smoother communication and coordination across projects.

Part 3 dives into practical applications of AI in everyday project management:

>> Chapter 8 shows how AI can improve project planning and scheduling by offering predictive insights and dynamic adjustments to timelines.

>> Chapter 9 explains how to predict and manage project risks using AI and foresee potential challenges.

>> Chapter 10 focuses on how AI can optimize budgeting and cost control, ensuring that projects remain financially viable.

>> Chapter 11 covers how AI improves tracking project performance and automating reporting processes for better transparency and oversight.

Part 4 addresses critical ethical, security, and change management considerations:

>> Chapter 12 explores the ethical use of AI in project management, helping you navigate fairness, transparency, and accountability when using AI tools.

>> Chapter 13 focuses on protecting data and ensuring security in AI-powered projects, offering strategies for keeping sensitive information safe.

>> Chapter 14 helps you manage AI adoption within your organization, outlining strategies for overcoming resistance to change and guiding your team through the transition.

Finally, Part 5 offers practical advice and tips for project managers:

- **»** Chapter 15 provides ten tips for getting started with AI, offering a roadmap for integrating AI tools into your workflow.

- **»** Chapter 16 highlights common mistakes to avoid when using AI in projects, ensuring you can steer clear of potential pitfalls.

- **»** Chapter 17 rounds out the book by introducing ten essential AI tools every project manager should know, giving you the resources to fully leverage AI's capabilities.

Whether you're new to AI or looking to refine your AI strategies, this book covers everything you need to know for successfully integrating AI into project management.

Understanding AI: The Basics

AI is fundamentally about simulating human intelligence within machines, enabling them to perform tasks that typically require human cognitive functions. These functions may include understanding language, recognizing patterns, making decisions, and solving complex problems.

AI is not a single entity but rather an umbrella term for a broad range of technologies and techniques that enable machines to learn from data and improve their performance over time. The idea behind AI is to allow machines to execute tasks that require judgment, insight, or creativity — things that were once thought to be exclusive to human abilities.

AI's relevance spans across various industries. In project management, AI offers ways to streamline operations, make data-driven decisions, and even anticipate challenges. While the concept of AI often conjures up images of highly autonomous systems that mimic human thinking, the reality is more nuanced. AI applications in project management typically involve specialized systems that optimize specific processes. Understanding these nuances helps you recognize where AI can be most effective in improving project outcomes.

The two major types of AI that are commonly discussed are narrow AI (also known as weak AI) and general AI (strong AI). Narrow AI refers to systems that are designed for specific tasks and can outperform humans in that domain. For example, speech recognition, image classification, and recommendation algorithms are typical examples of narrow AI. These systems are highly focused and excel in their designated tasks but lack the versatility of human intelligence. In contrast, general AI is the theoretical concept where machines could, in the long term, replicate human-like intelligence across a broad array of tasks. General AI is still a concept rooted more in science fiction than in practical reality.

In the realm of project management, narrow AI tools are most relevant. These tools help optimize specific aspects of projects, such as automating routine tasks, analyzing historical data to predict outcomes, or managing resources more efficiently. The true power of narrow AI in this context lies in its ability to process vast amounts of information quickly and provide actionable insights. This enables project managers to make informed decisions, enhance productivity, and mitigate risks effectively.

TIP

Recognize the distinction between narrow and general AI. When selecting AI tools for your projects, focus on those that specialize in optimizing specific areas of your workflow rather than trying to find a one-size-fits-all solution.

Defining Key AI Concepts

To effectively harness the power of AI in project management, it's crucial to grasp some of the key concepts that form the foundation of AI. These core ideas include machine learning, natural language processing, large language models, and robotics. (See Figure 1-1.) Each of these technologies serves a distinct purpose and contributes to different aspects of project management, from automating routine tasks to generating insights that guide decision-making. Understanding these concepts will enable you to better assess how you can integrate AI into your workflow to drive efficiencies and improve overall project outcomes. In this section, I explain these key AI concepts and explore their applications in project management.

Machine learning

Machine learning (ML) is a core subset of AI that enables computers to learn from and make decisions based on data. Unlike traditional programming, where specific instructions are given to perform tasks, ML allows systems to learn from examples and improve over time. This is achieved by training algorithms on large datasets, which helps the model recognize patterns and relationships within the data. The more data an ML model is exposed to, the more consistent it becomes in its predictions or classifications.

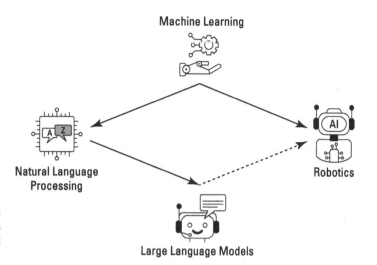

Machine Learning

Natural Language
Processing

Robotics

Large Language Models

FIGURE 1-1:
Relationships
between different
approaches to AI.

However, ML can't judge whether data is right or wrong. It simply detects what occurs more or less frequently in the data it's given. So, if the training data is biased, incomplete, or inaccurate, the ML model will learn and reinforce those errors, leading to flawed predictions or classifications. This concept is often summarized as "garbage in, garbage out" (GIGO); if the input data is flawed, the output will be as well. While ML models can improve with more data, their accuracy depends entirely on the quality, diversity, and reliability of the data they are trained on.

In the context of project management, machine learning can significantly enhance processes such as task scheduling, resource allocation, and risk management. By analyzing historical project data, ML can identify trends, predict delays, and recommend optimized resource allocation strategies. It can also forecast the success of different project timelines and help predict where bottlenecks are likely to occur. As a project manager, leveraging ML tools can help you make data-driven decisions that reduce uncertainty and increase project efficiency. Chapter 6 gives more details on how ML can be used to analyze data and enhance project decisions.

TIP

When implementing ML in your project, ensure you have access to clean, high-quality data. The quality of the data directly affects the accuracy of the model's predictions.

Natural language processing

Natural language processing (NLP) is a specialized area of AI that focuses on enabling machines to understand, interpret, and generate human language. NLP bridges the gap between human communication and computer understanding, allowing for smoother interaction between AI systems and users. This technology powers tools such as chatbots, language translation services, and speech recognition systems. It's also what enables you to have a conversation with certain AI tools that's very like a conversation you would have with another human. NLP enables AI to analyze text or speech, extract meaningful insights, and respond in a way that mimics human conversation.

In project management, you can use NLP to automate repetitive tasks like report generation, document analysis, or summarizations of meeting notes. Additionally, NLP-driven chatbots can assist teams by answering common questions, managing communication between departments, and even scheduling tasks. You can also use NLP tools to analyze team feedback, customer reviews, or stakeholder communications, which helps you gain deeper insights into project progress and areas that need attention.

TIP

Use NLP tools to automate routine communication tasks, such as responding to frequently asked questions or generating weekly project summaries, to save time and improve productivity.

Large language models

Large language models (LLMs) are a type of machine learning model that is particularly advanced in understanding and generating human language. Trained on vast amounts of text data, LLMs like OpenAI's GPT or Google's BERT are designed to process and generate highly coherent and contextually relevant text. These models use complex deep learning architectures, such as transformers, to analyze the context of words in a sentence and generate responses that sound highly human-like.

For project managers, LLMs can be particularly useful in automating complex communication tasks. For example, LLMs can draft detailed project reports, generate meeting notes, or even provide real-time answers to project team members' inquiries. By incorporating LLMs into project workflows, you can save significant time on administrative tasks.

TIP

Use large language models for tasks that require content generation, such as drafting project updates or summarizing large documents. Be sure to review the outputs for accuracy because LLMs can sometimes generate incorrect or irrelevant information.

Generative AI

Generative AI is a subset of ML that focuses on creating new content rather than just analyzing or classifying existing data. It relies on deep learning algorithms, which are a type of artificial neural network designed to recognize complex patterns in large datasets. These algorithms consist of multiple layers of interconnected nodes (neurons) that process and transform data through weighted connections, allowing the model to learn and generate realistic outputs. LLMs, such as GPT-4, are built using deep learning techniques and trained on vast amounts of text data to predict and generate coherent, contextually relevant content. This process is a key aspect of NLP, which enables AI to understand and generate human-like text.

Unlike traditional AI, which primarily classifies or analyzes structured data, generative AI actively produces original content by identifying and replicating patterns from unstructured data, such as text, images, or code. This ability makes it a powerful tool for applications such as automated content creation, brainstorming, and problem-solving, particularly in fields like project management where efficient communication and documentation are essential.

In project management, generative AI can be particularly useful for enhancing communication, automating documentation, and improving decision-making. For example, if a project manager needs to prepare a risk assessment report, a generative AI tool can analyze previous project risks, industry trends, and real-time data to generate a detailed, structured report with potential risks, mitigation strategies, and action plans. Additionally, generative AI can help draft project proposals, create stakeholder updates, and even generate task summaries from meeting notes, saving valuable time. By automating these repetitive yet critical tasks, project managers can focus more on strategy, collaboration, and problem-solving, making projects run more efficiently and reducing administrative burden.

Robotics

Robotics is another significant area of AI that deals with the creation of machines that can perform tasks autonomously or semiautonomously, often replicating or enhancing human physical abilities. Robotics integrates AI to allow machines to make decisions and perform complex tasks with minimal human intervention. These tasks can range from simple repetitive actions, such as picking and placing items in manufacturing, to more complex tasks like navigating environments or interacting with humans in service settings.

In industries such as manufacturing, logistics, or supply chain management, robotics plays a vital role in automating labor-intensive tasks, reducing errors, and improving efficiency. For project managers working in these industries, understanding robotics is crucial for overseeing projects that involve physical automation. Robotics may also have a role in projects related to construction, where robots are increasingly used to carry out tasks that are dangerous or difficult for human workers.

TIP

When working with robotics in project management, ensure that you thoroughly evaluate the integration of AI-driven robotics with existing systems to avoid disruptions and maintain smooth project operations.

Agentic AI

Agentic AI refers to artificial intelligence systems that can operate autonomously, make decisions, and take actions to achieve specific goals with minimal human intervention. The term *agentic* comes from the concept of agency, which refers to the ability of an entity to act independently and make choices. Unlike traditional AI models that passively generate responses or insights based on inputs, agentic AI actively engages with its environment, monitors changes, and adapts its behavior accordingly. These systems are designed to plan, reason, and execute tasks, often incorporating reinforcement learning, goal-directed reasoning, and real-time decision-making to improve their effectiveness over time. Because they can assess situations, weigh alternatives, and take initiative in achieving set objectives, they function more like intelligent agents rather than simple tools.

A defining characteristic of agentic AI is its ability to interact with external systems, coordinate multistep tasks, and optimize workflows autonomously. For example, in project management, an agentic AI could automatically adjust schedules, allocate resources, and send progress reports based on real-time data, reducing the need for manual oversight. In supply chain operations, such AI might predict disruptions, reroute shipments, and negotiate with suppliers without requiring human intervention. While this level of autonomy increases efficiency, it also raises questions about control, accountability, and ethical considerations because these systems must be designed to align with human objectives and prevent unintended consequences. The more autonomous and goal-driven AI becomes, the more critical it is to establish guidelines and safeguards that ensure it remains beneficial, transparent, and aligned with human values.

Mastering the Art of Prompt Engineering

Now that you're familiar with the key AI concepts, it's time to explore a critical aspect of working with AI: prompt engineering. A prompt is the input or instruction given to an AI system, typically in the form of a question or command, that directs the AI to generate a response. Not all AI systems interpret prompts the same way, and the quality of the AI's output largely depends on how the prompt is crafted. Prompt engineering — the process of designing precise and effective prompts to guide AI — is particularly valuable for NLP models and LLMs. This section explains how to use prompt engineering to maximize the value of these AI tools.

Understanding where prompt engineering fits

Prompt engineering is particularly important for AI systems that process human language, such as NLP models and LLMs, because they respond dynamically based on the prompt's content. This makes prompt engineering critical for tasks like summarizing reports, generating project plans, or brainstorming solutions.

TIP

Be specific. The clearer your prompt, the better the AI's response. Include details and context to guide the AI.

There are numerous schools of thought on how to write the best AI prompts. Here are some key points to keep in mind:

» Provide relevant context, a persona, or other key background information. Identify who you are in relation to the task. For example, "I am a project manager working on a large-scale real estate project" gives the AI tool helpful details, which will lead to better outputs.

» Give clear and concise instructions. Be specific about the task you want the AI to perform and provide. Rather than saying, "Help with project management," say, "List three ways AI can automate task assignments in a software project." This reduces ambiguity and directs the AI to deliver focused, relevant answers.

» Focus on what you want the AI tool to do rather than what you *don't* want it to do. This approach, known as positive instruction, offers a clear goal and direction, allowing the tool to generate more relevant and accurate responses. So, instead of saying, "Don't make the agenda too detailed," say, "Design an agenda with five discussion topics and one action item per topic." The latter prompt is more specific, helps the AI tool understand your intent better, and reduces the likelihood of unintended or negative outcomes.

» Consider specifying the audience you're speaking to. Are you writing for a cross-functional team, other project managers, executives, or someone else? Understanding who your audience is enables the AI tool to properly adjust the tone and level of detail included in the output.

» Describe the format you want in the output. You might be looking for a short email, a bulleted list, or a comprehensive project timeline. Specifying the structure tells the AI tool how to format the output for your needs.

>> Break down complex prompts into small, manageable chunks. This can help the AI tool better understand your intent and generate more accurate and relevant responses. For example, if you want to generate a comprehensive project plan for a new software development project, you could start by providing a brief overview of the project goals and scope. Then, you'd break down the project into smaller phases or milestones, such as requirements gathering, design, development, testing, and deployment. Providing a structured breakdown guides the AI tool's thought process and helps ensure that it generates a more complete and accurate project plan.

Refining prompts for NLP and LLMs

Don't be afraid to make mistakes with AI. Doing so is part of the learning process. Just like when you were learning to ride a bike, you probably fell a few times before you got the hang of it. Prompt engineering is nearly always iterative. After receiving an initial response, you will likely need to refine the prompt by adding context or rephrasing it. Through trial and error, you'll learn how to fine-tune your prompts to get more useful outputs. Over time, this skill will improve your ability to work with NLP-based AI systems effectively.

REMEMBER

For complex tasks, break your prompt into smaller questions to get more focused answers.

REMEMBER

In project management, prompt engineering enhances the use of AI for tasks such as drafting reports, summarizing meetings, or analyzing risks. For example, asking, "Summarize the key action items from the last project meeting" is more effective than a vague request for a summary. Similarly, prompts like "Generate a progress report that highlights task completion rates and identifies any project risks" can help streamline routine tasks.

Knowing the Difference between AI and Automation

AI and automation are often used interchangeably, but they are distinct concepts that serve different purposes in project management. While both technologies can enhance efficiency and reduce manual effort, their capabilities and applications vary significantly. Automation is designed to perform repetitive tasks following predefined rules, streamlining processes that do not require complex decision-making. In contrast, AI involves machines learning from data, adapting to new information, and making informed decisions based on patterns and insights. Understanding the difference between AI and automation is crucial for leveraging their strengths effectively and determining which tool is best suited for different tasks within project management.

Understanding automation in project management

Automation refers to the use of software or machines to execute predefined tasks without human intervention. In project management, automation typically involves systems that follow a set of rules to complete repetitive, predictable activities efficiently. These can be as simple as sending email reminders or as complex as automatically tracking time and expenses across multiple team members.

Automation excels in processes that require speed, consistency, and precision. For example, a project management tool might automatically generate weekly status reports based on task completion data, reducing the time spent on manual data entry. By automating routine administrative work, project managers can focus on more strategic decision-making and problem-solving.

However, the key limitation of automation is that it cannot adapt to changes or new information unless specifically programmed to do so. It follows strict guidelines and cannot handle unstructured problems or make decisions based on analysis beyond its preset capabilities. This is where AI surpasses traditional automation.

TIP

Start by automating repetitive tasks in your project management processes, such as scheduling meetings or generating status reports, to free up time for higher-level work.

Defining artificial intelligence in project management

Artificial intelligence involves machines that not only execute tasks but also learn and adapt based on data. AI systems are capable of analyzing information, identifying patterns, and making decisions without human intervention. AI can process vast amounts of data to recognize trends, optimize processes, and even predict outcomes, providing much more dynamic and flexible solutions than automation alone.

For project managers, AI has the potential to go beyond automating tasks. It can analyze historical project data to predict future risks, recommend the best course of action for resource allocation, or provide insights into how project timelines can be optimized. While automation handles repetitive tasks, AI helps in making smarter decisions by learning from past data and adjusting its actions accordingly.

AI's ability to handle complexity means it's ideal for managing unpredictable elements of projects, such as adjusting timelines when a project falls behind or recommending alternative vendors if supply chain disruptions occur.

TIP

Use AI to improve decision-making in your project management processes, such as predicting potential delays or risks based on historical data and real-time inputs.

Key differences between AI and automation

The main difference between AI and automation lies in the complexity of the tasks they handle and the level of decision-making involved. Automation operates on predefined rules and can execute tasks only as programmed. It is most effective for routine, repetitive activities that require speed and accuracy but do not involve decision-making or learning.

In contrast, AI mimics human intelligence, allowing it to learn from data and adjust its responses over time. AI can identify patterns, predict outcomes, and recommend actions, making it suitable for more complex tasks. For instance, AI can analyze the efficiency of a project team, recognize underperforming areas, and recommend improvements, whereas automation can only send reminders or track time spent on tasks.

AI's adaptability means it's ideal for managing uncertainty in projects. Automation, while useful, requires continuous updates to handle new scenarios. AI, on the other hand, can adjust its actions based on changing conditions without needing to be reprogrammed.

Both AI and automation have their places in project management, so knowing when to use each is key to optimizing project workflows. Automation is best suited for activities that require high efficiency and accuracy without the need for human judgment. For example, automating reminders for team members to submit status updates is simple, and effective AI should be implemented for tasks where data analysis and predictive insights are critical. For instance, if a project manager needs to predict resource constraints or identify the likelihood of meeting a deadline based on current progress, AI can provide valuable recommendations. AI is particularly useful in scenarios where the project environment is dynamic and quick, data-driven decisions need to be made.

Ultimately, a combination of both AI and automation will provide the most benefits. Automation can handle repetitive tasks efficiently, while AI can manage the more complex, decision-oriented aspects of project management, leading to better performance overall.

TIP

Use automation for repetitive tasks and AI for tasks that involve analyzing data, learning from patterns, and making decisions based on complex information. Figure 1-2 shows tasks automation and AI have in common and where they differ. Check out Chapter 5 for more on using AI to automate specific project management tasks.

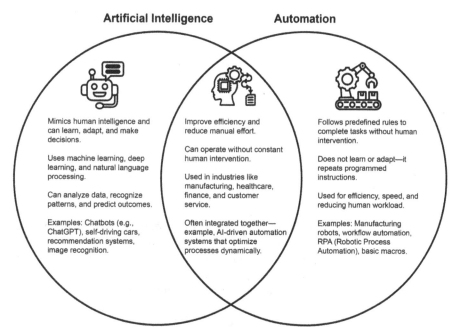

FIGURE 1-2:
A Venn diagram of AI and automation.

TIP

Implement automation to handle routine tasks first, and then explore AI tools to enhance your decision-making process, especially in areas like risk management and forecasting.

Managing the information value chain

To understand why generative AI is such a game changer, let's look at the information value chain, which is shown in Figure 1-3. It begins with data — simple facts like a phone number. By organizing data, we create information — for example, linking a name to a number. This information helps us make decisions and act.

When we further organize information — filtering and finding patterns — it becomes knowledge. Finally, by applying judgment and intuition, knowledge turns into wisdom.

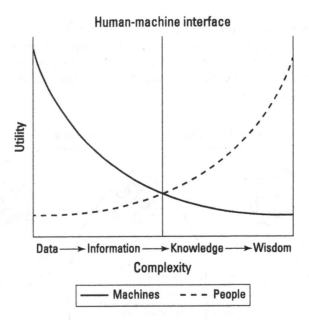

Computers excel at processing data quickly, but as we move up the value chain to tasks involving judgment, people outperform machines. For example, project management tasks like scheduling or tracking resources are ideal for automation because computers handle these better than humans. However, when it comes to decision-making, human judgment is essential.

The balance between people and machines is shifting with AI's growth. As AI improves, it takes on more advanced tasks, moving the human-machine interface further along the chain. This shift is driving digital transformation — where more tasks can be automated, leaving humans to focus on high-level decisions. To stay competitive, project managers need to strategically adopt these technologies and decide what to automate.

EMMA'S JOURNEY INTO PROJECT MANAGEMENT WITH AI

Emma is a project manager at a mid-sized marketing firm, known for her ability to juggle multiple projects while keeping her team on track. Recently, she started hearing more about the role of AI in project management. Colleagues mentioned AI-powered tools that could automate workflows, help with data analysis, and improve risk management. Curious, but unsure where to begin, Emma decided to explore how AI could benefit her work.

Her first challenge was simply understanding what AI actually is. She'd heard terms like machine learning and automation but didn't fully grasp the differences. Emma started by searching for articles and videos on the basics of AI, but quickly found herself overwhelmed by technical jargon. She realized she needed a structured approach to learning, starting with the fundamentals.

That's when she came across a comprehensive guide to AI in project management. This book laid out exactly what she needed, starting with an introduction to what AI is and how it's different from simple automation. Emma learned that AI goes beyond automating routine tasks. It can draft documents, predict risks, allocate resources, and provide data-driven insights that would allow her to make better decisions.

With a clearer understanding, Emma moved on to learning about the specific tools available. The book provided a roadmap for choosing the right AI tools for her projects. Emma started with AI-powered task automation tools, which helped her streamline repetitive tasks like sending reminders and generating reports. She then dived into AI tools for data analysis, which transformed how she planned her project timelines and resource allocation.

As Emma continued to apply AI, she faced resistance from some team members who worried AI might replace their jobs. However, using strategies she learned from the book, she addressed their concerns by explaining that AI would enhance their work rather than replace it. Emma also involved her team in testing new AI tools, helping them feel more engaged with the changes.

Within months, Emma was not only comfortable using AI but had transformed how her team approached projects. They were more efficient, made more informed decisions, and handled risks better. Emma's journey into AI started with confusion, but by seeking out the right resources and taking a step-by-step approach, she mastered AI's potential and led her team into a new era of project management.

IN THIS CHAPTER

» **Automating routine tasks**

» **Enhancing decision-making**

» **Improving monitoring and reporting**

» **Reducing risks**

» **Adapting AI tools across agile, waterfall, and hybrid methodologies**

Chapter **2**

Exploring the Evolution of Project Management with AI

rtificial intelligence (AI) has begun to reshape how people approach project management, offering new tools and capabilities that can enhance the way projects are planned, executed, and monitored. The use of AI marks a significant departure from manual, reactive methods. By automating routine tasks, offering real-time insights, and enhancing decision-making with predictive analytics, AI has begun to revolutionize how project managers approach their work, making projects more efficient, predictable, and successful.

As AI continues to evolve, project managers must understand its potential and how to integrate it into their methodologies. This chapter explores how AI is changing the project management landscape, the role of AI in different project management methodologies, and real-world examples of AI-driven success in project management.

Understanding the Evolution of Project Management before AI

Project management has long been a cornerstone of organizational success, driving projects to completion through effective planning, coordination, and resource management. Before the advent of AI, project management heavily relied on manual processes, human intuition, and static tools that, while functional, were often limited in scope. As industries evolved and projects became more complex, project managers had to juggle an increasing number of variables without the benefit of advanced automation or predictive analytics. To understand the transformative impact AI has on project management today, it's crucial to first examine how traditional project management functioned in the pre-AI era.

Before AI, collecting and reporting of project data were labor-intensive processes. Project managers manually compiled data from various sources, such as spreadsheets, time-tracking tools, and team reports. This often led to a lag in information flow, making it difficult for project managers to get real-time insights into project progress. Reports were typically generated weekly or monthly, meaning that any issues or delays often only came to light long after they had begun affecting the project. Moreover, human error in data entry or report generation was a common problem, further complicating decision-making.

TIP

Keeping detailed and consistent records of project data, including timelines, budgets, and resource usage, can help you identify patterns and improve forecasting.

Project managers typically used historical project data to forecast timelines and resource needs, but these predictions were far from precise. In the absence of real-time data, project managers had to rely heavily on their experience and gut instincts to identify risks, adjust timelines, and allocate resources. Although skilled project managers could make educated guesses about potential risks and how to mitigate them to successfully guide projects to completion, the reliance on manual reporting made it challenging to anticipate problems and react quickly to changing project dynamics. Delays in identifying bottlenecks or resource constraints were common, leading to cost overruns and missed deadlines. In general, risk management was reactive rather than proactive.

TIP

Focusing on early identification of risks and maintaining contingency plans are essential for minimizing the impact of unforeseen issues.

Although there were project management software tools before AI, the tools primarily functioned as repositories for project plans and task lists rather than dynamic systems that could adjust in real time. Gantt charts, task tracking systems, and resource allocation tools offered some degree of automation, but they required frequent manual updates. If a project team missed a deadline, project managers had to manually adjust timelines, reallocate resources, and communicate changes to stakeholders.

The limited flexibility of these tools made it difficult to manage complex or fast-moving projects. For instance, changes to project scope or unexpected resource shortages could disrupt an entire project plan, and it would take significant manual effort to update the project management tools to reflect the new reality. This was particularly challenging for projects with many interdependent tasks, where a delay in one area could cascade through the rest of the project, causing widespread disruption.

In the pre-AI landscape, human resource management was a critical yet time-consuming aspect of project management. Project managers had to coordinate team schedules, assign tasks based on availability and expertise, and monitor team workloads to ensure that no one was overwhelmed. This process was often done manually, with project managers relying on personal communication, emails, and meetings to track team progress and resolve conflicts. In larger teams or cross-functional projects, this coordination became increasingly complex, making it difficult for project managers to have a clear picture of who was working on what and how resources were being utilized.

Resource allocation was another area where the absence of AI made project management more difficult. Without tools that could dynamically adjust resource allocation based on project needs, project managers often struggled to balance workloads and ensure that resources were being used efficiently. This often led to underutilized resources in some areas and overburdened team members in others, affecting both productivity and team morale.

Before the widespread adoption of AI, communication and collaboration in project management were primarily done through email, phone calls, and in-person meetings. While effective, these methods often created silos of information and made it challenging to keep all stakeholders aligned in real time. For distributed teams or projects that spanned multiple time zones, keeping everyone informed and on the same page was a significant challenge. Delays in communication often led to confusion, misalignment on priorities, and duplication of efforts, which slowed progress and increased the likelihood of mistakes.

TIP

Frequent check-ins and clear communication channels are critical for avoiding misalignment and ensuring that all team members stay on track with project goals.

Tools like instant messaging and cloud-based project management software helped alleviate some of these challenges, but they were far from the real-time, AI-driven collaboration tools available today. Teams often had to wait for scheduled meetings to resolve issues or make decisions, which hindered project delivery.

Examining How AI Is Changing the Project Management Landscape

The integration of AI into project management is transforming how teams manage their projects. While project management has always been about handling processes, people, and resources effectively, AI offers a new level of support. It enables project managers to streamline workflows, reduce human error, and provide a data-driven approach to decision-making.

TIP

One of the most significant changes AI brings is the automation of routine tasks that previously consumed much of a project manager's time. Now, tasks such as scheduling, updating project plans, and generating reports can be automated, freeing up project managers to focus on more strategic decisions and responsibilities. This shift in focus allows for greater efficiency in managing the project life cycle, and project managers can dedicate their attention to problem-solving and stakeholder management.

AI's strength for enhancing decision-making lies in its ability to analyze massive datasets quickly and extract meaningful insights. By analyzing historical project data and real-time project metrics, AI helps project managers predict potential bottlenecks, allocate resources more efficiently, and identify risks before they become significant issues. This data-driven decision-making enables project managers to anticipate challenges and proactively address them, significantly reducing the likelihood of project failure. For example, predictive analytics powered by AI can help forecast project timelines, budget needs, and potential risks based on historical data, resulting in better planning and execution. It's like having a crystal ball for your project, but without the tarot cards and mystical mumbo-jumbo.

AI also enhances real-time monitoring and reporting of project progress. Traditionally, project managers relied on periodic updates to track milestones and assess overall project health. With AI, project teams can receive real-time insights into project status, allowing for immediate adjustments. AI-powered tools can automatically generate reports, track key performance indicators (KPIs), and monitor progress without human intervention, ensuring that stakeholders always have access to the latest information. This transparency reduces the chances of surprises or project delays because any discrepancies or issues can be addressed as they arise rather than after they have escalated.

Risk management, a critical aspect of project management, is also significantly improved with AI. AI uses past project data and real-time project variables to identify potential risks early in the project life cycle. These risks could range from budget overruns and resource shortages to delays in key milestones. AI's predictive capabilities allow project managers to develop contingency plans and implement preventive measures to mitigate risks before they affect the project's success. In this way, AI not only helps identify risks but also suggests solutions.

Understanding AI's Role in Industry 4.0

To understand AI's impact on project management, it helps to look at the evolution of industry itself. The first industrial revolution introduced mechanization through water and steam power, transforming manual labor into machine-assisted production. The second industrial revolution built on this with the introduction of electricity, enabling mass production and assembly lines. The third industrial revolution, also known as the digital revolution, brought electronics, computers, and automation to manufacturing processes, further enhancing productivity and efficiency.

Then came Industry 4.0, also known as the fourth industrial revolution. This revolution is defined by the integration of advanced digital technologies — like AI, the internet of things (IoT), big data, robotics, and cyber-physical systems — into industrial and manufacturing processes. The key to Industry 4.0 is the connection between physical systems (machines, equipment, and production lines) and the digital world, allowing for smart, self-regulating systems that optimize performance, reduce downtime, and improve efficiency. AI plays a central role in Industry 4.0, driving intelligent automation and predictive analytics. AI-powered systems analyze vast amounts of data collected from connected machines, identify patterns, and optimize operations without human intervention.

For example, AI enables predictive maintenance, where machines detect early warning signs of failures and notify operators before they break down. This minimizes downtime and improves operational efficiency. AI also enhances supply chain management, resource allocation, and production quality, helping industries make data-driven decisions in ways that weren't possible before.

While many organizations are still adopting Industry 4.0 technologies, some experts believe we're already entering Industry 5.0 — a shift that focuses on collaboration between humans and intelligent machines. Unlike Industry 4.0, which emphasizes automation and efficiency, Industry 5.0 prioritizes human-centric innovation, sustainability, and resilience. Instead of replacing workers with

AI-driven automation, Industry 5.0 aims to enhance human capabilities by integrating AI, robotics, and smart technologies in ways that support creativity, personalization, and ethical decision-making.

For example, in an Industry 5.0 environment, AI doesn't just automate production lines; it works alongside human workers, assisting with complex problem-solving, enhancing decision-making, and adapting to unique customer needs. In manufacturing, this could mean AI-powered robots collaborating with skilled workers to customize products in real time. In project management, AI might automate repetitive tasks while providing project managers with real-time insights and predictive recommendations, but the final decisions remain in human hands.

For project managers, AI's role is critical in both Industry 4.0 and Industry 5.0. As industries become smarter and more connected, AI helps manage the increasing complexity of modern projects by

>> Automating data-heavy tasks like scheduling, resource allocation, and risk analysis

>> Providing intelligent insights to optimize decision-making

>> Predicting risks and suggesting mitigation strategies before they escalate

Projects that incorporate Industry 4.0 and 5.0 technologies, such as smart factories, AI-driven production lines, or human-machine collaboration, require a more dynamic approach to planning, execution, and oversight. By embracing AI, project managers can stay ahead of industry trends, enhance collaboration between humans and machines, and lead successful projects that drive the next wave of digital and human-centered transformation in their organizations.

Incorporating AI with Agile, Waterfall, and Hybrid Methodologies

Project management methodologies provide structured approaches to organizing and executing projects, and each offers unique strategies to manage time, resources, and risks. Agile, waterfall, and hybrid methodologies are three of the most used frameworks. (See Figure 2-1.)

>> Agile is characterized by its flexibility, iterative development, and focus on continuous feedback, making it ideal for fast-paced environments that require adaptability.

>> Waterfall follows a linear and structured approach, progressing through predefined phases in sequence. This method is more suited for projects with well-defined requirements.

>> Hybrid methodologies combine elements of both agile and waterfall, offering the flexibility of agile with the structured phases of waterfall.

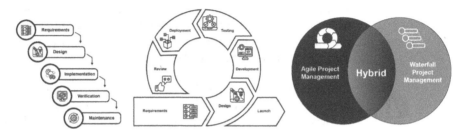

FIGURE 2-1: Waterfall, agile, and hybrid project management frameworks.

Waterfall
- Iterative and incremental
- Flexible and adaptive
- Customer collaboration
- Frequent releases
- Best for dynamic projects

Agile
- Waterfall project management
- Linear and sequential
- Fixed requirements
- Heavy documentation
- Limited flexibility
- Best for stable projects

Hybrid
- Combination of waterfall and agile
- Tailored to project needs
- Balanced approach
- Phased execution with iterative development
- Best for complex or large-scale projects

Each methodology presents its own challenges, but AI's versatility makes it a valuable tool in enhancing efficiency, decision-making, and risk management across all three approaches.

The role of AI in agile methodology

Agile project management emphasizes flexibility, adaptability, and continuous feedback, making it a natural fit for AI-powered tools. In an agile environment, teams work in iterative cycles or sprints, constantly adjusting their priorities based on new insights and customer feedback. AI can enhance agile practices by automating many of the routine tasks that come with each sprint. For example, AI can assist with sprint planning by analyzing historical data on team performance, helping project managers allocate tasks more efficiently and avoid burnout. AI-powered tools can suggest optimal workloads for each team member, balancing their tasks to maximize productivity without causing overcommitment.

AI can also play a role in dynamic task prioritization, a core aspect of agile. With real-time data analysis, AI can continuously adjust task priorities based on their impact on project goals or customer feedback. By identifying patterns in past project performance, AI tools can help teams focus on the most critical tasks while deprioritizing or delaying lower-impact tasks. This ensures that teams always focus on delivering the most value to customers, allowing agile methodologies to function more smoothly.

Furthermore, AI can assist in creating user stories and defining acceptance criteria. By analyzing data from previous projects and current customer feedback, AI can suggest user stories and acceptance criteria that align with the project's goals. This reduces the manual effort needed from team members, allowing them to focus on refining these stories rather than drafting them from scratch. AI-generated insights can also ensure that acceptance criteria are consistent across the project, improving the quality of deliverables.

WARNING

It's important to remember that AI models can perpetuate and even amplify existing biases and stereotypes that are present in the data they're trained on, which can lead to prejudiced or biased outcomes in the user stories and acceptance criteria they generate. Therefore, careful human oversight of these AI outputs is essential to ensure fairness, inclusivity, and alignment with ethical guidelines.

Additionally, AI facilitates continuous feedback loops in agile by gathering and analyzing feedback from both customers and team members in real time. It can process data from surveys, user interactions, or internal communications to highlight potential areas for improvement. This feedback loop is critical to agile's iterative nature because it enables teams to make timely adjustments and maintain alignment with customer needs throughout the project life cycle.

TIP

Use AI-driven tools to automate sprint planning and task prioritization in agile projects, helping your team focus on high-value activities and reduce manual work.

The role of AI in waterfall methodology

The waterfall methodology is more rigid and structured than agile, with its linear approach where each phase of the project must be completed before the next phase begins. While AI might seem more suited to flexible methodologies like agile, it can still provide valuable benefits in waterfall project management.

One of the key advantages AI brings to waterfall is its ability to improve predictive analytics during the planning phase. AI can analyze large datasets from previous projects to improve the accuracy of project timelines, budget forecasts, and resource allocations. This results in more reliable project plans, reducing the risk of delays and budget overruns later in the project.

AI can also enhance risk management in waterfall projects. By using predictive analytics, AI can identify potential risks early in the project life cycle. This allows project managers to implement proactive risk mitigation strategies, such as allocating additional resources or adjusting timelines to avoid potential issues. This is particularly important in waterfall methodology, where adjustments can be more difficult to make once a phase is completed.

In terms of collaboration and reporting, AI-powered tools can automate much of the manual work associated with scheduling updates and tracking progress at the end of each project phase. AI can automatically generate detailed reports based on project data, providing stakeholders with insights into progress, challenges, and milestones. This eliminates the need for project managers to manually compile reports, saving time and reducing the risk of errors.

Moreover, AI's ability to process large datasets means it can track and manage resource dependencies more effectively. In waterfall projects, where dependencies between tasks are often tightly linked, AI can predict where bottlenecks might occur and suggest solutions to ensure that resources are utilized optimally. This helps keep the project on track and ensures smooth transitions between phases.

TIP

Implement AI tools in the early planning stages of waterfall projects to enhance forecasting and minimize risks, allowing for smoother project execution.

The role of AI in hybrid methodology

Hybrid methodologies, which blend aspects of both waterfall and agile approaches, offer a structured yet flexible project management framework. AI can play a pivotal role in managing the complexities that arise from using a hybrid methodology. It's like a Swiss Army knife, with AI as the extra blade that makes the hybrid strategy even more versatile.

One of the main challenges of hybrid project management is balancing flexibility with structure, and AI helps by dynamically allocating resources and making real-time adjustments as the project evolves. AI can assess the different needs of agile iterations and waterfall phases, ensuring that resources are appropriately allocated at each stage of the project.

Hybrid methodologies often require frequent adjustments based on real-time feedback. AI's ability to provide data-driven insights ensures that these adjustments are timely and accurate. Whether it's reallocating resources or adjusting timelines, AI can make recommendations based on real-time data, helping project managers adapt quickly to changes in project scope, customer requirements, or team performance.

Workflow management is another area where AI proves benefits in hybrid methodologies. Different phases require different levels of flexibility, and AI can automate workflows to ensure smooth transitions between agile iterations and waterfall phases. For example, AI can automate handoffs between teams working in different methodologies, ensuring that tasks are completed on time and dependencies are managed effectively.

AI also supports better decision-making in hybrid projects by providing predictive insights across both agile and waterfall phases. Whether you're deciding how to allocate resources, managing project timelines, or addressing risks, AI-powered tools offer data-driven recommendations that improve the efficiency and success of hybrid projects. This ensures that teams can adapt to changing circumstances while maintaining the structure necessary for large-scale project goals.

TIP

Check out Chapter 4 to help select tools based on specific project management methodologies.

Managing Change and AI Integration

Introducing AI into project management workflows requires careful change management because it influences not only the tools and processes teams use but also the way they think about their work. Successfully managing change during AI integration means overcoming resistance, ensuring that teams are adequately trained, and communicating the benefits of AI to all stakeholders. This section explores how to manage these challenges and set your organization up for a smooth transition to AI-powered project management.

Overcoming resistance to AI adoption

Resistance to AI adoption is common, particularly among team members who fear that AI might replace their jobs or fundamentally change their work. To overcome this resistance, it's important to involve teams early in the AI adoption process and communicate clearly how AI will enhance — not replace — their roles.

TIP

Following are some recommended areas of focus to ease concerns about AI:

>> **Address fears and misconceptions:** Explain that AI is not meant to replace human workers but to assist them by taking over repetitive tasks, which allows employees to focus on more meaningful, value-added work. Highlight examples of how AI has been used to improve job satisfaction by reducing administrative burdens. You can find more suggestions for addressing these concerns in Chapter 14.

>> **Foster a culture of innovation:** Encourage employees to view AI as a tool for innovation and improvement. Create an environment where experimentation with AI tools is encouraged and demonstrate how AI can unlock new opportunities for creativity and strategic thinking.

>> **Involve team members in decision-making:** Allow them to participate in the selection and implementation of AI tools. This inclusiveness gives them more ownership of the changes and reduce feelings of uncertainty.

By addressing concerns head-on and promoting a culture of innovation, project managers can help ease the transition to AI and foster a more open attitude toward its adoption.

Training teams for AI integration

Successful AI integration depends on the ability of team members to understand and use new AI tools effectively. Training is a critical component of this process and requires more than just a one-time session. Ongoing support and opportunities for continuous learning are essential for maximizing the benefits of AI.

Consider the following factors in preparing training for your team:

>> **Conduct hands-on training sessions:** Provide practical, hands-on training sessions where team members can learn how to use AI tools relevant to their daily tasks. This helps build confidence and reduces any anxiety around using new technology.

>> **Offer tiered learning experiences:** Different team members may require different levels of AI proficiency depending on their roles. Provide introductory courses for those unfamiliar with AI and more advanced training for those who will be managing the tools or interpreting the insights they provide.

>> **Encourage a continuous learning mindset:** AI technology evolves quickly, so it's important to promote a culture of continuous learning. Offer ongoing workshops, online resources, or AI learning paths through platforms like LinkedIn Learning or Coursera to help team members stay up to date on the latest AI developments.

TIP

Investing in proper training ensures that employees feel empowered and capable of integrating AI into their workflows rather than overwhelmed or uncertain.

Communicating the benefits of AI to stakeholders

To gain buy-in from all levels of the organization, project managers must effectively communicate the benefits of AI to stakeholders. Different stakeholders may have different priorities, so it's important to tailor your message to their specific concerns. When it comes to AI, it's all about storytelling: Paint a picture of a future where your projects are more efficient, more profitable, and less stressful.

As you're crafting your message, consider the following things:

>> **Highlight efficiency gains:** For executives or business leaders, emphasize how AI can drive efficiency, cut costs, and improve project outcomes. Provide data-driven examples of how AI has helped similar organizations reduce project delays, improve resource allocation, or optimize budgeting.

>> **Showcase tangible benefits for teams:** When communicating with teams, focus on how AI will make their day-to-day work easier. Share how AI can automate routine tasks like reporting or scheduling, allowing them to focus on more meaningful work.

>> **Demonstrate value to clients:** If clients or external stakeholders are involved, highlight how AI will lead to better project outcomes, such as more accurate timelines, improved risk management, and greater transparency through real-time reporting.

REMEMBER

By aligning AI benefits with each stakeholder's goals and concerns, project managers can help ensure broader support for AI adoption.

Building a long-term strategy for AI integration

Effective AI integration requires a long-term strategy that goes beyond the initial adoption phase. As AI tools evolve, the opportunities for innovation and improvement in project management processes will also evolve. A long-term strategy includes the following tasks:

>> **Create a phased AI adoption plan:** Start small by identifying a few key areas where AI can provide the most immediate value, such as automating scheduling or improving resource allocation. Once AI has proven its benefits in these areas, gradually expand its use to other aspects of project management.

>> **Monitor and iterate:** Continuously assess how well AI is meeting your team's and stakeholders' needs. Collect feedback regularly, analyze performance data, and adjust your AI strategy as needed to ensure it remains aligned with project goals and organizational objectives.

>> **Stay informed about AI trends:** The AI landscape is evolving rapidly. Stay informed about the latest AI tools and trends to ensure that your organization is taking advantage of the most effective technologies. Encourage teams to experiment with new AI tools as they emerge to foster a culture of innovation.

TIP

For more in-depth strategies on managing AI adoption and change, read Chapter 14.

Best Practices for Integrating AI in Project Management

Integrating AI into project management can dramatically enhance efficiency, decision-making, and overall project outcomes. However, to maximize the benefits, project managers need a strategic approach to incorporating AI into their workflows. This section discusses some best practices for starting to leverage AI effectively in your project management processes.

Identifying repetitive tasks for automation

One of the most immediate and practical ways to integrate AI into your projects is by automating repetitive, time-consuming tasks. AI can handle a wide range of administrative activities like those in the following list, enabling project managers to focus on higher-value strategic work.

>> **Automate scheduling:** Use AI tools to automatically assign tasks based on availability, skills, and workload, optimizing your team's efficiency.

» **Streamline reporting:** Leverage AI to generate regular project reports and updates, saving time on manual report preparation.

» **Automate reminders and notifications:** Set AI-powered reminders to keep team members on track with deadlines and deliverables.

Employing data-driven decision-making

AI excels at analyzing large datasets and providing actionable insights. Project managers can use AI to improve decision–making by relying on data rather than assumptions:

» **Analyze historical data:** Use AI tools to review data from past projects and identify trends that could inform future decision-making, such as common causes of delays or resource constraints.

» **Predict outcomes:** Implement AI-driven predictive analytics to forecast project timelines, budget needs, and potential risks, helping to mitigate issues before they arise.

» **Allocate resources effectively:** AI can analyze real-time data and optimize resource allocation, ensuring that team members are working on the most critical tasks at the right times.

TIP

Check out Chapter 6 for more on using predictive analytics and AI-powered insights.

Using AI tools to monitor progress in real time

AI can give you real–time updates on project performance, allowing for quick adjustments to keep everything on track. AI-powered monitoring tools make it easier to stay informed about the status of various aspects of your project, such as the following:

» **Track KPIs automatically:** Use AI to monitor KPIs continuously to ensure you have up-to-date information on project progress and performance.

» **Set up real-time alerts:** Configure AI tools to alert you to any deviations from the project plan, such as missed milestones, budget overruns, or underutilized resources.

>> **Adjust timelines and workloads dynamically:** AI can adjust schedules and reallocate resources automatically based on real-time progress data, ensuring the project stays aligned with deadlines.

Focusing on enhancing collaboration and communication

AI tools can play a significant role in improving team collaboration, especially in distributed or remote environments. Project managers can use AI to streamline communication and ensure everyone stays on the same page. The following are some ways you can use AI for collaboration and communication:

>> **Use AI-powered chatbots:** Deploy chatbots to answer routine project questions or provide updates, enabling team members to get the information they need without waiting for a response from the project manager.

>> **Generate meeting summaries:** AI tools can automatically generate summaries and action items from meetings, ensuring key information is captured and shared with the team.

>> **Facilitate collaboration across time zones:** AI can help manage global teams by automating the coordination of handoffs and ensuring that critical updates are communicated in real time.

Starting small and scaling gradually

AI implementation doesn't need to happen all at once. Starting with a few targeted AI tools and expanding usage over time allows for smoother integration:

>> **Pilot AI in specific areas:** Start by introducing AI in areas with the highest potential for impact, such as task automation or resource allocation.

>> **Monitor AI performance:** Keep an eye on how AI tools are performing and gather feedback from your team. This will help you refine your approach and ensure the AI is meeting project needs.

>> **Scale AI usage:** Once the benefits of AI become evident in one area, begin expanding its use to other aspects of project management, like risk management or budgeting.

Training your team on AI tools and workflows

Introducing AI requires some level of training and adaptation for your team. Ensuring that team members understand how to work with AI in the following ways makes the integration smoother and more effective:

>> **Provide training sessions:** Organize training sessions that cover how to use new AI tools, what data they leverage, and how to interpret AI-driven insights.

>> **Encourage experimentation:** Allow team members to explore AI tools and workflows on their own to identify opportunities for improvement or innovation.

>> **Create an AI knowledge base:** Develop a centralized resource hub that provides ongoing support, troubleshooting guides, and FAQs for working with AI in your project.

Prioritizing data security and ethics

As you integrate AI into your project management processes, it's critical to ensure that data is handled securely and ethically. Following are some ways to do that:

>> **Implement data protection measures:** Use AI tools that include encryption and other security features to protect sensitive project data.

>> **Monitor AI for bias:** Continuously assess AI-driven decisions for any signs of bias, especially in areas like resource allocation or risk assessment.

>> **Comply with regulations:** Ensure that your use of AI complies with industry regulations and data protection laws, particularly when handling customer or employee data.

Regularly reviewing and optimizing AI performance

AI systems improve over time with the right inputs and optimizations. Continuously review the performance of your AI tools to ensure they are providing the most value to your project.

>> **Track AI effectiveness:** Measure the impact of AI on your project outcomes, including reductions in manual work, improved efficiency, and better decision-making.

>> **Iterate based on feedback:** Collect feedback from your team on AI integration and make adjustments to ensure that the tools are fully meeting the project's needs.

>> **Update AI systems:** Regularly update AI tools and algorithms to take advantage of new capabilities, improved analytics, and enhanced security features.

AI-POWERED PROJECT MANAGEMENT AT INNOVATETECH

InnovateTech, a mid-sized tech company specializing in software development, was struggling to keep up with the increasing complexity of its projects. Their project management team often faced delays, unexpected risks, and misallocated resources, leading to missed deadlines and cost overruns. As the company grew, these issues began to hinder their ability to scale efficiently and compete in the market. Determined to solve these problems, InnovateTech's leadership decided to integrate AI into their project management processes.

One of the first areas where InnovateTech implemented AI was in automating routine tasks. The project management team used AI-powered tools to handle scheduling, send reminders, and generate progress reports. Previously, these tasks took hours of manual effort, but AI now accomplished them in seconds. This freed project managers to focus on higher-level strategic decisions and stakeholder management. As a result, InnovateTech saw a 30 percent reduction in time spent on administrative tasks, improving team efficiency and enabling more focus on innovation.

AI's real-time data analysis capabilities transformed InnovateTech's decision-making process. By leveraging machine learning algorithms, the company could analyze historical data and current project conditions to predict risks and resource needs. AI provided actionable insights into which areas of the project were likely to face delays or require additional resources. This led to more data-driven decisions, minimizing guesswork and helping InnovateTech allocate resources more effectively. In one instance, AI predictions helped InnovateTech realize that to avoid a significant project delay, they needed to allocate development resources to a critical task two weeks earlier than planned.

At InnovateTech, projects often combined both agile and waterfall approaches, requiring flexibility while maintaining a structured process. AI tools were able to adapt to both methodologies seamlessly. For their agile teams, AI assisted in sprint planning by predicting optimal workloads for each team member based on previous sprints.

(continued)

(continued)

Meanwhile, for waterfall phases, AI improved the accuracy of resource allocation and timeline forecasts. This hybrid AI approach helped InnovateTech reduce overcommitment in agile teams and increased efficiency in their waterfall projects by improving accuracy in long-term planning.

Risk management was another key area where AI made a difference. InnovateTech used AI to monitor real-time project data and identify risks before they could escalate into critical issues. In one of their large software rollouts, AI detected an emerging risk related to potential budget overrun early in the project life cycle. The system analyzed historical data from past rollouts and flagged spending patterns that matched those associated with budget overruns. With this early warning, the project manager was able to adjust the budget and mitigate the risk before it impacted the project's timeline.

By integrating AI into their project management processes, InnovateTech was able to automate routine tasks, enhance decision-making, improve risk management, and adapt AI to their hybrid methodology. The company saw measurable improvements in project efficiency, risk mitigation, and resource allocation, leading to a higher success rate in their projects. InnovateTech's leadership now considers AI an essential tool for their ongoing growth and innovation, setting a new standard for how they manage projects in an increasingly competitive market.

Looking Ahead: What's Next for AI in Project Management?

As AI continues to evolve, it's poised to have a dramatically expanded role in project management. Emerging technologies such as advanced natural language processing, deep learning, and AI-driven automation will allow AI tools to take on more sophisticated tasks, transforming the way projects are managed. One promising development is the rise of AI-powered virtual project assistants, which can act as support systems for project managers by handling routine tasks, providing real-time insights, and even answering questions from team members. These assistants can anticipate needs, offer suggestions, and keep projects on track, allowing project managers to focus on high-level decision-making and strategy.

In the near future, AI may also take on more independent roles in managing low-risk projects autonomously. As AI becomes more capable of understanding project goals, tracking progress, and adjusting, they could manage entire projects without human intervention, particularly in cases where tasks are well-defined, and data is plentiful. For example, AI might autonomously manage software updates, marketing campaigns, or standard operational projects, continuously optimizing resource allocation, monitoring timelines, and identifying potential risks. This will free up project managers to oversee more complex, strategic initiatives while AI handles the more routine, predictable work.

TIP

Stay informed about emerging AI technologies and continuously evaluate how you can integrate them into your project management practices to enhance efficiency and innovation, while freeing up time for strategic tasks.

Looking further ahead, the integration of AI into project management will likely become more seamless as the technology continues to improve. You could say that the versions of AI that we are working with today are the worst ones we'll ever have to use because AI is getting better so quickly. We can expect AI to move beyond its current capabilities, offering more nuanced decision-making, helping with creative problem-solving, and even anticipating the needs of team members before they arise. This evolution will redefine the role of project managers, allowing them to become even more focused on leadership, innovation, and guiding the organization through complex, high-stakes projects. The future of AI in project management promises to drive efficiency, reduce risks, and enable teams to achieve more with fewer resources.

Real-World Examples of AI in Project Management

The integration of AI into project management is not just theoretical; it's being applied in real-world scenarios across various industries. Companies like IBM, Microsoft, and Google are leveraging AI to optimize workflows, enhance decision-making, and streamline project processes. From construction projects to software development, AI-driven tools are providing project managers with the insights they need to deliver successful outcomes. This section explores how different organizations are using AI in practical applications, offering a glimpse into how AI can transform project management in diverse settings.

IBM Watson for project management

IBM Watson has long been a leader in the AI space, and its application to project management is no exception. IBM Watson's Project Manager tool utilizes AI to analyze project data, predict risks, and offer recommendations for optimizing performance. This tool integrates with existing project management systems, analyzing massive amounts of data from past projects, current progress, and even industry trends. By using predictive analytics, Watson provides project managers with insights that allow them to adjust resources and timelines in real time, ensuring projects stay on track.

For example, IBM Watson can detect patterns that may indicate potential delays or resource bottlenecks before they happen. This allows managers to proactively adjust, either by reallocating resources or adjusting project timelines. Watson's AI capabilities also automate routine tasks such as report generation, allowing project managers to focus on more strategic issues. The real-time feedback loop created by Watson ensures that no issue remains hidden for too long, giving managers the opportunity to mitigate problems early.

TIP

Consider integrating AI tools like IBM Watson early in your project planning phase to benefit from predictive analytics from the start, giving you a clear roadmap and identifying potential risks before they become critical.

Microsoft Project with AI insights

Microsoft Project, a widely used tool in project management, has enhanced its capabilities with AI-driven insights. The AI functionalities in Microsoft Project offer predictive analytics, helping project managers forecast timelines, optimize resource allocation, and spot bottlenecks before they disrupt progress. AI-powered scheduling can automatically adjust timelines and allocate resources based on historical project data and real-time updates, reducing the manual workload for project managers.

In practical use, Microsoft Project's AI insights can analyze past project performance and generate recommendations for future projects. For instance, if historical data shows that similar projects tended to go over budget when certain resource constraints were present, the AI can flag this early on and suggest alternative resource strategies. It also helps managers compare project progress to predetermined milestones, making necessary adjustments to keep things moving smoothly.

TIP

Use AI insights from tools like Microsoft Project not only for ongoing project management but also for post-project analysis. This can help you refine your methodologies for future projects, based on data-driven findings.

Asana's AI-powered workflows

Asana, known for its user-friendly project management platform, has integrated AI to automate workflows and enhance team collaboration. One of its standout features is task prioritization, where the AI can automatically suggest which tasks should take precedence based on deadlines, team capacity, and project milestones. The platform can also predict potential delays by analyzing team workloads and project progress, allowing managers to reallocate resources more effectively.

In addition to task prioritization, Asana uses AI to balance workloads across teams, ensuring that no team member is overburdened while another has available capacity. The AI also generates automated reminders and task updates, ensuring that nothing falls through the cracks. The integration of AI has led many organizations to report increased project delivery speed and better team productivity because AI handles mundane tasks, freeing up human resources for high-value work.

TIP

Take advantage of Asana's AI features to create automated workflows that reduce time spent on task management. This will help ensure your team stays focused on more critical, high-level project goals.

Google's use of AI in project management

Gemini, a large language model from Google, can be a valuable tool for various aspects of project management. While Gemini doesn't directly manage projects in real time like a dedicated project management platform, its capabilities can significantly enhance project workflows and outcomes. For instance, Gemini can analyze project-related documents, such as requirements, specifications, and reports, to identify potential risks, inconsistencies, or areas for improvement. It can also assist in generating project documentation, like meeting minutes, status reports, and even initial drafts of project plans. Gemini's natural language processing capabilities can be leveraged to summarize lengthy email threads or chat logs related to a project, quickly bringing project managers up to speed on key discussions and decisions. Furthermore, Gemini can help with communication by drafting emails to stakeholders, summarizing project updates, or even generating creative content for project presentations. While human oversight remains crucial for effective project management, Gemini can act as a powerful assistant, automating tasks, improving communication, and providing valuable insights to support informed decision-making.

TIP

Incorporate AI-driven transparency tools in your project management process to keep stakeholders updated in real time and prevent communication delays that could derail your project.

Construction industry: AI for risk management

In the construction industry, AI has become an essential tool for risk management, which is critical in large-scale, high-risk projects. AI tools, such as Alice Technologies, use data from past construction projects to predict risks that may occur during current or future projects. This includes identifying potential delays, cost overruns, and safety hazards. AI helps construction companies mitigate these risks early by suggesting alternative actions or resource reallocations.

For example, AI can predict that adverse weather conditions may delay construction by analyzing weather patterns and local conditions. It can then recommend adjusting timelines or sourcing backup materials in anticipation of supply chain issues. Construction managers can use these AI-driven insights to make informed decisions that reduce the likelihood of costly delays or accidents on site.

TIP

In industries like construction, where delays and risks can have huge financial implications, AI-driven risk management tools can be invaluable. Make sure to incorporate these into your planning stages to preemptively address any risks.

Chapter **3**

Measuring the Benefits of Using AI

This chapter focuses on how to effectively measure the benefits of using artificial intelligence (AI) in project management. By providing frameworks and key performance indicators (KPIs), you can assess AI's impact on time savings, cost reduction, risk mitigation, and overall project outcomes. The goal is to ensure that AI integration not only improves project execution but also aligns with broader business objectives, driving value and efficiency across the organization.

Defining Success in AI-Driven Projects

The use of AI in project management has become a game-changer, transforming how tasks are executed, decisions are made, and projects are completed. AI's ability to streamline workflows, analyze vast amounts of data, and improve real-time monitoring has had a significant impact on project success rates.

However, as organizations increasingly integrate AI into their project management processes, it's essential to understand how to measure the tangible benefits AI brings. Without clear metrics, it's challenging to evaluate whether AI truly delivers value or is simply a trendy addition to the toolbox. This section examines how to choose KPIs, pinpoint areas where artificial intelligence can deliver the most value, and ensure alignment between AI-driven outcomes and overarching business objectives.

Setting clear objectives and KPIs

One of the first steps to measuring the success of AI in project management is setting clear objectives and KPIs. Defining what you aim to achieve with AI ensures that its use is purposeful and aligned with your project goals. Are you looking to improve team productivity, speed project delivery, or reduce errors in decision-making? Without well-defined objectives, it's impossible to measure success accurately.

KPIs allow you to track progress in real time and evaluate whether AI is contributing to the desired outcomes. For example, KPIs for AI-driven projects might include the reduction in time spent on manual tasks, improvements in project timelines, cost savings through automation, or higher resource efficiency. By establishing these metrics early on, you can ensure that AI tools are being used effectively and are delivering measurable value.

TIP

Establish both quantitative KPIs (for example, project completion time, cost reduction) and qualitative KPIs (things like improved team collaboration, better stakeholder engagement) to fully assess AI's impact.

Identifying key areas where AI adds value

AI's benefits in project management typically fall into a few key areas: time savings, cost reduction, risk mitigation, and enhanced decision-making. Identifying these areas early helps focus efforts and ensures that AI is being leveraged where it has the most impact.

For instance, AI-driven tools excel at automating repetitive tasks such as scheduling, reporting, and resource management. By automating these processes, AI can save significant amounts of time, freeing you to focus on strategic activities like stakeholder communication and problem-solving. AI also enables more accurate cost forecasting by analyzing historical data and predicting resource needs, which can reduce the likelihood of budget overruns. Check out Chapter 8 to see how AI can help you manage project timelines and improve planning accuracy.

Risk mitigation is another area where AI shines. By analyzing data from past projects and current performance metrics, AI can predict potential risks and suggest mitigation strategies before those risks become critical. These capabilities allow you to proactively manage issues that may have otherwise gone unnoticed until too late. Check out Chapter 9 for a detailed explanation of how AI can help you identify and mitigate project risks.

To maximize AI's value, focus on areas that offer the highest return, such as reducing manual effort or improving accuracy in forecasting and risk management.

Aligning AI outcomes with overall business goals

For AI to truly be successful in project management, its benefits must align with broader organizational goals. While AI might improve specific project metrics, such as speed or cost savings, the real value comes when these improvements support larger business objectives, such as increasing market competitiveness, enhancing customer satisfaction, or driving innovation.

To align AI outcomes with business goals, you should ensure that the KPIs they track not only measure project-specific outcomes but also connect to strategic business objectives. For example, if a company's goal is to improve customer satisfaction, you can use AI to optimize timelines and ensure faster delivery of products or services, which ultimately benefits the customer.

Regularly review project KPIs in the context of overall business goals to ensure AI-driven improvements contribute to long-term organizational success.

INNOVATEX'S AI-DRIVEN TRANSFORMATION IN PROJECT MANAGEMENT

InnovateX, a mid-sized software development firm, was struggling with project inefficiencies, rising costs, and slow decision-making. As the company scaled, their manual processes, such as scheduling, reporting, and resource allocation, became increasingly time-consuming and prone to error. Recognizing these bottlenecks, InnovateX's leadership decided to integrate AI into their project management processes to improve efficiency and reduce costs.

(continued)

(continued)

Before implementing AI, project managers at InnovateX spent significant time manually scheduling tasks, updating project timelines, and generating reports. These tasks slowed down overall project execution, often resulting in delays. After adopting AI-driven project management tools, such as automated scheduling and reporting software, InnovateX saw an improvement in workflow speed. AI tools streamlined task assignment, tracked progress in real time, and provided instant project updates, enabling managers to focus on high-priority activities like problem-solving and stakeholder engagement.

In addition to improving efficiency, InnovateX saw tangible cost savings by using AI to optimize resource allocation. Before AI adoption, the company often overallocated resources to certain tasks, leading to unnecessary expenses. With AI's predictive analytics, InnovateX gained real-time insights into resource utilization, allowing them to allocate staff and tools more accurately. By avoiding overstaffing and preventing resource shortages, InnovateX reduced project overhead, freeing up budget for other strategic initiatives.

The biggest game-changer for InnovateX was how AI enhanced decision-making. The AI tools analyzed historical project data, identified patterns, and predicted potential risks, allowing managers to make informed decisions. For example, when launching a new software development project, AI detected potential bottlenecks in resource availability two months before they could impact delivery. Armed with this data, InnovateX proactively adjusted timelines and shifted resources, ensuring the project stayed on track. The company also used AI-generated insights to improve project planning accuracy, reducing timeline deviations.

By leveraging AI-driven automation, InnovateX significantly improved its project efficiency, reduced overhead costs, and made more informed, data-driven decisions. The AI integration transformed how the company managed projects, allowing them to scale operations without sacrificing quality or increasing costs.

Considering Quantitative Metrics for Measuring AI Benefits

Measuring the benefits of AI in project management requires a clear understanding of how AI-driven changes affect time efficiency, cost savings, and team productivity. By focusing on these three key areas, you can track improvements and ensure that AI is delivering value to your projects. This section examines the importance of establishing a baseline for comparison to measure progress over time and how to quantify time savings, cost reductions, and productivity improvements using AI.

TIP

To effectively measure the impact of AI, it's essential to establish a baseline. This involves tracking key metrics before AI implementation, such as task completion times, resource utilization, and project costs. Once AI is in place, you can measure improvements in these areas over time. Using tools like time-tracking software, task management systems, and project performance dashboards helps collect the necessary data to make informed comparisons. With a clear baseline, you can quantify how much AI has improved your process and make data-driven decisions to optimize its use further.

One of the most immediate advantages of AI in project management is the time saved through automation. Tasks like scheduling, reporting, and data entry are often time-consuming, and by automating these tasks with AI, you can shift your focus to higher-level strategy and decision-making. To measure this impact, you should track how much time your team spends on routine tasks both before and after AI implementation. For example, if scheduling previously required two hours of manual work each week but now takes only ten minutes with AI, the time savings are substantial. Additionally, task management tools can help you monitor how long it takes to complete specific tasks, providing real-time data to assess AI's impact.

Another important area to evaluate is cost savings. AI can significantly reduce project costs by improving resource allocation and minimizing human errors. It's the ultimate budget-friendly project manager, like having a personal accountant and cost-cutter all in one. AI-driven resource management tools can optimize the use of personnel and materials by analyzing data from past projects and predicting future needs. By doing so, AI prevents overstaffing and underutilization, which can lead to budget overruns. You can track cost savings by comparing the actual resource usage after AI adoption with previous manual methods. Furthermore, AI reduces the risk of errors that often lead to rework. Tracking the frequency and cost of errors before and after AI adoption shows how much AI is helping to reduce these costly mistakes.

Beyond time and cost savings, AI impacts productivity and team performance. When routine tasks are automated, teams have more time to focus on creative and strategic work. AI can improve collaboration by facilitating real-time communication, automating status updates, and enabling task prioritization. Measuring productivity involves tracking key metrics like task completion rates, collaboration frequency, and overall project timelines. Additionally, evaluating how AI improves team output during specific project phases, such as planning or risk management, can provide insights into how AI is improving overall performance. You should compare performance metrics, such as team output or project milestones met, before and after integrating AI to ensure that its contribution to productivity is clearly understood.

TIP

Use productivity tools to measure team output and performance, ensuring that AI adoption leads to measurable improvements in collaboration and project delivery.

Considering Qualitative Metrics for AI Success

Qualitative metrics play a crucial role in evaluating the success of AI implementation in project management. These metrics provide valuable insights into how AI impacts stakeholder satisfaction, risk reduction, and decision-making quality. Qualitative outcomes may be harder to measure in numbers than quantitative measures, but they reveal how AI can enhance overall project experiences and outcomes.

Measuring stakeholder satisfaction

One of the key qualitative metrics for AI success is stakeholder satisfaction, which encompasses feedback from clients, team members, and other project stakeholders. AI can impact how effectively communication flows, how transparent the project is, and whether stakeholders feel their expectations are being met. You should actively gather feedback throughout the project life cycle using surveys, interviews, and feedback forms to assess how stakeholders perceive the influence of AI on project performance. For example, clients may appreciate real-time updates facilitated by AI-driven reporting tools, or team members may feel more confident when AI assists with workload management.

Assessing stakeholder satisfaction requires looking beyond immediate results and focusing on the long-term relationships built through improved communication and transparency. AI-powered tools that automate reporting or provide real-time data can enhance visibility into project progress, thus promoting greater trust and clarity for all parties involved. Clients who are consistently updated and informed about a project's status are more likely to feel satisfied, resulting in fewer misunderstandings or conflicts later.

Additionally, AI can enable more open channels of communication between project teams and stakeholders. Chatbots or AI-driven project management platforms that streamline communication workflows reduce the friction of manual updates and interactions. By ensuring that stakeholders are kept in the loop and information is readily accessible, AI helps foster a collaborative and transparent project environment.

Regularly collect feedback from stakeholders at key milestones to understand how AI-driven tools are improving communication and then adjust your AI implementation based on this feedback.

Measuring risk reduction

AI's potential to mitigate risks is another essential qualitative metric to evaluate. AI tools can anticipate risks before they escalate, such as budget overruns, missed deadlines, or resource shortages. It's like a crystal ball, but instead of predicting the future, it predicts project disasters before they happen. By leveraging predictive analytics and data from previous projects, AI can provide early warnings of potential issues and suggest preventative measures. For instance, AI may flag that a certain phase of the project is under-resourced, allowing you to reallocate resources before it impacts the timeline.

To effectively measure risk reduction, you should keep track of the types of risks identified by AI tools, along with the number and severity of risks that were avoided or mitigated due to AI intervention. This data can be collected in post-mortem reports, where the project team reviews what risks were identified and how they were successfully handled. By analyzing risk reduction metrics, you can gain insights into how AI helps maintain control over project variables that could lead to failure if not managed proactively.

Furthermore, AI can reduce uncertainty by providing data-driven insights into potential risk factors that may not be immediately apparent. For example, AI may detect trends such as a pattern of delayed deliveries from a supplier, helping the project team address the issue before it affects the project timeline. Over time, AI systems "learn" from the data they collect, improving their ability to predict and mitigate risks more effectively.

Incorporate AI tools early in the planning phase to identify potential risks upfront and develop contingency plans to prevent project delays or overruns.

Measuring decision quality

Decision quality is another qualitative metric that reflects AI's impact on the project management process. AI can dramatically improve the accuracy and timeliness of decision-making by analyzing vast datasets and providing insights that a human might miss. For example, AI can assess multiple scenarios to determine the best course of action, helping you make informed decisions more quickly and with greater confidence.

To measure improvements in decision quality, analyze whether decisions influenced by AI led to better results, such as improved resource allocation, more accurate budget forecasting, or faster issue resolution. Documenting case studies where AI helped avert potential failures or enhanced project performance is also useful. For instance, an AI system may have highlighted a critical risk that would have otherwise gone unnoticed, leading to the project team implementing an early course correction.

AI tools can also reduce your cognitive load, allowing you to focus on higher-level strategic decisions rather than getting bogged down in data analysis. The use of AI for real-time reporting and forecasting means that project leaders have the right data at their fingertips, enabling you to adapt quickly to changes in project scope or conditions. Over time, this leads to a more agile and adaptive project management style, reducing the likelihood of costly mistakes or oversights.

Tracking AI's Return on Investment

As AI continues to transform project management processes, calculating its return on investment (ROI) becomes essential for understanding the value AI brings to an organization. Measuring AI's ROI helps justify the initial investment and provides a clear picture of how AI-driven solutions contribute to long-term project success. This section covers how to calculate AI ROI, explores the difference between short-term and long-term gains, and examines how financial tools can help measure the monetary value of AI in project management.

ROI calculation

Calculating the ROI of AI in project management begins with establishing a simple yet effective formula. A basic ROI formula measures the net gain from AI against the total cost of investment. To calculate ROI, subtract the initial AI investment (including both implementation costs and ongoing maintenance) from the performance gains attributable to AI. Divide that result by the initial investment, then multiply by 100 to express the outcome as a percentage. This provides a clear percentage that represents how much value AI has added to the project.

In the case of AI in project management, the investment includes not only the cost of AI tools but also training, integration time, and any additional resources required to support the AI system. On the benefits side, you would include increased efficiency, time savings, reduced project delays, and any tangible gains, such as cost savings from fewer human errors. It's essential to capture all relevant variables, so you can see the full picture of AI's financial impact on your projects.

Here's an example that shows how to calculate ROI. A construction company is planning to invest in AI-powered software to optimize their project scheduling and resource allocation.

Initial AI investment, which includes the cost of the software, implementation, and initial training for employees: $20,000

Performance gains expected from AI (through optimized scheduling, the company was able to reduce project delays, leading to cost savings and increased revenue.): $30,000

Net Gain: $30,000 (performance gains) – $20,000 (initial investment) = $10,000

ROI: ($10,000 / $20,000) * 100 = 50%

Result: The ROI of the AI investment in this scenario is 50 percent. This means that for every dollar invested in AI, the company gained 50 cents back.

REMEMBER

You should also account for performance gains over time when calculating ROI. While AI may require a substantial upfront investment, the cumulative benefits over multiple projects often far exceed the initial costs. Improvements in task automation, predictive analytics, and resource allocation, for instance, can lead to significant gains in project efficiency and reduce long-term expenses.

TIP

Regularly update your ROI calculation as your AI system evolves. This will help you refine your understanding of AI's value over time and make informed decisions about further AI investments.

Short-term versus long-term gains

AI delivers benefits in both the short and long term, though these gains differ in scope and impact. In the short term, organizations may notice immediate improvements in project management metrics such as reduced task completion time, increased accuracy in scheduling, and improved reporting. These instant benefits arise from automating repetitive tasks like data entry, scheduling, and generating reports.

Short-term gains also include enhanced decision-making capabilities because of AI's ability to quickly analyze large amounts of project data and provide insights that might take a team days to gather. This allows for quicker adjustments and real-time course corrections, reducing the chances of project delays. You should document these quick wins as part of your ROI evaluation to demonstrate the immediate value AI brings to the table.

However, the real potential of AI lies in its long-term value. AI's learning capabilities allow for continuous improvement in project strategies, earlier identification of risks, and adaptation to the evolving needs of the business. Over time, AI systems become more attuned to the specific needs of the organization, allowing for better resource allocation, scalability, and overall efficiency. Long-term gains also manifest in reduced operational costs, improved client satisfaction, and more consistent project success.

When assessing AI's ROI, balance short-term results with the potential for long-term gains. A successful AI integration should offer immediate improvements but also provide sustained value as the system matures.

Cost-benefit analysis tools

One effective way to measure AI's monetary value in project management is by leveraging cost-benefit analysis tools. These tools can help quantify both direct and indirect benefits of AI, such as reduced labor costs, increased productivity, and minimized project risks. Financial tools can also provide projections for future savings, which is especially useful when evaluating AI's long-term impact on business scalability.

Start by creating detailed cost-benefit models that factor in all aspects of AI adoption, from software and hardware costs to training and ongoing maintenance. These tools allow you to compare different AI systems and their potential returns before making any major investments. It's also important to consider hidden costs, such as the time required to train your team on new AI tools or the potential integration challenges that might slow down initial deployment.

Many financial tools can simulate different scenarios, helping you anticipate the ROI under various conditions, such as scaling AI across multiple projects or expanding its capabilities. This allows you to make informed decisions about future AI upgrades or scaling based on hard data rather than assumptions. Furthermore, these tools help track ROI over time, offering insights into how AI's performance evolves as the organization becomes more familiar with the technology.

Incorporate hidden costs, such as time spent on training or integration challenges, into your cost-benefit analysis to get a more accurate picture of AI's ROI. Overlooking these expenses can skew your analysis and lead to incorrect assumptions about AI's value.

Regularly tracking and adjusting AI ROI measurements

AI ROI is not a static figure; you need to measure it continuously and refine it as you implement and improve AI systems over time. Initially, you may need to set conservative ROI targets as the organization adjusts to the new technology. As the AI tool becomes more integrated into the workflow, you should revisit and revise ROI calculations to reflect updated performance metrics, new data, and improved processes.

Tracking ROI on an ongoing basis allows you to quickly identify areas where AI is underperforming and where it may be overdelivering. For example, if task automation leads to significant time savings but integration challenges slow down the overall workflow, adjustments to how AI is used or how teams are trained may be necessary. Similarly, regular tracking can help identify opportunities for expanding AI's role in the organization.

TIP

As your AI tools become more refined, consider creating a feedback loop that incorporates lessons learned from previous projects. This not only helps improve your ROI calculations but also provides valuable insights for optimizing AI use in future projects. The goal is to ensure that AI continues to offer value well after its initial implementation.

REMEMBER

Revisit your AI ROI metrics regularly — at the end of each project phase or quarterly — to ensure you are capturing the most accurate representation of AI's value to your organization.

Examining Tools and Methods for Measuring AI Performance

As you incorporate AI into your workflow, it becomes increasingly important to track AI's performance to ensure it delivers the expected benefits. Various tools and methods help you measure the effectiveness of AI in driving results, enhancing efficiency, and providing actionable insights. This section examines three essential categories of tools for measuring AI performance: AI performance dashboards, predictive analytics tools, and survey tools for feedback.

AI performance dashboards

AI performance dashboards provide a centralized hub for monitoring AI-driven processes and tracking real-time data. These dashboards give you an overview of key AI metrics, helping you visualize the impact AI has on specific aspects of project management. Tools like Power BI and Tableau allow you to create customized dashboards that display relevant data such as task completion rates, resource utilization, risk mitigation progress, and AI-driven forecasts.

One of the key advantages of using dashboards is their ability to offer real-time insights. With AI performance dashboards, you can track how well AI is automating tasks or how accurately it's predicting project timelines. By pulling data from various sources into one dashboard, you can have a holistic view of how AI is impacting your projects.

Customization is a critical feature of AI performance dashboards. You can tailor these dashboards to focus on specific AI metrics that align with you project goals, such as time savings, budget tracking, or task efficiency. For example, a project manager focused on resource allocation might customize their dashboard to emphasize metrics that show resource distribution patterns and AI's influence on reducing resource shortages.

TIP

When setting up your AI performance dashboard, choose metrics that align with your project's objectives — for example, time savings, efficiency, or cost reduction. This will ensure that you're tracking AI's performance in ways that matter most to your goals.

TIP

Dashboards also allow for better communication with stakeholders. Instead of manual updates or reports, you can share live dashboard links, giving stakeholders immediate access to the latest data. This transparency fosters trust and enables quicker decision-making when adjustments are needed.

Predictive analytics tools

While the potential of AI-driven predictive analytics in project management is huge, it's still a field that's developing rapidly. You'll find that cloud providers like Google, IBM, and Microsoft all offer tools that can be used to build these kinds of solutions. However, you shouldn't expect to find a perfect, ready-made AI project management tool just yet.

For example, Google Cloud offers services like Vertex AI and BigQuery ML, which you can use to analyze your project data and start building predictive models. IBM has Watson Studio and other AI services within its cloud platform that you might find helpful for similar data analysis and forecasting tasks. And if you're looking at Microsoft's offerings, Azure Machine Learning is a service you should explore.

WARNING

Effectively applying these tools requires careful planning. You'll need to think about your data, how to prepare it, and you might even need to do some custom development. Don't jump in without a clear strategy!

So, what should you do? You need to carefully evaluate the available options from each provider. Don't just pick the first shiny new AI tool you see.

With AI-powered predictive analytics, you can measure how well your AI solutions are identifying risks or opportunities. For example, if an AI tool is analyzing previous projects to predict likely delays in a new project, its success in anticipating and avoiding those delays can be measured as part of its performance. Similarly, predictive analytics can assess resource demand, budgetary constraints, or potential bottlenecks, allowing you to make data-driven decisions proactively.

One of the real-world applications of predictive analytics tools is in construction projects, where AI has been used to forecast potential weather-related delays. By predicting when certain weather conditions are likely to affect progress, these tools help you adjust timelines or allocate resources accordingly. These forecasts often prevent expensive delays and keep projects running smoothly.

TIP

Predictive analytics also help quantify AI's impact on decision-making quality. By tracking how often AI-powered predictions lead to better outcomes, you can measure AI's direct contribution to project success. The more accurate the predictions, the more valuable the AI tool is for future projects.

Survey tools for feedback

While quantitative metrics provide a solid foundation for assessing AI performance, qualitative feedback from team members and stakeholders is just as important. Survey tools like Google Forms, SurveyMonkey, and Qualtrics can be used to gather feedback on how AI is influencing team performance, communication, and overall project satisfaction. By asking specific questions about AI's role in automating tasks or improving decision-making, you can gain insights into how AI impacts your team.

These surveys should focus on gathering qualitative data regarding AI's influence on collaboration, transparency, and workflow. For example, asking team members if AI tools have improved their productivity or helped them focus on higher-level tasks can provide a deeper understanding of AI's benefits. Client satisfaction can also be gauged by inquiring about how AI has improved project outcomes, such as faster delivery times or better project transparency.

Interpreting this feedback is key to measuring AI's success. For example, team members reporting increased ease of communication or fewer manual processes due to AI integration is a sign that AI is enhancing the project life cycle. On the other hand, negative feedback may reveal gaps in AI implementation, such as a lack of training or unclear integration processes. Either way, insights provide valuable information on how to improve AI tools or processes.

TIP

Track your survey results over time to assess how perceptions of AI evolve. Early resistance to AI might decrease as team members become more familiar with its benefits, leading to higher satisfaction and improved project performance. This qualitative data is crucial in providing a balanced view of AI's role in project management, complementing the quantitative metrics gathered from dashboards and predictive analytics tools.

Overcoming Challenges in Measuring AI Impact

When integrating AI into project management, measuring its true impact presents several challenges. Factors like attribution, resistance to AI adoption, and data quality can obscure AI's benefits, making it difficult to fully assess its value. This section discusses strategies to overcome these challenges, ensuring that AI-driven success is measured accurately and effectively.

Attribution of AI benefits

One of the biggest challenges in measuring the impact of AI is isolating its benefits from other project factors. AI tools are often implemented alongside other new systems or processes, making it difficult to pinpoint exactly which improvements are due to AI and which are the result of other changes. For example, a team might adopt AI tools around the same time they introduce new team collaboration practices, making it hard to distinguish whether improved project timelines are the result of AI or better teamwork.

To ensure accurate attribution of AI's success, you can create a baseline before AI implementation. This involves measuring KPIs such as project timelines, resource utilization, and error rates before the AI tools are introduced. By comparing these metrics with post-implementation results, managers can better assess the specific areas where AI made a difference. However, it's important to remember that AI doesn't work in isolation. It amplifies human capabilities, so improvements may often be the result of both AI and human intervention.

Another approach is to conduct pilot programs with control groups, where AI is implemented in one team while another team continues with traditional methods. This kind of A/B testing allows for clearer attribution of AI's contributions and identifies the exact benefits AI brings in comparison to non-AI workflows.

Resistance to AI adoption

Resistance to AI adoption is another significant factor that can distort the measurement of AI success. If team members or stakeholders are resistant to AI or reluctant to use the tools as intended, the full potential of AI won't be realized. This lack of adoption can skew performance metrics, making it appear as if AI is less effective than it actually is. For example, a project manager might implement an AI scheduling tool, but if team members continue to rely on manual methods, the time savings and efficiency gains of the AI tool will be diminished.

To address resistance, it's essential to engage the team early in the AI adoption process. Educating staff on the benefits of AI and offering hands-on training can ease concerns about job displacement or unfamiliarity with new technology. Resistance should be viewed not as a failure of AI but as a temporary hurdle that can be addressed with proper change management techniques.

AI adoption rates can be a metric of success, so measure AI adoption over time. Low initial adoption may mask the benefits of AI, but as teams become more comfortable and the tools are integrated into everyday workflows, their true value will become more apparent. Tracking adoption metrics helps identify whether resistance is a temporary barrier or a sign of deeper issues that need to be addressed. For a tool with a high adoption rate that's being fully utilized, any improvements can more accurately be attributed to the AI itself.

Data quality and availability

For AI tools to perform optimally and for their impact to be measured accurately, clean and reliable data is essential. Incomplete or inconsistent data can hinder AI's ability to provide valuable insights, leading to skewed performance results. One common issue is the existence of data silos, where information is stored in separate systems that don't communicate with each other. Without a unified dataset, AI cannot function at its full capacity, leading to inaccurate forecasts or recommendations.

Ensure that your AI tools are connected to a unified data source to avoid the pitfalls of data silos. When all project data is accessible, AI can provide better, more accurate insights.

To overcome this challenge, you should establish data governance practices that prioritize data cleanliness and accessibility. This involves regular data audits, ensuring that the data fed into AI systems is up to date and accurate. Moreover, teams should establish protocols for data entry to maintain consistency across different departments and projects. By improving the quality of data, the insights generated by AI will be more accurate, leading to better decision-making.

Data availability is another challenge, particularly in organizations where historical data might be incomplete. For AI to be effective, it needs a significant amount of past project data to train its algorithms. When this data is missing, you should explore external datasets or industry-specific benchmarks to supplement their internal information.

Establish regular data audits and governance practices to ensure clean, consistent data for AI tools. Good data quality is the foundation for accurate AI insights and performance tracking.

The challenge of incomplete or inconsistent data

When dealing with incomplete or inconsistent data, AI's ability to generate accurate forecasts and recommendations can be compromised. This can be particularly problematic when trying to track AI's impact on project performance. In these situations, you should focus on improving data collection processes and standardizing data entry methods across the organization. This ensures that all teams are working with the same set of standards, leading to better-quality data that AI tools can effectively utilize.

One strategy for dealing with incomplete data is to implement AI solutions gradually, focusing on specific areas where data is more reliable. For example, start by implementing AI tools for resource allocation, where data on past resource usage is likely to be more consistent. As data quality improves in other areas, AI can be expanded to more complex aspects of project management, such as risk management and forecasting.

Adopting Best Practices for AI Measurement

To effectively measure AI's impact in project management, it's essential to adopt best practices that allow for continuous monitoring and improvement. AI is not a one-time solution but a tool that evolves and grows over time, making it crucial that you stay engaged with its performance. This section covers key strategies for evaluating AI, including regular reviews and audits, adapting metrics to keep pace with AI advancements, and establishing a continuous feedback loop from stakeholders and teams.

Conducting regular reviews and audits

One of the most effective ways to ensure that AI continues to deliver value in your projects is by scheduling regular performance reviews and audits. AI tools can sometimes degrade in effectiveness over time due to changes in project requirements, shifts in data quality, or technological advancements. Establishing a cadence for these reviews helps identify performance dips and areas for improvement. For example, scheduling quarterly reviews allows teams to evaluate whether AI is meeting set KPIs and fine-tune any parameters that need adjustment.

These audits should not only focus on the technical performance of AI but also on how well the AI tools align with business goals. You should gather input from all relevant departments to gain a comprehensive view of AI's overall impact. The "Survey tools for feedback" section earlier in this chapter provides recommendations on ways to streamline the process of gathering this input. AI performance audits can also reveal areas where AI could be underutilized, providing an opportunity for expanding its role in project management tasks like risk mitigation or resource allocation.

TIP

Set a quarterly or annual review schedule to assess the performance of your AI tools. This routine evaluation will help maintain AI's effectiveness and ensure it aligns with project and business goals.

In addition to quarterly reviews, consider conducting an annual deep dive into AI performance metrics. This allows for a more strategic assessment of long-term AI impacts, including how the AI tools have contributed to overall project efficiency, cost savings, and risk management over the year. By documenting these findings, you can create a historical performance record that serves as a benchmark for future AI integrations.

Adapting metrics as AI evolves

As AI technologies continue to evolve, the metrics used to measure their success should evolve as well. AI tools today may be focused on automating routine tasks or providing data-driven insights, but as they grow more sophisticated, their contributions to projects may expand to more complex areas like decision-making or autonomous project management. You need to ensure that their measurement strategies can keep pace with these advancements.

TIP

One way to adapt metrics is to periodically revisit the KPIs used to gauge AI performance. What may have been an appropriate metric when AI was first implemented may no longer apply as the tools evolve and improve. For example, early AI adoption metrics might focus on the time saved through task automation, but as AI matures, you might start measuring its impact on decision accuracy or its role in improving team collaboration.

You should also stay informed about new AI technologies that may impact your current systems. Being aware of emerging AI capabilities can prompt an early adjustment to the metrics you're using. If a new AI tool provides better predictive analytics, for example, then you might shift from measuring time savings to tracking improved project forecasting accuracy.

TIP

Staying updated on new AI technologies and their potential impact on your projects helps you adjust your metrics to capture the evolving benefits of AI.

Maintaining a continuous feedback loop

An essential aspect of measuring AI performance is regularly incorporating feedback from stakeholders and team members. AI may be an advanced technology, but its effectiveness still depends on how well it integrates with human processes and systems. Establishing a continuous feedback loop (see Figure 3-1) allows you to adjust AI tools based on real-world usage rather than purely relying on technical metrics.

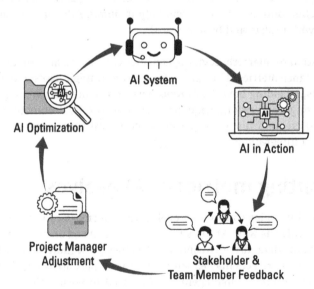

FIGURE 3-1:
A continuous
feedback loop.

REMEMBER

This feedback can come from different sources. Team members using AI daily may have valuable insights into how the tools could be better optimized for their specific workflows. Clients and external stakeholders can provide input on how AI is impacting communication, reporting, and overall project transparency. Gathering this feedback consistently allows you to make incremental improvements to AI deployment.

TIP

Try establishing regular team meetings where AI performance is discussed openly. These sessions should encourage users to highlight both successes and challenges they've encountered with AI tools. By creating a culture of continuous feedback, you can make data-driven decisions about improving AI's integration into the project life cycle.

Building this feedback into a scalable system for tracking AI performance over time is crucial. As projects grow or become more complex, having a well-established feedback loop ensures that the AI systems are continually optimized, enhancing both their short-term and long-term contributions.

2

Implementing AI Tools and Techniques

Choose the right AI tools for different stages of your project and find out how to integrate them into your workflows.

Automate routine tasks such as scheduling, task assignments, and status reporting to improve productivity.

Use AI to enhance decision-making with predictive analytics and scenario planning.

Streamline communication and collaboration, especially for remote or global teams, using AI-powered tools.

Integrate AI with existing project management software to optimize performance.

IN THIS CHAPTER

» **Using AI to automate meeting transcriptions**

» **Generating project documents and risk registers with LLMs**

» **Creating schedules and making plans using AI tools**

» **Using AI to manage resources**

» **Leveraging AI for risk management and forecasting**

Chapter **4**

Choosing the Right AI Tools for Your Projects

A rtificial intelligence (AI) is rapidly becoming a vital component in project management, making it essential that you choose the tools tailored to your specific needs. Whether you're focused on planning, scheduling, managing resources, or handling risks, AI can significantly improve efficiency and decision-making. However, with countless tools available, selecting the ones that align with your project's goals, team structure, and technological requirements is key.

In this chapter, I walk you through how to choose the best AI tools for the projects you're working on so that you make well-informed decisions.

Using AI to Transcribe Meeting Minutes

Taking meeting minutes can be one of the most tedious tasks in project management, yet it's critical for keeping track of decisions, action items, and stakeholder updates. Fortunately, AI tools can handle this task efficiently by automatically transcribing meetings in real time, allowing project managers to focus on leading discussions rather than jotting down every detail.

With AI transcription tools like Otter.ai or built-in transcription features in Microsoft Teams, you can record a meeting and have the AI tool generate a nearly accurate transcript almost immediately. This means no more scrambling to capture every word during fast-paced discussions. The AI tool listens, processes, and delivers a written version of the conversation — complete with speaker identification and time stamps.

Imagine you're in a meeting with multiple stakeholders, brainstorming ideas, assigning tasks, and discussing timelines. AI transcription tools can provide a full transcript, which you can scan through after the meeting to highlight key points or extract action items. The transcript can also serve as a reference for anyone who missed the meeting, ensuring that everyone stays aligned. But remember that AI transcription tools can make mistakes. It's a good idea to review the transcript right after a meeting and make corrections as needed to ensure that the transcript captures everyone's comments accurately.

TIP

Check out Chapter 7 to find out how transcription tools also support team communication.

Here are some of most popular AI tools for transcribing meetings:

>> **AssemblyAI** (www.assemblyai.com): AssemblyAI is primarily used by developers. It offers transcription via application programming interface (API) to provide a customizable solution for companies integrating transcription services into their platforms.

>> **Descript:** (www.descript.com): This powerful tool provides real-time transcription and editing capabilities. Descript also allows for easy editing of both audio and text, making it ideal for producing podcasts, videos, or meeting summaries.

>> **Fireflies.ai** (https://fireflies.ai): If you need a robust AI meeting assistant that automatically records and transcribes meetings in real time, Fireflies.ai may be a good option. It integrates with Zoom, Google Meet, Microsoft Teams, and more, making collaboration and review easy.

>> **Google Meet** (https://meet.google.com): Google Meet isn't strictly a transcription service, but when you use it for virtual meetings, it offers live captions during video calls, and the transcript can be saved automatically after meetings. Third-party integrations, like Otter.ai, can be used for more advanced transcription features.

- **Happy Scribe** (www.happyscribe.com): This AI transcription service supports more than 120 languages and offers subtitles and captions for video content, along with an intuitive text editor.

- **Microsoft Teams** (https://teams.microsoft.com): This is another meeting platform that includes built-in transcription — including speaker attribution — during video calls. Teams can save the transcript for future reference, making it easy to revisit key discussions.

- **Notta** (www.notta.ai): Notta, which is designed for remote teams, provides automated meeting notes and transcription for Zoom, Google Meet, and Microsoft Teams. It also offers collaborative note-taking features.

- **Otter.ai** (https://otter.ai): Otter is known for its capability to manage real-time transcription with automatic speaker identification. It integrates with online meeting tools for seamless transcription and provides searchable, editable transcripts.

- **Rev** (www.rev.com): This speech-to-text service offers professional transcription services powered by a combination of AI and human review for high accuracy. Rev also offers automatic transcription for faster results, with human editing available for a fee.

- **Scribie** (https://scribie.com): This AI-based transcription service offers a combination of machine and human-verified transcription for higher accuracy. Scribie also provides options for manual edits after transcription.

- **Sonix** (https://sonix.ai): This AI-powered transcription service supports multiple languages and provides editing tools for refining transcripts. Sonix integrates with Zoom and other platforms.

- **Temi** (www.temi.com): Temi supports automatic speech-to-text transcription with editing tools for refining and exporting transcripts. It's a fast and affordable option.

- **Trint** (https://trint.com): This option has additional features like text editing, translation, and collaboration tools. Trint is popular for journalists and video producers and integrates well with media platforms.

- **Zoom (with Otter.ai Integration)** (https://marketplace.zoom.us/apps/): The Zoom meeting platform allows integration with Otter.ai to provide automatic transcription during meetings. The transcript can be viewed in real time and shared with attendees after the meeting. Visit the Zoom Marketplace to integrate the Otter app with Zoom.

TIP

If your online meeting platform doesn't offer built-in transcription, consider integrating Otter.ai or Fireflies.ai to automatically record and transcribe meetings in real time.

AI transcription tools work best when used in quiet environments with minimal background noise.

Have you ever tried to record the notes for a meeting while you were also actively participating in the discussion? If so, then you know how hard it is to capture everything accurately, especially when you're speaking or when the conversation is moving fast. AI-generated transcripts aren't just about saving time; they also help with accuracy. In fast-moving discussions, details can be missed or misinterpreted, but AI does its best to ensure that your words are captured verbatim, which takes the pressure off project managers and team members and allows them to engage more fully in discussions. You can even set the AI to summarize key decisions and actions, making it easier to pull out essential information for follow-up.

Always review AI-generated transcripts for accuracy, especially when important decisions are discussed.

Using Large Language Models (LLMs) to Draft Project Documents

AI is changing the game in project management, and large language models (LLMs) like ChatGPT, Copilot, and Gemini are now helping project managers with tasks that go beyond scheduling and risk analysis. One of the coolest things LLMs can do is help generate draft documents like project charters, task lists, and risk registers. Instead of spending hours drafting these yourself, LLMs can handle the heavy lifting and give you a solid starting point.

Creating project charters with LLMs

A project charter is one of the most critical documents when kicking off a new project, but drafting it from scratch can be time-consuming. LLMs can make this process much faster by generating a well-structured draft in just a few minutes. All you need to do is provide some basic information — such as the project's goals, timeline, and key team members — and the AI will produce a complete project charter.

For example, if you're starting a new software development project, you could type, Create a project charter for building an e-commerce platform. The LLM will generate a document with sections covering objectives, scope, stakeholders, deliverables, and more. You'll need to refine and tailor the document to fit the specific details of your project, but the hardest part — getting the structure down and not starting from a blank page — is done for you.

The real power of LLMs makes itself known when you provide more detailed inputs. The more specific you are with your prompt, the better the AI can assist you. Here's how additional details can enhance the usefulness of the generated draft:

>> **Stakeholders:** Including information about your stakeholders (such as key clients, department heads, or external partners) helps the LLM create a more targeted project charter. For instance, you might specify, `Create a project charter for a marketing automation platform that includes key stakeholders from the marketing, IT, and legal teams`. This way, the draft reflects how different parties need to be involved, such as identifying who will approve different project phases or which stakeholders should be kept in the loop.

>> **Requirements and constraints:** Adding specific requirements or constraints makes the draft more relevant to your project. If you know your project must meet certain industry regulations, or if there are resource limitations, providing these details helps the LLM draft a more realistic project charter. For example, `Create a project charter for building a healthcare app that meets HIPAA compliance requirements` ensures the AI includes regulatory concerns and project constraints right in the draft.

>> **Timelines:** Incorporating clear deadlines or milestones into your prompt helps the LLM provide a more precise timeline for deliverables in the charter. Instead of just saying, `Create a project charter for a website redesign`, you could say, `Create a project charter for a website redesign to be completed in six months, with key milestones at three and four months for design approval and content migration`. The result is a charter that outlines deliverables in line with your specific time frame.

>> **Budgets:** If budgetary concerns are central to your project, including them in your prompt improves the charter draft's accuracy. For example, `Create a project charter for developing a CRM system with a budget of $100,000` guides the LLM to generate a draft that includes budget tracking and financial considerations, making it more aligned with your project's financial reality.

REMEMBER

The quality of the AI-generated documents heavily depends on the level of detail you provide in your input prompt.

By feeding the LLM all these elements — stakeholders, requirements, constraints, timelines, and budgets — you enable the tool to create a first draft that's not only faster but also far more useful. The AI can tailor the document more closely to your actual project, allowing you to make more minor tweaks rather than a full overhaul. This gives you a huge time-saving advantage and ensures you have a professional, well-organized starting point for your project documentation.

Using AI to automate project documentation

From generating task lists to managing risk registers and even drafting routine project communications, LLMs are revolutionizing how project managers handle documentation. Let's look at how AI can automate these key tasks.

LLMs can help organize your project by creating task lists or work breakdown structures (WBSs). Just give it a general description of the project, and the AI breaks everything down into a list of tasks or milestones. Need a detailed breakdown for a mobile app development project? You can input something like Generate a task list for developing a mobile app, and the LLM gives you a structured list with steps like designing the interface, building the backend, and testing the app.

Risk management can be tricky, but LLMs can make it easier by drafting initial risk registers. Just tell the AI about your project, and it can generate a list of potential risks, along with some ideas for how to deal with them. For instance, if you're managing a construction project, the AI might flag risks like weather delays, material shortages, or budget overruns, and even suggest mitigation strategies.

LLMs aren't just useful for official project documents; they can help you with everyday communication, too. Need to draft a meeting agenda, a project update, or a report for stakeholders? LLMs can create a first draft in minutes, leaving you more time to focus on the actual meeting or decision-making. Check out Chapter 5 to learn more about automating repetitive document management tasks.

Translating documents and correspondence into different languages

In today's globalized business environment, project managers often work with international teams, clients, and stakeholders who speak different languages. LLMs can play a pivotal role in bridging language barriers by translating project documents and correspondence into various languages quickly and accurately. Instead of relying on manual translations, which can be time-consuming and sometimes imprecise, LLMs can produce high-quality translations in seconds.

For instance, if you're working with a supplier in a non-English-speaking country, you can use an LLM to translate your project charter, task list, or contract into their native language. Similarly, the tool can help translate incoming correspondence or technical documents into your preferred language. By translating documents into team members' preferred languages, you ensure that all parties have a clear understanding of the project's requirements and goals, reducing the risk of miscommunication and errors.

What's more, LLMs can handle nuanced language, adjusting for formal or informal tones based on the context, to help make sure that translations are not only accurate but also culturally appropriate. This capability is invaluable in correspondence where tone and professionalism can impact relationships with clients or partners. With LLMs, you can streamline communication and ensure that your international projects move forward smoothly, without language becoming a stumbling block.

Be cautious when using AI for legal or contract translations; always have a human review for accuracy.

Using project documents to create custom GPTs

Custom GPTs (generative pretrained transformers) offer project managers an innovative way to leverage their project's specific documentation for a more tailored AI experience. By feeding GPTs project charters, requirements, contracts, and other key documents, you can create a custom AI tool that you and your colleagues can use to better understand the project, automate responses, and even predict project risks.

To build a custom GPT, you first need to gather and structure relevant project documentation, ensuring that key documents are well organized and free of unnecessary or redundant information. Next, upload these documents into a custom GPT. Once your custom GPT is trained on project-specific data, team members can interact with it to extract insights, generate reports, and streamline communication by asking questions like, "What are the key milestones in the project plan?" or "What risks were identified in previous stakeholder meetings?" Over time, as the AI processes more updates and feedback, it becomes increasingly refined and useful for automating responses, summarizing changes, and identifying potential risks before they escalate.

For example, imagine you're managing a complex construction project. You upload the project charter, requirements documents, and relevant contracts into a custom GPT. This AI then becomes familiar with the specifics of your project — such as deadlines, deliverables, and constraints. If any team member has questions about the project's scope or contractual obligations, they can query the GPT directly. Instead of combing through pages of documents, the GPT can instantly provide answers to questions like, What are the main deliverables due in phase two? or What are the penalties for late delivery?

Creating custom GPTs is also a powerful way to ensure consistency in how your team interprets and adheres to project guidelines. This is especially helpful when you're working on large, multistakeholder projects, where everyone may not be familiar with the project2019s intricacies. Instead of scheduling a meeting or reaching out to multiple people for clarification, team members can simply interact with the custom GPT to get real-time answers that align with the project's documentation.

Moreover, custom GPTs can be trained to spot potential risks or inconsistencies within your project's scope, helping you flag issues before they become problems. For instance, if a new task is added that seems to conflict with the original project requirements, the custom GPT could alert you, ensuring you remain aligned with the original scope and contract terms.

In short, by using LLMs to create custom GPTs, project teams can enhance their efficiency, reduce misunderstandings, and ensure they stay on track with the project's goals and constraints. It's a powerful tool that transforms static project documentation into a dynamic resource, accessible anytime.

Using LLMs to handle these kinds of tasks does more than save time; it also helps ensure consistency across documents, making everything easier to manage. With AI handling the drafts, you can focus on what really matters — keeping your project on track and your team moving forward. Plus, you won't have to start every document from scratch, which is always a win!

HOW A PM USED AN LLM TO DRAFT PROJECT DOCUMENTS

Sarah just kicked off a new software development project with a tight timeline. Typically, she would spend hours drafting the project charter, task lists, and risk registers, but this time, she turns to an LLM for help.

Sarah starts by feeding the LLM a few key details about the project: its objectives, timelines, and team members. In minutes, the AI generates a structured project charter, including sections on scope, deliverables, and stakeholders. She reviews the draft, makes a few tweaks, and moves on.

Next, she asks the LLM to generate a preliminary task list for developing the software. The AI provides a breakdown of major tasks like designing the interface, building the backend, and performing quality assurance testing. Instead of starting from scratch, Sarah now has a solid task list to work with, which she can adjust to fit her team's specific workflow.

Finally, Sarah uses the LLM to draft a risk register. The AI generates a list of potential risks, like integration challenges or budget overruns, along with suggested mitigation strategies. This saves her hours of brainstorming and ensures she doesn't overlook common risks.

By using the LLM to handle these first drafts, Sarah can focus on refining the details and strategy rather than getting bogged down in the initial writing process. This not only saves time but also ensures she can quickly provide her team with organized, structured documents that get the project off to a strong start.

Examining top AI tools for drafting project documents

With the increasing integration of AI into project management, drafting key project documents has never been easier. AI tools powered LLMs can help project managers save time by generating first drafts of essential documents like project charters, task lists, risk registers, and more. Here are some of the top AI tools for drafting project documents:

>> **ChatGPT** (https://chatgpt.com)**:** You can use this highly versatile AI model to draft a variety of project documents. By feeding the model prompts and key project details, you can generate structured drafts for documents such as project charters, meeting agendas, and risk assessments. ChatGPT's ability to produce human-like text makes it an excellent tool for creating detailed, professional documents in minutes. The drafts are customizable, allowing project managers to refine the output based on specific needs.

>> **Copy.ai** (www.copy.ai)**:** Though it's primarily known for content generation, Copy.ai is useful for drafting project-related documents. It offers prebuilt templates that you can customize for project management tasks, such as writing project plans, reports, and documentation summaries. It's especially helpful for project managers who want to generate multiple types of documents quickly; It provides an AI-driven starting point that you can tailor to fit the project's specific goals.

>> **Google Gemini** (https://gemini.google.com)**:** Gemini is Google's AI-powered tool that can assist project managers by generating drafts of

project documents, answering questions, and even summarizing project information. It leverages Google's vast knowledge graph and pulls from a wide array of data to provide accurate and useful drafts for project charters, task lists, and risk registers. Its real-time capabilities make it ideal for quick turnarounds on documents that require up-to-date information.

>> **Grammarly Pro** (www.grammarly.com/business): Grammarly is primarily known for grammar and style improvements, but Grammarly Pro offers AI-powered writing assistance that can help polish and draft project documents. It ensures your documents are professional, clear, and error-free, making it an excellent secondary tool to refine drafts created by other AI models.

>> **Jasper AI** (https://jasper.ai): Jasper AI is another powerful tool for generating content quickly. While commonly used for marketing and content creation, Jasper AI can be adapted for project management purposes. It helps project managers draft initial documents, such as task lists, project timelines, and status updates. The AI's templates and user-friendly interface make it easy to generate concise, well-organized documents with just a few inputs.

>> **Microsoft Copilot** (https://copilot.microsoft.com): Microsoft's AI-powered Copilot integrates with tools like Word and Excel to assist project managers in drafting documents directly in the Microsoft ecosystem. Whether you need to generate a detailed project charter or outline a risk management plan, Copilot uses AI to speed up document creation by suggesting formatting and content based on the initial inputs provided. This AI tool is particularly valuable for teams already working within the Microsoft suite.

>> **Miro AI** (https://miro.com): Miro AI enhances collaboration by automating brainstorming, organizing ideas, and offering suggestions in real time. It's particularly useful for remote teams working on visual planning and ideation tasks.

>> **Notion AI** (www.notion.com): Notion AI enhances project management by enabling users to automate document creation within the Notion workspace, generating task lists, meeting minutes, and project summaries in real time. Unlike standalone tools, it works seamlessly within Notion, allowing teams to collaborate, edit, and refine documents without switching platforms. Through Notion's API, it integrates with tools like Slack, Jira, Google Calendar, and Trello, ensuring automatic updates, synchronized deadlines, and centralized project tracking. By combining AI-powered content generation with system connectivity, Notion AI streamlines workflows, enhances collaboration, and reduces administrative overhead for project managers.

>> **QuillBot** (https://quillbot.com): QuillBot is an AI-driven writing assistant known for its paraphrasing and summarizing abilities. It can help project

managers quickly revise or improve the clarity of their drafted documents, such as meeting notes, project updates, or summaries. It's great for condensing lengthy documents into concise, clear formats.

» **Rytr** (https://rytr.me): Rytr is another AI tool that helps create content, including project-related documents like charters, timelines, and status updates. Rytr's ease of use and quick turnaround time makes it a good option for project managers who need to produce high-quality drafts in a short period.

» **Tome** (https://tome.app): Tome is a unique AI tool designed for storytelling and presentation, which makes it useful for project managers to draft project pitches, high-level charters, or stakeholder presentations. It can automatically create slides or written presentations based on prompts, helping turn rough ideas into structured, visually appealing documents.

» **Writesonic** (https://writesonic.com): Writesonic is an AI tool built for generating high-quality written content quickly. Project managers can leverage Writesonic to create drafts for project plans, task lists, and reports. It's especially handy for generating long-form documents, and it offers various templates to structure content according to specific project requirements.

» **Zoho Zia** (www.zoho.com/zia): This AI assistant, which is part of the Zoho suite, helps with more than just writing. Zia can analyze project data and suggest content for reports, task lists, and documentation. It's particularly useful for teams that already use the Zoho platform for their project management needs because it integrates seamlessly with the broader Zoho ecosystem.

REMEMBER

Each AI tool has its strengths, and some work better in different project management environments. For instance, Gemini's integration with Google's extensive knowledge base can provide up-to-date information in a document, whereas tools like Grammarly and QuillBot can ensure that the text is polished and professional. Combining multiple tools could give you the best of both worlds — fast content generation and high-quality output.

Selecting AI Tools for Planning and Scheduling

Planning and scheduling are the backbone of any successful project. AI tools can improve the accuracy of your project plans and help automate scheduling tasks, ensuring that your projects stay on track.

Understanding your planning and scheduling needs

Before selecting an AI tool, assess your project's specific planning and scheduling requirements. Are you dealing with complex timelines involving multiple teams? Do you need real-time updates to accommodate dynamic project environments? Understanding your project's unique needs will help you identify the right AI tools.

TIP

Projects with rigid timelines may benefit from AI tools that provide predictive scheduling, whereas projects with more flexible timelines might require tools that prioritize real-time adjustments and collaboration features.

Whether you're handling a small project or a large-scale operation, the right features can significantly improve accuracy, optimize resource allocation, and ensure real-time adaptability. The following list outlines some key features to consider when evaluating AI planning and scheduling tools:

- >> **Predictive scheduling:** AI tools that analyze historical data to forecast project timelines and potential bottlenecks can help improve planning accuracy. Predictive scheduling features are especially useful for complex projects where delays can cascade.

- >> **Automated task scheduling:** Some AI tools automatically assign tasks to team members based on availability, skills, and workload, reducing the need for manual scheduling and balancing team productivity.

- >> **Dynamic adjustments:** AI-powered scheduling tools can make real-time adjustments to project plans when new variables arise, such as scope changes or resource constraints. This ensures that your schedule remains optimized throughout the project lifecycle.

Selecting AI tools for planning and scheduling

Here are some of the top AI tools for planning and scheduling:

- >> **Accelo** (www.accelo.com): Accelo is an AI-powered project and client management tool that streamlines operations, automates repetitive tasks, and provides real-time insights into project health. Its AI features help monitor progress, manage resources, and predict project outcomes.

- >> **Asana** (https://asana.com): Asana uses AI to help manage tasks, track progress, and streamline workflows. The AI engine provides recommendations on task prioritization and workload balancing, ensuring team members aren't overburdened while maintaining efficiency.

- >> **Bitrix24** (www.bitrix24.com): Bitrix24 is an all-in-one project management and collaboration platform that uses AI for workflow automation, task scheduling, and performance tracking. It also offers AI-driven customer support tools for managing client interactions.

- >> **ClickUp** (https://clickup.com): ClickUp is a flexible project management tool that incorporates AI to automate workflows, track project progress, and predict task completion times. Its AI-powered features help teams stay organized by dynamically adjusting priorities and timelines based on task dependencies.

- >> **Hive** (https://hive.com): Hive uses AI to automate project updates, manage workflows, and optimize resource allocation. It also includes predictive analytics to anticipate project bottlenecks before they happen, ensuring projects stay on time and within budget.

>> **Jira** (www.atlassian.com/software/jira): Jira is a powerful tool for planning and scheduling, especially for agile and scrum-based projects. It offers AI-driven features called Atlassian Intelligence that help write user stories, prioritize tasks, manage team workloads, and track project progress. With real-time data analysis, Jira assists in adjusting sprint timelines, allocating resources dynamically, and identifying bottlenecks in workflows. Its built-in reporting and forecasting tools enable project managers to plan more efficiently, ensuring that tasks are completed on schedule and teams stay productive.

>> **Microsoft Project** (https://project.microsoft.com): Microsoft Project incorporates AI to improve scheduling by analyzing historical data to predict timelines and resource needs. It can also adjust schedules in real time based on changes in project progress or scope and provides dynamic updates to keep projects aligned.

>> **Monday.com** (https://monday.com): Monday.com is an AI-powered project management tool with features like automated task scheduling and resource allocation. It can analyze project data to optimize workflows, helping teams stay organized and on track.

>> **Nifty Orbit AI** (https://niftypm.com/ai): Nifty Orbit AI is an AI-powered project management platform that combines task management, communication, and reporting. Its AI features help automate progress tracking, predict project timelines, and optimize workflow efficiency.

>> **OnePlan** (https://oneplan.ai): This AI-driven platform excels in strategic portfolio and project management. It offers seamless integration with tools like Microsoft Project, Jira, and Smartsheet, providing a comprehensive view of all work across an enterprise. OnePlan's AI-powered insights assist with project planning, resource allocation, and financial forecasting. Additionally, it enables real-time updates and scenario planning, allowing project managers to adapt to changing business needs. OnePlan's AI assistant, Sofia GPT, streamlines resource management and stakeholder communication.

>> **Oracle Primavera Cloud** (www.oracle.com/erp/project-portfolio-management-cloud/): This tool is often used for large-scale projects and construction. It uses AI to forecast project timelines and risks, helping project managers make informed decisions about scheduling and resource allocation. Primavera P6 also integrates with specialized AI solutions such as Doxel and Whippy, enabling enhanced project tracking, automated progress updates, and predictive analytics for more informed decision-making throughout the project life cycle.

>> **Planview** (www.planview.com): Planview, formerly known as Clarizen, integrates advanced AI tools to streamline resource allocation, manage task dependencies, and optimize project timelines. By automating task

assignments based on team members' availability and skills, it prevents overallocation and ensures efficient use of resources. Its real-time analytics offer insights into project progress, enabling dynamic adjustments to keep schedules on track and mitigate potential risks before they escalate.

>> **Portfolio Manager** (www.tempo.io/products/portfolio-manager): Portfolio Manager, formerly known as LiquidPlanner, uses AI-driven predictive scheduling to forecast project completion dates, automatically update timelines based on changes, and help project managers identify bottlenecks before they arise.

>> **Smartsheet** (www.smartsheet.com): Smartsheet is designed for larger, more complex projects and includes AI capabilities for predictive analytics, dynamic resource allocation, and task prioritization. Its AI features help with managing dependencies and adjusting schedules based on real-time data.

>> **Trello with AI Integrations** (https://trello.com): Trello is known for its easy-to-use project management boards, and it offers AI integrations like Butler, which automates repetitive tasks. Butler allows you to set rules, triggers, and actions based on your project's workflow, making task automation a breeze.

>> **Wrike** (www.wrike.com): Wrike uses AI to optimize project scheduling and resource management. The tool helps in workload balancing and task assignment, ensuring tasks are distributed efficiently across teams. It also provides insights for improving project timelines and adjusting to changes in scope.

WHY HISTORICAL AND REAL-TIME DATA ARE CRUCIAL FOR AI IN PROJECT MANAGEMENT

AI in project management relies on both historical data and real-time data to function effectively. Each type of data serves a unique role in predicting risks, optimizing workflows, and ensuring project success.

Historical data provides AI with a foundation of past performance, enabling it to identify patterns, trends, and potential pitfalls that may arise in a project. By learning from conditions in previous projects — such as delays, resource bottlenecks, or budget

(continued)

(continued)

overruns — AI can predict similar risks in current projects and suggest preventive actions. For example, if past projects consistently experienced delays during a specific phase, the AI can flag this and recommend adjustments before issues arise.

Real-time data allows AI to make dynamic, on-the-fly adjustments to projects. As tasks progress, team workloads shift, or unexpected delays occur, real-time data gives AI the ability to adapt quickly. It provides up-to-the-minute insights into resource availability, task completion, and emerging risks, enabling AI to suggest instant solutions, like reallocating resources or adjusting timelines. This ability to monitor and react in real time ensures that projects stay on track and respond to challenges as they happen.

In short, historical data helps AI anticipate potential issues based on past experiences, while real-time data empowers AI to manage and mitigate risks as they emerge in the present. The combination creates a powerful tool for effective and proactive project management.

Finding AI Tools for Resource Management

Effective resource management is critical to ensuring that your project has the necessary personnel, equipment, and materials to meet its objectives. AI-powered resource management tools can analyze vast amounts of data to optimize how resources are allocated and ensure that your team and materials are used efficiently. By automating resource allocation and providing real-time insights, AI can help you make better decisions about how to manage your project's resources.

AI tools for resource management not only save time but also maximize the efficiency of your team and assets. With AI's ability to optimize resource allocation, your project is more likely to stay on schedule and within budget.

This section explores how to find the right AI tools for resource management.

Assessing your resource management needs

Resource management varies greatly depending on the project. For large-scale projects, you may need AI tools that optimize both human and material resources. For smaller teams, AI tools that focus on task allocation and workload balancing may suffice.

Understanding your project's resource management needs will help you select AI tools that can optimize how your resources are utilized.

After you've assessed what you need, keep the following key features in mind as you look for resource management tools:

» **Workload balancing:** AI-powered resource management tools can analyze team members' workloads and redistribute tasks to ensure that no one is overburdened. This helps prevent burnout and improves productivity across the team.

» **Resource allocation optimization:** AI can optimize the allocation of both human and material resources, ensuring that each resource is used effectively. This includes managing physical assets, such as equipment, and ensuring that the right team members are assigned to the right tasks.

» **Capacity Forecasting:** AI tools can predict future resource needs based on project timelines and progress. This allows project managers to plan and ensure that resources are available when they're needed most.

Selecting AI tools for resource management

Here are some of the top AI tools for resource management:

» **Airtable** (www.airtable.com)**:** Airtable combines the power of a spreadsheet with a database and offers AI-driven features like task automation, intelligent project tracking, and real-time collaboration. Its AI automations are customizable to support complex workflows, making it versatile for project managers.

» **Asana** (https://asana.com)**:** Asana's AI-powered resource management features allow you to balance workloads, automate task assignments, and forecast capacity. The AI can help ensure that no team member is overworked while optimizing the allocation of resources for project efficiency.

» **ClickUp** (https://clickup.com)**:** ClickUp incorporates AI to manage resources dynamically. Its AI capabilities help distribute tasks based on team members' workloads and skill sets, ensuring optimal performance and resource use. It also provides insights into capacity planning and resource forecasting.

» **Float** (www.float.com)**:** Float is an AI-powered resource management tool that focuses on real-time scheduling and forecasting. It helps project managers allocate resources efficiently by providing insights into team availability and automatically adjusting schedules when changes occur.

>> **Forecast** (www.forocast..app): Forecast is an AI-powered resource and project management tool that predicts project timelines, automates scheduling, and optimizes resource allocation based on historical project data. It's designed to help reduce manual oversight and improve project outcomes.

>> **Kantata** (www.kantata.com): Kantata, formerly known as Mavenlink, uses AI to optimize resource planning by analyzing project data and recommending the best use of available resources. It tracks resource utilization and helps forecast future needs, ensuring that the right people and materials are available at the right time.

>> **Monday.com** (https://monday.com): Monday.com, which is known for its flexibility, uses AI to help manage resources by automating task assignments and optimizing workflows. It analyzes team availability and workload to make sure tasks are distributed efficiently and bottlenecks are prevented.

>> **RescueTime** (www.rescuetime.com): RescueTime is an AI-powered productivity tool that helps project managers track how time is spent on different tasks. It uses AI to analyze work habits, identify distractions, and offer recommendations for improving focus and productivity. By automatically tracking application and website usage, RescueTime provides insights into team performance and time management, making it easier to optimize workflow and ensure project deadlines are met.

>> **Resource Guru** (https://resourceguruapp.com): Resources Guru is specifically designed for resource management. It uses AI to track resource availability and optimize allocations. The tool ensures that teams, equipment, and other resources are scheduled effectively, helping avoid conflicts and underutilization.

>> **SAP S/4HANA** (www.sap.com/products/erp/s4hana.html): SAP's AI-powered resource management features provide robust tools for optimizing human and material resources. It's particularly useful for large enterprises that need to manage resources across multiple departments or regions, offering AI-driven insights into allocation and utilization.

>> **Smartsheet** (www.smartsheet.com): Smartsheet offers AI-powered resource management that helps project managers optimize both human and material resources. The tool analyzes team capacities and adjusts resource allocation based on real-time data, ensuring that resources are utilized effectively without delays.

>> **Timely** (www.timely.com): Timely uses AI to automatically track work hours, manage project timelines, and ensure that resources are utilized effectively. The tool provides insights into where time is being spent to help project managers ensure deadlines are met while avoiding burnout.

- **Wrike** (www.wrike.com): Wrike's AI-driven resource management tool helps track team availability and reallocates resources based on workload and task priority. It can forecast future resource needs, allowing you to plan and avoid overloading team members or underutilizing resources.

- **Zoho Projects** (www.zoho.com/zia): Zoho integrates AI to manage workloads and resources, providing real-time updates on team capacity and resource availability. It automates task assignments based on skill sets and availability, making sure projects remain on track without overburdening team members.

Identifying AI Tools for Risk Management and Forecasting

Risk management is one of the most critical aspects of project management, and AI can help project managers predict and mitigate risks. AI-driven risk management and forecasting tools analyze data and provide real-time insights to anticipate risks and help you plan for various scenarios, which enables you to protect your project from unexpected disruptions and increase the likelihood of success. AI tools can help you stay ahead of potential issues that could derail your project.

This section dives into how to choose AI tools for risk management and forecasting.

Understanding your risk management needs

Risk management requirements can vary depending on your project's complexity, industry, and external factors. Before selecting an AI tool, consider what types of risks are most relevant to your project. Are you dealing with supply chain risks, technical risks, or market risks? Understanding the risks that could impact your project will help you choose the right AI tools to address them.

With your list of needs in hand, you can begin to look at risk management and forecasting tools that have these key features:

- **Predictive risk analysis:** AI tools that use predictive analytics can identify potential risks before they become problems. By analyzing data from previous projects, these tools can predict risks and suggest mitigation strategies.

>> **Real-time risk monitoring:** AI-powered risk management tools can continuously monitor project data to identify emerging risks. This allows project managers to take immediate action to address issues before they escalate.

>> **Scenario planning and forecasting:** AI tools can help project managers create what-if scenarios to forecast potential outcomes based on different variables. This allows you to plan for various contingencies and make more informed decisions.

Selecting AI tools for risk management and forecasting

Here are some of the top AI tools that project managers can use for risk management and forecasting:

>> **@RISK** (https://lumivero.com/products/at-risk): @RISK is an add-on to Microsoft Excel that uses AI to perform Monte Carlo simulations and other probabilistic forecasting methods. It helps project managers assess the likelihood of risks and their potential impacts, giving a clear view of possible project outcomes.

>> **Domo** (www.domo.com): Domo offers AI-based risk forecasting by analyzing project data to detect potential risks and trends. Its predictive analytics feature helps project managers stay ahead of emerging risks by providing insights into factors that could derail projects, such as market changes or supply chain disruptions.

>> **Kensho** (https://kensho.com): Kensho is an AI platform that uses natural language processing (NLP) and machine learning to analyze vast amounts of unstructured data, such as market news and reports, to forecast potential risks. It's commonly used in financial services and industries where market conditions heavily influence project risk.

>> **Microsoft Azure Machine Learning** (https://azure.microsoft.com/en-us/products/machine-learning): With AI-driven risk analysis capabilities, Azure Machine Learning helps project managers identify and mitigate risks by using machine learning models to analyze patterns from historical project data. It can forecast future risks based on a range of variables, allowing for proactive risk management.

>> **Oracle Primavera Cloud** (www.oracle.com/erp/project-portfolio-management-cloud/): Oracle Primavera Cloud is designed for large-scale projects and offers AI-powered risk management capabilities. It performs risk analysis and scenario planning, allowing project managers to forecast

potential risks and their impact on the overall project timeline and budget. It also provides what-if simulations for better risk mitigation planning.

» **Proggio** (www.proggio.com)**:** Proggio's AI-driven risk management capabilities allow for real-time risk tracking and forecasting. It provides early warnings of potential delays or bottlenecks and offers suggestions on how to mitigate these risks before they impact the project.

» **Safe** (https://safe.security)**:** Safe, formerly RiskLens, is an AI-powered risk management tool specifically designed to quantify and prioritize risks. It uses data-driven insights to help project managers assess the financial impact of risks and make informed decisions. It also allows for scenario planning and real-time monitoring of risk factors.

» **RiskWatch** (www.riskwatch.com)**:** RiskWatch uses AI to assess project risks in areas such as cybersecurity, compliance, and operations. It provides real-time risk scores based on current data and past incidents, helping project managers monitor potential threats and develop mitigation plans.

» **Tara AI** (https://app.tara.ai)**:** This tool uses machine learning to automate product management workflows, enabling project managers to plan sprints, track progress, and manage product releases efficiently. It analyzes project data to predict potential roadblocks and optimize task completion.

» **Workday Adaptive Planning:** (www.workday.com/en-us/products/adaptive-planning/overview.html)**:** Workday Adaptive Planning, formerly Adaptive Insights, offers AI-driven forecasting capabilities to help project managers identify financial risks and adjust project budgets accordingly. The tool analyzes financial data and provides real-time forecasts of budget overruns, revenue losses, or other financial risks.

Chapter 5

Automating Tasks and Workflows with AI

Automation is one of the most powerful applications of artificial intelligence (AI) in project management. By automating routine tasks, optimizing workflows, and integrating AI into existing project management tools, you can reduce manual effort, improve productivity, and ensure that your projects run smoothly. This chapter explores how AI can help automate routine project management tasks, optimize task allocation and workflows, and integrate with your existing project management tools to maximize efficiency.

Automating Routine Project Management Tasks

Project management often involves a series of repetitive tasks that, while necessary, can consume a significant portion of your time. Automating these routine tasks with AI can free valuable time and energy for more strategic work. Here, I share some common project management tasks AI can streamline and automate:

>> **Scheduling and reminders:** Scheduling is a key element of project management, but it's also a repetitive task that can be time-consuming. AI-powered

tools can automatically schedule meetings, set deadlines, and send reminders to team members. For example, tools like Microsoft Project and Monday. com can automatically schedule tasks based on team availability and workload, and tools like Asana can automate reminders to ensure that team members meet deadlines.

» **Status updates and reporting:** Generating status updates and reports is another routine task that AI can automate. AI-powered project management tools can automatically track progress and generate real-time status updates and reports for stakeholders. Tools like Smartsheet and Wrike use AI to gather data from ongoing tasks and compile comprehensive reports, saving you the effort of manually compiling data. Check out Chapter 11 for more information about how AI can automate the generation of performance reports.

» **Task assignments:** AI can automate task assignments based on team members' skills, availability, and workload. For example, AI can assign tasks to the most suitable team members, ensuring that work is distributed efficiently. Tools like Jira and ClickUp offer AI-powered task assignment features that analyze team members' past performance and current workload to ensure tasks are allocated optimally. Check out Chapter 6 to find out how predictive analytics helps optimize resource allocation.

TIP

When using AI to optimize task allocation, ensure that the data you input — such as team member skills, performance history, and current workload — is accurate and up to date. AI's effectiveness depends on the quality of the data it processes, so regular updates help maintain efficient and balanced task distribution.

» **Document management:** AI-powered systems can automate the organization, tagging, and retrieval of project documents. For example, AI tools can automatically categorize project files, making them easier to search and access. This automation can reduce the time spent on administrative tasks and ensure that important documents are always available when needed.

» **Time tracking:** Time tracking is often a tedious but necessary part of project management. AI tools can automatically track time spent on tasks, freeing team members from manual time entry. Tools like Harvest and Toggl use AI to track time automatically, providing accurate data for billing, payroll, and productivity analysis.

Integrating AI with Your Existing Project Management Tools

Adopting AI doesn't mean overhauling your entire project management system. Instead, AI can be integrated into your existing project management tools to enhance your workflows and processes. This covers how to integrate AI with your current tools and maximize the benefits of both.

Choosing the right AI integrations

When selecting AI integrations, consider the specific needs of your project and team. Do you need AI to handle scheduling, resource management, risk forecasting, or communication management? Identifying your top priorities helps you choose AI integrations that address those specific needs without disrupting your existing processes. By aligning AI solutions with your unique project goals, you can avoid the pitfalls of adding unnecessary complexity to your system.

Many popular project management tools, such as Microsoft Project, Asana, Jira, and Trello, offer built-in AI features or integrations with third-party AI platforms like Zapier and Automate.io or AI-driven reporting tools like Power BI. These integrations can enhance your existing workflows by automating manual tasks, generating insights from data, and streamlining communication. AI integrations can act as extensions of your current tools rather than requiring a complete system overhaul.

TIP

When integrating AI into your existing project management tools, start by identifying the specific needs of your team — whether it's scheduling, resource management, or reporting. Select AI integrations that align with these priorities to avoid overwhelming your current system and maximize efficiency without major disruptions.

Consider the following questions before selecting AI integrations:

>> What pain points does my current system have? Is there too much manual effort in task tracking, scheduling, or reporting?

>> What integrations are my team already comfortable with? Understanding your team's familiarity with AI tools like Slack bots or automated scheduling assistants can smooth the transition to AI-driven workflows.

>> How scalable is the AI integration? If your project grows, will the AI integrations grow with it?

Here are some of the top tools that project managers can use for AI integration:

>> **Apache Camel** (https://camel.apache.org): Apache Camel is an open-source integration framework that enables developers to route, transform, and mediate data between different applications using a variety of protocols and technologies.

>> **Boomi** (https://boomi.com): Boomi is a cloud-based integration platform that allows businesses to connect applications, synchronize data, and automate workflows using an intuitive drag-and-drop interface.

>> **Jitterbit** (www.jitterbit.com): Jitterbit is an integration platform that helps businesses connect cloud and on-premise applications, automate workflows, and manage APIs efficiently.

>> **Make** (www.make.com): Make, formerly Integromat, is a visual automation platform that allows users to connect apps, automate workflows, and transfer data between systems without coding, which enables seamless integration across various business tools and services.

>> **Microsoft Power Automate** (https://powerautomate.microsoft.com): Microsoft Power Automate helps users create automated workflows between applications and services to streamline repetitive tasks and improve productivity.

>> **MuleSoft Anypoint Platform** (www.mulesoft.com/platform/enterprise-integration): MuleSoft's Anypoint Platform provides API-led integration solutions that allow businesses to connect applications, data, and devices across cloud and on-premise environments.

>> **n8n** (https://n8n.io): n8n is an open-source workflow automation tool that enables users to connect different services and applications while allowing full control over data processing.

>> **Node-RED** (https://nodered.org): Node-RED is a low-code programming tool for wiring together APIs, IoT devices, and services to create automation flows in a visual manner.

>> **Pabbly Connect** (www.pabbly.com/connect): Pabbly Connect is a workflow automation tool with a simple, affordable pricing model that allows users to connect multiple apps and automate tasks.

>> **Tray.io** (https://tray.io): Tray.io is a low-code automation platform that helps businesses connect applications, automate workflows, and scale integrations with enterprise-level security.

>> **Workato** (www.workato.com): Workato is an enterprise-grade automation platform that allows businesses to integrate applications and automate processes using AI-powered workflow management.

>> **Zapier** (https://zapier.com): Zapier is an automation tool that connects apps and services, allowing users to create workflows (Zaps) that automate repetitive tasks without coding, improving efficiency across various platforms.

Ensuring compatibility with your current tools

Compatibility is key when integrating AI with your project management software. The last thing you want is to adopt an AI tool that conflicts with your existing platform, causing workflow disruptions or requiring significant reconfigurations. To avoid this, it's essential to evaluate AI tools based on how well they integrate with your current software stack and team workflows. Seamless integration helps ensure a smooth transition to AI-powered automation without the need for a full overhaul of your processes.

Before adopting an AI tool, conduct a thorough assessment of the tools you're already using. Identify key software that your team relies on daily, such as project management systems (Trello, Asana, Jira), communication platforms (Slack, Microsoft Teams), and analytics tools (Power BI, Tableau, Google Data Studio). Determine whether the AI tool you're considering can integrate natively with these systems or if it will require third-party connectors. For instance, if your team heavily relies on Trello for task management, you'll want to seek out AI tools that work natively with Trello's boards and cards, offering features like automated task prioritization, deadline reminders, and real-time status updates.

WARNING

Ensure the AI tools you're considering can integrate with your company's cloud services and data storage solutions (for example, Google Workspace, Microsoft 365, Dropbox). Otherwise, you may not be able to access critical documents and data across systems.

If your team uses Slack or Microsoft Teams for communication, it's crucial to ensure the AI tools you choose are compatible with these platforms. The right AI tool can enhance team collaboration by automating routine tasks such as scheduling meetings, generating status updates, or even answering common questions through chatbots. For example, an AI assistant integrated into Slack can automatically schedule meetings, remind team members of upcoming deadlines, or generate quick reports on project progress, saving time and reducing manual tasks. Additionally, some AI tools can automatically share updates in Slack whenever a task in Asana or Trello is completed, keeping everyone in the loop.

REMEMBER

By integrating AI with communication tools, you can streamline team interactions, ensure seamless collaboration, and keep all stakeholders informed without needing to switch between platforms manually.

Another important area of compatibility is with your data analysis and reporting tools. Platforms like Power BI, Tableau, and Google Data Studio offer AI-driven insights that can analyze project performance data, generate automated reports, and create dashboards. These tools can integrate with project management platforms like Jira or Asana to pull real-time data, offering valuable insights into resource allocation, project timelines, and performance metrics. Ensuring that the AI tools you choose can feed data into these platforms allows you to automate reporting and minimize manual data entry, while delivering real-time project visibility to stakeholders.

For example, when integrating Power BI with Jira, project managers can easily generate dashboards that show project milestones, bottlenecks, and team performance that are updated instantaneously using AI-driven analytics. This removes the need for manual reporting and ensures that the team can focus on strategic decisions rather than administrative tasks.

AI platforms like Zapier and Make (formerly Integromat) offer hundreds of integrations with popular project management tools, making it easy to connect AI features to your existing workflows. These platforms act as bridges between different tools, enabling you to automate complex workflows without requiring extensive technical reconfiguration.

For example, you can use Zapier to integrate Google Sheets, Trello, and Slack into a seamless workflow: When data is updated in Google Sheets, Zapier can automatically create a task in Trello and notify relevant team members in Slack. Similarly, Make can automate approval processes across tools like Google Drive, Microsoft Teams, and Asana, ensuring that workflows move efficiently from one stage to the next without human intervention.

These integration platforms allow teams to create sophisticated workflows across different systems without writing any code, making them highly effective for organizations with existing project management software that want to add AI without major disruptions.

Integrating custom APIs with your existing tools

If you have specific project needs that are not addressed by out-of-the-box AI tools or integration platforms, consider building custom application programming interface (API) integrations. Many AI tools and project management systems provide open APIs, allowing you to build custom integrations that meet your team's unique requirements. For example, if you need to connect Salesforce with Asana for task automation based on customer data, a custom API solution can ensure seamless communication between these platforms.

Custom APIs allow for deeper and more precise integrations, especially for organizations with complex or highly specialized workflows. While they require a bit more technical expertise, the payoff is significant because you can tailor the AI integration to meet specific project demands, resulting in enhanced efficiency and a smoother overall process.

TIP

If your team has complex workflows, consider using custom APIs for AI integration. While they require technical expertise to create, custom APIs offer precise, tailored solutions that can significantly enhance efficiency and streamline your processes.

Automating routine communication with AI

AI can do more than just optimize workflows — it can also significantly enhance team collaboration by automating communication, ensuring that everyone stays aligned and informed throughout a project's lifecycle. AI-powered chatbots and virtual assistants integrated into your communication tools can handle routine tasks, such as scheduling meetings, answering FAQs, and providing real-time status updates. These AI tools can improve communication efficiency and collaboration within both small teams and large, distributed organizations.

AI-powered chatbots can be integrated into tools like Slack, Microsoft Teams, or Zoom to streamline team interactions. These bots act as virtual assistants, managing common requests and administrative tasks, such as setting up meetings, sending reminders, or delivering progress updates. For example, if your team uses Slack, an AI chatbot can schedule a meeting based on the availability of key team members, send reminders for upcoming deadlines, and even provide automated responses to frequently asked questions (FAQs) about the project.

By automating these routine interactions, chatbots can drastically reduce the back-and-forth communication that often slows down team efficiency. Instead of spending time on administrative tasks or chasing after team members for updates, you can rely on AI to ensure these tasks are handled in real time with minimal manual intervention.

Scheduling and managing meetings can often take up significant time, especially in remote or distributed teams. AI tools integrated with platforms like Zoom or Microsoft Teams can automate many aspects of meeting management. For example, AI can analyze calendar availability, suggest optimal meeting times, and even send out automated invites and reminders to participants.

Beyond scheduling, AI-powered transcription services can capture and transcribe entire meetings in real time, ensuring that key discussions, action items, and decisions are accurately recorded and easily accessible for later review. These transcription tools, discussed in Chapter 4, use speech recognition and natural language processing (NLP) to generate searchable, structured transcripts, allowing team members to quickly reference important points without replaying entire meetings. By reducing administrative burdens and improving documentation, AI-driven meeting management tools enhance collaboration and ensure nothing gets lost in communication.

By reducing the time spent organizing meetings and capturing notes, AI ensures that teams spend more time focused on collaboration and problem-solving rather than logistical details. AI meeting assistants can also provide real-time summaries of meetings, action items, and follow-ups, ensuring nothing gets lost in communication.

In project management, timely communication is critical to ensure that tasks are progressing as planned and that everyone stays aligned. AI tools integrated with project management platforms can automatically provide real-time status updates to team members without needing manual input. For instance, when a task in Asana or Trello is completed, an AI assistant can automatically send a notification to the project's Slack or Microsoft Teams channel, informing everyone of the progress. This automation helps to keep all stakeholders in the loop, ensuring that projects move forward smoothly without miscommunication or delays.

AI tools like Intercom and Drift are designed to handle both team and customer communication efficiently. These tools can be integrated into your project management ecosystem to provide continuous, real-time updates to both internal teams and external stakeholders, such as clients or vendors. By doing so, AI ensures that key information is shared as soon as it's available, reducing the chances of delays due to miscommunication.

Enhancing collaboration in remote and cross-functional teams

In today's global business environment, many organizations operate with remote or distributed teams spread across different time zones. This can lead to challenges in maintaining consistent communication, especially when teams are located in different parts of the world. AI-powered communication tools can help bridge this gap by facilitating asynchronous communication. For example, AI assistants can send out updates and notifications even when certain team members are offline, ensuring that no one misses critical information when they return to work.

For large remote teams or multistakeholder projects, AI communication tools can help to centralize project discussions and status updates, allowing everyone to access important information in one place. By reducing the need for real-time coordination, AI ensures that work continues to flow efficiently, even when team members don't work on synchronous schedules.

In complex projects involving multiple teams from different departments or functional areas, AI tools can serve as a bridge, facilitating smoother cross-functional collaboration. By integrating AI tools into existing communication platforms like Slack or Microsoft Teams, different departments can receive tailored updates or notifications relevant to their specific tasks. For example, marketing, engineering, and design teams may all be working on different parts of the same project. AI tools can help ensure that updates, changes, and decisions made by one department are automatically communicated to the relevant teams, helping everyone stay aligned.

This automation reduces the likelihood of information being siloed within one team and enhances transparency and coordination across the project, leading to a more unified approach.

REMEMBER

AI tools can facilitate cross-functional collaboration in complex projects by automatically communicating updates and decisions between departments through platforms like Slack or Microsoft Teams, ensuring alignment and reducing information silos.

Reducing delays and improving information flow

One of the most significant benefits of AI-powered communication tools in project management is the reduction of delays caused by miscommunication. Traditional communication methods often rely on individuals to manually send updates, follow-ups, or notifications, which can be time-consuming and prone to error. AI tools can automate these communication tasks, ensuring that all relevant parties are notified instantly when a milestone is reached or a task is completed.

Additionally, by using AI tools to automate FAQs or respond to routine inquiries, you can reduce the time spent answering the same questions repeatedly. AI chatbots can ensure that teams have access to the information they need, when they need it, reducing the chance of miscommunication and keeping projects on track.

Automating data analysis and reporting

One of the most powerful applications of AI in project management is in the automation of data analysis and reporting. Rather than relying on manual data collection and report generation, AI can continuously analyze project data in real time, providing valuable insights and automatically generating reports tailored to different stakeholders. By leveraging AI-powered analytics tools such as Power BI, Tableau, and Google Data Studio, you can gain a deeper understanding of the project's status and performance without the time-consuming process of compiling information manually.

AI tools have the unique ability to analyze project data in real time, giving you a continuous, up-to-date view of key metrics such as task completion rates, resource utilization, budget adherence, and risk factors. Instead of waiting for periodic updates, AI can track changes as they happen, providing immediate feedback on project health. For instance, if certain tasks are falling behind or resources are being overallocated, AI-powered analytics tools can highlight these issues in real time, enabling you to make timely adjustments and prevent bottlenecks before they escalate.

Real-time analysis ensures that decision-makers have access to the most current information, empowering them to react swiftly to challenges and seize opportunities that might otherwise go unnoticed in traditional reporting cycles. This capability is especially valuable in complex or fast-moving projects where rapid decision-making is critical to maintaining momentum.

Centralizing data from multiple sources

One of the greatest strengths of AI in data analysis is its ability to pull and consolidate data from multiple sources. Project managers typically work with a variety of tools for different aspects of project management, such as task tracking (Trello, Asana), budgeting (QuickBooks, Excel), resource management (Mavenlink, Smartsheet), and risk tracking (Jira). Manually gathering data from each of these systems can be a time-consuming and error-prone process, not to mention laborious.

AI-powered analytics tools can automatically pull data from these disparate systems into a centralized platform. For example, Power BI and Tableau can connect with multiple project management platforms to aggregate data related to task progress, budget performance, team utilization, and other key performance indicators (KPIs) into a single dashboard. This comprehensive view allows project managers to have a holistic understanding of the project's status without needing to toggle between different systems.

Once AI tools collect and analyze the data, they can automatically generate visually rich dashboards tailored for different stakeholders. These dashboards not only display project metrics in an easy to-understand format but can also be customized for the needs of each stakeholder. For instance, a project sponsor might need high-level information about timelines, budget, and overall progress, whereas team leads may require more detailed reports about resource allocation, task completion rates, and potential risks.

Reports are also not a one-size-fits-all solution. Many AI analytics tools allow reports to be highly customized, providing different views and insights based on the needs of various teams within the organization.

For example, a finance team might need detailed breakdowns of project spending, cost projections, and budget adherence, while the operations team may focus on task progress, resource allocation, and team performance. With customizable dashboards and reports, each team can focus on the data that matters most to them, improving overall project efficiency. By visualizing data through intuitive charts, graphs, and heat maps, AI analytics tools like Google Data Studio make it easier for stakeholders to grasp complex data trends and insights. This improves transparency and keeps all stakeholders informed, ensuring alignment across teams and reducing the chances of miscommunication or delays caused by lack of information. Additionally, these tools can be set to automatically refresh data at regular intervals or on-demand, ensuring that stakeholders always have access to the most up-to-date information without needing to request manual updates.

Automating reports and forecasting project risks

In addition to reporting on current project status, AI tools can play a significant role in risk management and forecasting. By analyzing historical data and current project conditions, AI can predict potential risks and bottlenecks before they occur. For example, if previous projects showed that a certain type of task often causes delays, the AI tool can flag similar tasks in the current project, prompting you to allocate additional resources or adjust deadlines to mitigate the risk.

AI can also forecast future project performance based on current trends. If the project is ahead or behind schedule, AI can project whether it will finish on time or over budget, allowing you to take corrective action proactively. These predictive insights help teams manage uncertainties more effectively, leading to better project outcomes.

AI's automation capabilities also help reduce the risk of human error in reporting. Manual data entry and reporting can lead to inconsistencies, especially in complex projects with multiple data sources. By automating data collection, analysis, and reporting, AI minimizes the risk of errors that could arise from manual processes. This ensures that stakeholders receive accurate, reliable, and consistent information, contributing to better-informed decisions throughout the project lifecycle.

Moreover, automated reporting can be scheduled to occur at regular intervals, ensuring that stakeholders always receive timely updates without having to manually request reports. This not only reduces the workload for project managers but also increases accountability, as stakeholders can be confident that the information they are receiving is both up-to-date and accurate.

The integration of AI-powered analytics tools with project management software frees up project managers from the tedious task of manually compiling reports, allowing you to focus on higher-level strategic decision-making. Instead of spending hours pulling together data and formatting reports, you can spend your time analyzing the insights generated by AI and using those insights to drive project success.

For example, rather than compiling task completion data manually, you can review AI-generated reports that highlight areas where the team is excelling or where bottlenecks are occurring. This allows you to address challenges more quickly and effectively, leading to smoother project execution and better outcomes.

REMEMBER

AI-powered analytics tools can automate real-time data analysis and reporting, consolidating information from multiple sources into customizable dashboards, allowing project managers to focus on strategic decision-making while ensuring stakeholders receive accurate and timely updates.

Streamlining routine tasks with workflow automation

Workflow automation is one of the most effective ways to integrate AI with your project management tools, enabling teams to automate repetitive tasks and reduce manual effort. AI-powered automation can significantly enhance project efficiency by ensuring that routine tasks are completed automatically and on time, without requiring constant oversight from team members. This allows you to focus on higher-level strategy and problem-solving while leaving mundane tasks to AI.

With tools like Zapier, Make, and Automate.io, you can create sophisticated automated workflows that connect different tools, applications, and systems across your organization. For instance, Zapier enables workflows, or "Zaps," that can integrate hundreds of apps. If a task is completed in Asana, a notification can be sent automatically to your team's Slack channel, keeping everyone up to date without manual input. Similarly, when a document is approved in Google Drive, a task can be automatically created in Trello for the next team member to review, ensuring that your project moves forward without delays.

Here are some ways routine tasks can be automated:

>> **Automating approval processes:** AI can streamline approval workflows by automating the routing of documents, tasks, or decisions to the appropriate team members. For example, when a document reaches the review stage, AI can ensure that it's automatically forwarded to the correct approver, and, once approved, it can trigger the next step in the process, such as sending the document to the legal team or initiating the next phase of development. This eliminates the need for manual oversight and follow-ups, reducing bottle-necks in the approval process and ensuring that projects stay on schedule.

>> **Automating reminders and deadlines:** One of the most common uses of workflow automation is for automating reminders and managing deadlines. AI-powered tools like Microsoft Power Automate, Monday.com, or Trello can send automated reminders to team members when tasks are approaching their deadlines. These tools can track task progress in real time and send notifications to individuals or teams when tasks are behind schedule, helping to ensure accountability and reducing the chances of missed deadlines. For example, AI can automatically remind a team member of an upcoming deadline or trigger a notification if a task hasn't been updated in a certain amount of time.

>> **Tracking task status across multiple platforms:** AI can also play a vital role in tracking task status across multiple platforms, which is especially valuable in teams using a variety of project management and communication tools. For instance, AI-driven platforms like Wrike and ClickUp can consolidate data from different project management systems and provide real-time updates on the status of tasks. This allows you to monitor project progress without needing to manually check multiple systems. By aggregating data and automating status updates, AI helps prevent duplication of work and keeps everyone aligned with the project timeline.

>> **Reducing human error and enhancing workflow consistency:** Automating routine workflows with AI reduces the risk of human error, particularly in tasks that are repetitive and prone to mistakes, such as data entry or manu-ally transferring information between tools. By eliminating the need for human intervention in these areas, AI ensures greater accuracy and

consistency. For example, automating a workflow that moves data from a form submission in Google Forms to a spreadsheet in Google Sheets ensures that no data is missed or entered incorrectly. Additionally, automating routine tasks establishes standardized processes that can be applied consistently across projects, improving overall workflow reliability.

>> **Integrating multiple platforms for seamless workflow automation:** AI-driven workflow automation is particularly powerful when integrating multiple platforms. Tools like Zapier and Make provide an extensive library of integrations, enabling teams to automate workflows across software suites like Google Workspace, Microsoft 365, Salesforce, and many others. For instance, when a customer submits a form through Typeform, AI can automatically create a task in Asana, send an acknowledgment email through Gmail, and log the details in a Salesforce CRM record. No manual input required!

By automating these connections, teams can reduce the need for constant switching between platforms and systems, saving time and improving overall efficiency. This integration not only enhances productivity but also improves collaboration by ensuring that relevant stakeholders are kept in the loop with real-time updates from connected platforms.

REMEMBER

AI-powered workflow automation can significantly enhance efficiency by automatically completing routine tasks like approvals, reminders, and status tracking across multiple platforms. This allows teams to focus on high-value activities, reduces manual oversight, and ensures tasks are completed on time.

HOW TANINA USED AI TO AUTOMATE TASKS AND WORKFLOWS

Tanina, a project manager at a mid-sized software company, was tasked with overseeing a critical software development project. The project involved multiple teams — developers, designers, and testers — working in different time zones. With tight deadlines, numerous tasks, and a need for seamless collaboration, Tanina quickly realized that manually managing workflows, tracking progress, and generating reports would consume a significant amount of her time. She needed a solution to streamline these repetitive tasks and ensure the project stayed on track.

Initially, Tanina was managing the project using standard project management tools like Asana for task tracking and Slack for communication. However, she found herself spending hours on manual tasks such as

- Assigning tasks to team members based on availability.

- Sending follow-up reminders to ensure deadlines were met.

- Generating weekly progress reports for stakeholders.

- Tracking time spent on tasks to ensure the project stayed within budget.

As the project progressed, it became clear that manual management was leading to inefficiencies. Tasks were occasionally overlooked, deadlines were missed due to miscommunication, and Tanina found herself spending more time on administrative work than on higher-level project strategy.

To address these challenges, Tanina decided to integrate AI tools into her existing project management workflow. After researching various options, she implemented several AI-powered tools to automate routine tasks and optimize workflows:

- **Zapier:** Tanina used Zapier to automate task assignments and follow-up reminders. For example, whenever a task was marked complete in Asana, Zapier automatically created a new task in Trello for the next team member in the workflow. It also sent reminders through Slack as deadlines approached, ensuring team members stayed on schedule without Tanina needing to chase them.

- **ClickUp:** Tanina integrated ClickUp's AI-powered task assignment features. The AI analyzed team members' availability, current workload, and past performance to assign tasks to the most suitable team members. This eliminated the manual process of task allocation and ensured that no one on the team was overloaded.

- **Power BI:** For data analysis and reporting, Tanina adopted Power BI, an AI-driven analytics tool. Power BI automatically pulled data from Asana and Google Sheets, creating dynamic dashboards that provided real-time project progress, resource allocation, and budget tracking. These reports were shared with stakeholders weekly without Tanina needing to manually compile them.

- **Toggl:** To track the time spent on tasks, Tanina introduced Toggl, which used AI to automatically log the time team members spent on different tasks. This ensured accurate billing and helped Tanina monitor productivity without requiring team members to log their hours manually.

By integrating these AI tools, Tanina saw immediate improvements in the project's efficiency:

- **Reduced administrative work:** Tanina was able to cut down the time spent on manual task assignments and follow-ups.

(continued)

(continued)

- **Improved task management:** The AI-driven task assignment tool in ClickUp ensured that tasks were distributed based on each team member's skills and availability, leading to faster completion times and better workload balance.

- **Automated reporting:** Power BI's real-time dashboards provided stakeholders with up-to-date project reports that improved stakeholder satisfaction and allowed for better decision-making.

- **Accurate time tracking:** Toggl's automatic time-tracking feature eliminated manual timesheets, ensuring accurate tracking of hours for billing and helping Tanina keep the project within budget.

- **Enhanced collaboration:** With Zapier automating the flow of tasks between Asana, Trello, and Slack, team members were always up to date with their next steps, and miscommunications were minimized.

By using AI tools to automate repetitive tasks and workflows, Tanina was able to streamline the management of her software development project. The automation not only reduced her administrative burden but also improved team collaboration, task management, and stakeholder communication. With AI handling routine tasks like reminders, task assignments, and reporting, Tanina could focus on higher-level project goals, ensuring the project was completed on time and within budget. This case highlights how AI can transform project management by enhancing productivity and efficiency.

Monitoring and optimizing AI integration

Once AI is integrated into your project management tools, it's critical to monitor its impact on your workflows and productivity. Regularly evaluate how well the AI tools are enhancing your processes and be prepared to adjust if necessary. AI is not a one-size-fits-all solution, and its effectiveness may vary depending on the specific needs of your team and project.

Most AI tools provide usage reports, which can offer valuable insights into how they are being used and whether they are delivering the expected benefits. By analyzing this data, you can determine whether AI is improving task allocation, optimizing resource use, and enhancing communication. If certain features aren't adding value, consider adjusting the settings or even exploring different tools that better meet your evolving project requirements.

For example, if AI-powered task assignment in Jira is not as effective as expected, you can adjust the algorithm's inputs or integrate additional tools to further refine the results. Regular monitoring and optimization of AI usage will help ensure you are consistently reaping the maximum benefits from your AI integrations.

By integrating AI with your existing project management tools, you can unlock higher levels of efficiency, collaboration, and decision-making without overhauling your current system. Whether you're automating routine tasks, optimizing workflows, or improving communication, AI integration can empower your team to work smarter, faster, and more effectively, ensuring project success.

REMEMBER

AI integration is not a one-size-fits-all solution. Regularly monitor its impact on your workflows, adjust settings as needed, and ensure the AI tools are delivering value based on the specific needs of your team and project.

IN THIS CHAPTER

» Using predictive analytics to forecast timelines and anticipate risks

» Turning data into insights for decision-making

» Simulating scenarios to prepare for challenges

» Optimizing resource allocation

» Enhancing communication with AI-driven dashboards

Chapter **6**

Making Data-Driven Decisions with AI

Data-driven decision-making is a critical element of modern project management. In today's fast-paced, complex environments, relying solely on intuition or historical approaches is no longer sufficient to manage projects efficiently. With the vast amount of data available, project managers are now expected to make informed decisions based on real-time insights. AI plays a key role in this transformation by providing the ability to analyze vast datasets, predict future outcomes, and identify potential risks long before they escalate. By incorporating AI into their toolkit, project managers can leverage its power to optimize resource allocation, anticipate bottlenecks, and streamline processes, ensuring that projects stay on track and within scope.

The capabilities of AI extend beyond simple data analysis. Through predictive analytics, project managers can forecast timelines, resource needs, and potential risks with greater accuracy. AI also supports scenario planning and forecasting, allowing teams to simulate different project outcomes and make contingency plans for a variety of challenges. By integrating AI into your decision-making process, you can confidently navigate uncertainties, improve overall project outcomes, and make more strategic, informed decisions. This chapter explores the practical ways in which you can use AI to enhance your project management efforts, enabling you to tackle even the most complex projects with greater precision and foresight.

Using AI for Predictive Analytics in Project Management

Predictive analytics is one of the most powerful applications of AI in project management. By analyzing historical data and identifying patterns, AI can predict future outcomes, enabling you to make proactive decisions that improve the likelihood of success. Rather than relying solely on experience or intuition, AI provides a data-driven foundation that enhances accuracy and foresight. With predictive analytics, you can not only forecast what might happen during a project but also take actionable steps to ensure things go according to plan. Whether you're dealing with complex projects or simply want to ensure your team works efficiently, predictive analytics allows you to stay one step ahead.

At its core, predictive analytics uses AI to analyze past project data, identify trends, and forecast potential outcomes. AI looks for patterns in historical projects, allowing it to predict critical aspects such as timelines, resource needs, and risks. For instance, AI can analyze data from previous projects to estimate how long a similar project will take or whether certain team members may face challenges with their tasks. It can even predict the likelihood of budget overruns based on past performance. This predictive power helps you plan more accurately and create contingencies for potential risks that might otherwise be missed.

TIP

AI tools can help forecast resource availability and simulate scenarios, ensuring you assign the right resources to the right tasks without causing burnout.

Tools like Microsoft Project with AI Insights and Smartsheet use data from past projects to help estimate timelines and resource needs, ensuring that your project starts on the right foot. AI can provide detailed insights into whether your project is likely to stay on track or encounter delays, and what resources might be needed at various stages to prevent those delays.

A major advantage of AI-powered predictive analytics is its ability to identify risks early in the project lifecycle. Instead of reacting to problems as they occur, AI helps you take proactive measures by flagging potential issues before they arise. AI can analyze past project data to highlight common risks, such as delays caused by supply chain disruptions or budget overruns due to unforeseen expenses. Tools like RiskLens and Oracle Primavera take this a step further by not only forecasting risks but also suggesting mitigation strategies. This allows you to be more prepared and respond swiftly to potential challenges, minimizing the impact on the project's success. Check out Chapter 9 for more on using predictive analytics to anticipate risks.

To address resource allocation, AI tools analyze past performance data to forecast when certain team members or resources will become available, which enables you to assign tasks more efficiently. For instance, AI can predict if a team member will be free for a task in the near future or if additional resources might be needed to complete a job without causing delays. Tools like Wrike and Asana use these predictions to optimize workload distribution and ensure that your team operates at maximum efficiency, without risking burnout or underutilization. This not only keeps your project moving forward smoothly but also prevents issues such as overburdening key team members or facing unexpected shortages in resources. Chapter 8 covers how AI can assist in mapping dependencies and resource allocation.

REMEMBER

Using AI-powered predictive analytics from the beginning of a project allows you to forecast potential risks, timelines, and resources, ensuring you can proactively manage your projects from the outset.

Making Informed Decisions with AI-Powered Insights

In today's data-rich environment, making informed decisions requires more than just intuition. It demands actionable insights derived from data. AI-powered tools can analyze vast amounts of data and provide insights that help you make smarter, more informed decisions. This section explains how AI can support data-driven decision-making in your projects.

AI-powered tools can process large datasets about project performance data, team productivity, or resource utilization and identify patterns and trends that might not be immediately apparent to human project managers. A human data analyst may be able to accomplish this same task, but it would take significantly longer than the time it takes the AI-powered tool.

REMEMBER

Although AI provides valuable data-driven insights, it's important to combine them with human expertise to make well-rounded decisions. Here's an example: AI can analyze project data to identify which tasks are consistently causing delays, which team members are underperforming, or which resources are being underutilized. Then you can take these insights to make informed decisions about how to improve efficiency in task execution, work with team members to improve performance, and reallocate resources to improve the project outcome.

One of the key advantages of AI is its ability to provide real-time insights so you can make decisions quickly and confidently with less delay in the project. Tools like Smartsheet and Monday.com offer AI-driven real-time reporting, providing project managers with up-to-date information that supports timely decision-making.

AI's ability to analyze data more accurately and thoroughly than humans ensures that your decisions are based on solid evidence rather than assumptions. For example, AI can analyze project financial data to predict budget overruns or assess team performance data to recommend reallocating tasks for maximum efficiency. Without AI, a human project manager would need to manually review spreadsheets, compare historical budgets, and analyze resource utilization reports — a process that could take hours or even days. In contrast, AI can process vast amounts of data instantly, providing insights that allow project managers to take corrective action before issues escalate, rather than reacting after delays or cost overruns have already occurred.

Tools like Power BI and Tableau provide AI-powered analytics that deliver precise, data-driven insights, helping you make decisions that are backed by reliable data.

WARNING AI is only as good as the data it processes, so ensure your datasets are clean, accurate, and up to date to avoid flawed insights or predictions.

Supporting Scenario Planning and Forecasting with AI

Scenario planning and forecasting are essential for managing uncertainty in project management. AI can enhance these processes by simulating different scenarios, predicting potential outcomes, and helping you prepare for a range of possibilities. Here's how AI can support scenario planning and forecasting in your projects.

AI tools can create "what-if" scenarios that simulate different project outcomes based on various inputs and variables. For example, you can use AI to model what would happen if a key team member is unavailable, if a supplier experiences a delay, or if your budget is cut by 10 percent. These scenarios allow you to plan for contingencies and make more informed decisions about how to respond to potential challenges.

Tools like Oracle Primavera and RiskLens offer AI-powered scenario planning features that allow you to simulate different project outcomes and prepare for various contingencies.

Tools like Microsoft Project with AI Insights and Smartsheet use AI to generate accurate forecasts that help you plan more effectively and stay ahead of potential challenges.

Tools like Wrike and Asana use AI to simulate resource allocation scenarios, helping you make informed decisions about how to distribute resources most effectively. AI can help you simulate different resource allocation scenarios to anticipate bottlenecks, balance workloads, and optimize efficiency. For example, if you're managing a construction project, AI-powered simulations can predict how reallocating workers from one phase (such as site preparation) to another (like structural assembly) would impact the overall timeline. If a material shortage causes a delay, AI can model alternative scheduling options, such as resequencing tasks or bringing in additional subcontractors, to keep the project moving. By using these simulations, you can make data-driven adjustments in real time, ensuring that you maximize efficiency, minimize delays, and stay within budget.

AI-powered simulation modeling is useful for more than construction projects; it can help you optimize resources and timelines across various industries. If you're managing a software development project, AI can simulate the impact of shifting developers between feature development and bug fixes, helping you maintain a balance between innovation and stability. In a marketing campaign, AI can model different budget allocation strategies, predicting which channels — such as social media, email marketing, or paid ads — will yield the highest return on investment based on real-time performance data. For event planning, AI can analyze factors like venue availability, vendor scheduling, and attendee registration trends to suggest the most efficient timeline and resource allocation. No matter the industry, AI-powered simulations allow you to test different strategies before making decisions, reducing risk and improving overall project outcomes.

AI can also help you prepare for external factors that could impact the project, such as market changes, supply chain disruptions, or regulatory shifts. Rather than purely speculating, AI-driven simulation tools use actual data — such as economic indicators, supplier performance metrics, weather forecasts, or industry regulations — to predict how these external factors might influence your project. For example, if you input current supply chain data, AI can model the potential impact of delayed shipments, fluctuating material costs, or supplier failures, allowing you to identify alternative suppliers or adjust your project timeline proactively. Similarly, for regulatory changes, AI can analyze past compliance data and new policy updates to estimate the costs and time required to adapt to new requirements. By integrating historical and up-to-date data into these simulations, AI provides data-backed insights rather than guesses, helping you develop contingency plans that keep your project on track even when faced with uncertainty.

Tools like RiskLens and Oracle Primavera offer AI-driven scenario planning that accounts for external factors, helping you prepare for a wide range of possibilities and ensuring that your project remains on track.

TIP

Run multiple what-if analyses so you can identify the most efficient resource allocation and be better prepared for external disruptions, such as supply chain issues or regulatory changes. The speed at which AI is able to evaluate situations means you don't have to limit yourself to evaluating only one contingency plan. You can examine several scenarios.

REMEMBER

By supporting scenario planning and forecasting with AI, you can navigate uncertainty more effectively than you would without the assistance of these tools. You can ensure that your project is prepared for any challenges that arise. AI-powered scenario planning and forecasting tools provide the insights you need to make informed decisions, optimize resource allocation, and stay ahead of potential risks.

USING AI TO MANAGE SUPPLY CHAIN RISKS IN A LARGE CONSTRUCTION PROJECT

A project management team overseeing a large-scale construction project faced significant challenges in managing supply chain risks, controlling costs, and ensuring timely material availability. The project required importing wood from Canada, cement from Mexico, steel from India, and electrical components from China, making it highly vulnerable to trade policy changes and international market fluctuations. Concerns over a potential trade war raised the possibility of sudden tariff increases on imported materials, which could severely impact the project budget and schedule.

To address these uncertainties, the project manager leveraged AI-driven simulation tools to assess the potential impact of different trade scenarios and develop proactive risk mitigation strategies. The AI system analyzed historical trade policies, economic indicators, and geopolitical trends to predict the likelihood of tariffs being imposed. Using scenario planning, the AI modeled multiple possible futures, such as the following:

- **No tariffs:** The project proceeds as planned with stable material costs.

- **Partial tariffs:** Tariffs increase on certain materials (for example, steel and electrical components), requiring budget adjustments.

- **Full tariffs:** All imported materials become significantly more expensive, forcing a complete reevaluation of suppliers and budget allocations.

For each scenario, the AI evaluated cost impacts, alternative sourcing options, and timeline adjustments. If tariffs on steel from India became too high, the AI suggested potential domestic or alternative international suppliers. If electrical components from China were affected, the AI identified vendors in countries with lower trade barriers or recommended prefabrication strategies to reduce dependency on imports.

In addition to cost modeling, AI-powered supply chain risk-assessment tools monitored real-time trade policy updates, currency fluctuations, and supplier reliability metrics. This allowed the project team to receive instant alerts if geopolitical risks escalated, enabling rapid decision-making to adjust procurement strategies before financial impacts became critical.

By integrating AI-driven scenario planning, cost modeling, and supply chain analytics, the project team minimized financial uncertainty and maintained control over procurement risks. As a result, they were able to proactively adjust contracts, explore alternative suppliers, and create contingency budgets, ensuring that the project remained on schedule and within budget despite potential trade disruptions. This case highlights how AI can empower project managers to navigate global supply chain risks with data-driven insights, reducing the impact of unforeseen geopolitical changes.

Optimizing Team Performance and Workflows with AI

AI optimizes team performance and workflow management by analyzing multiple data sources to determine the best way to allocate tasks efficiently. Instead of manually assessing availability and workload, AI-powered project management tools like Asana, Monday.com, or Wrike integrate with calendars, time-tracking software, and performance management systems to make data-driven decisions.

AI considers several key data points to optimize task delegation:

>> **Availability and capacity:** AI pulls calendar data (from Google Calendar, Outlook, or internal scheduling tools) to see if a team member is available or already scheduled for meetings, vacations, or personal leave.

>> **Workload and current assignments:** AI integrates with task-tracking systems (Jira, Trello, or Wrike) to analyze how many tasks each team member is handling and whether they are nearing capacity.

>> **Productivity and performance statistics:** AI may reference historical performance metrics from time-tracking apps (Toggl, Clockify) or internal analytics tools to identify who completes tasks efficiently and which team members may need additional support.

>> **Skills and expertise:** AI pulls from HR databases or project history to match tasks with individuals who have the right expertise (for example, assigning a complex coding task to a senior developer rather than a junior one).

>> **Deadlines and priorities:** AI can synchronize task dependencies and due dates to ensure that critical milestones are met before assigning lower-priority work.

TIP

For AI to effectively manage task allocation, it often needs to interface with project management tools, calendar and scheduling tools, time-tracking and productivity apps, and HR systems and employee databases.

By combining these data sources, AI-powered automation ensures that task assignments are not only balanced but also optimized to match skills and deadlines, reducing bottlenecks, burnout, and inefficiencies. This allows you to focus on strategic leadership rather than constantly managing workloads.

AI can provide insights into your team's performance by pulling data from various project management and productivity tools, helping you identify potential issues before they cause delays. Instead of waiting until a task falls behind schedule, AI can monitor task completion rates, individual progress, and time spent on specific activities to detect early warning signs of bottlenecks. Team members typically track their progress by updating their task status in project management apps like Asana, Monday.com, Wrike, or Jira, marking tasks as In Progress, Blocked, or Completed. Additionally, some organizations use time-tracking tools like Toggl, Clockify, or RescueTime, where employees either manually log hours or allow software to track time automatically. AI can analyze this information to compare actual time spent on tasks with estimated durations, helping you understand where slowdowns may be occurring.

Beyond tracking task progress, AI can also integrate with collaboration and communication tools like Slack or Microsoft Teams, analyzing team discussions and meeting logs to identify potential delays due to unclear requirements or dependencies. In software development projects, issue tracking systems like Jira or Trello can provide further insights by flagging recurring blockers or high-risk tasks that frequently cause slowdowns. By combining data from these different sources, AI can generate proactive alerts when a task or team member is falling behind, enabling you to reassign work, adjust timelines, or allocate additional resources before minor setbacks escalate into major project delays. This data-driven approach helps teams stay on track and reduces the need for last-minute crisis management.

AI's ability to track and analyze performance also makes it easier to spot inefficiencies. For instance, if a certain process is slowing your team down, AI can suggest improvements, such as automating repetitive tasks or reallocating resources to team members who have more capacity. This level of optimization ensures that your team is always working at peak performance, and it gives you the confidence that you're making decisions based on real-time data, not just gut instinct.

REMEMBER

By leveraging AI, you're not just improving your team's day-to-day efficiency. You're ensuring that every member is contributing their best and that the project is moving smoothly toward its goals. It's about working smarter, not harder, and using the best tools available to ensure your projects succeed.

Automating Project Reporting with AI

Creating and distributing project reports is a vital task for project managers, but it often consumes a significant amount of time and effort when done manually. Gathering data from multiple sources, formatting it correctly, and ensuring all stakeholders receive accurate updates can take hours. It's also very prone to human error.

Fortunately, AI can streamline this process by automating project reporting. AI-powered tools pull up-to-date data from project management platforms such as Asana, Jira, or Microsoft Project and automatically generate comprehensive reports. These reports provide key insights into progress, resource allocation, budget utilization, and risk management, giving you a complete and accurate overview at all times. The efficiency of AI reporting tools means that you can run multiple reports per day if needed, providing frequent updates when a project is at a critical stage. This ensures that decision-makers have continuous access to the latest project insights, allowing for faster response times and better-informed decisions.

For example, imagine a healthcare organization launching a new hospital wing. The project involves coordinating medical equipment procurement, staffing schedules, regulatory approvals, and construction timelines. As the opening date approaches, the project manager needs frequent updates to ensure that beds, diagnostic machines, and surgical tools arrive on time; staffing levels align with operational needs; and final safety inspections are completed as scheduled. With AI-powered project reporting, the system can automatically pull data from procurement software, HR scheduling systems, and compliance tracking tools, generating multiple reports per day that highlight potential bottlenecks. If a shipment of MRI machines is delayed or a critical certification is still pending, the AI alerts the project manager immediately, allowing you to escalate issues, adjust staffing plans, or prioritize alternative suppliers before the delay impacts the grand opening. This real-time visibility ensures that decision-makers can quickly address challenges, keep stakeholders informed, and maintain project momentum.

In addition to saving time, AI-driven reporting allows for a high level of customization. Reports can be tailored to specific stakeholder needs. Executives may need a high-level summary of timelines and budgets, whereas team leads require more detailed insights into task progress and resource distribution. AI handles these nuances effortlessly, eliminating the need for manual formatting and content adjustments.

Reports can also be scheduled to be sent automatically at regular intervals or triggered by important project milestones, ensuring stakeholders receive timely updates. With AI automating the reporting process, you can eliminate errors, enhance the quality of communication, and deliver critical information faster. This automation not only increases efficiency but ensures everyone involved has access to the most relevant and accurate data, leading to better decision-making across the board.

Communicating with stakeholders is essential to keeping a project on track, but the manual process of gathering data, preparing reports, and distributing updates can be both time-consuming and inefficient. AI has the power to transform this aspect of project management by automating the creation and distribution of real-time reports, dashboards, and status updates. By integrating AI-powered tools like Power BI and Tableau into your project management workflow, you can ensure that stakeholders always have access to the most current data. These tools pull data from various project platforms, providing a comprehensive view of the project's performance, risks, timelines, and overall progress. This automation removes the need for constant manual updates, significantly reducing the time you spend on communication tasks while improving the accuracy of the information being shared.

Another major benefit of AI-enhanced stakeholder communication is the ability to create dynamic, visual dashboards that provide stakeholders with a real-time interface for monitoring project key performance indicators (KPIs). Stakeholders no longer need to rely on static reports or sift through spreadsheets; AI-generated dashboards offer an intuitive way to see project performance at a glance. These dashboards can be customized to highlight the most important metrics for each stakeholder group, ensuring that everyone — from the finance team tracking budget to department heads monitoring resource utilization — receives the insights they need. This level of transparency not only builds trust but allows for more proactive decision-making because stakeholders can identify potential issues early and collaborate on solutions before they escalate. By using AI to automate and enhance communication, you can ensure smoother project execution, reduce miscommunication, and keep all parties aligned with the project's goals.

Tools like ClickUp and Wrike offer AI-driven reporting and dashboards that can be shared with stakeholders, ensuring that everyone has access to the same data and insights.

Chapter **7**

Enhancing Collaboration with AI Tools

As AI continues to reshape the workplace, its role in enhancing collaboration is becoming more essential than ever. From streamlining communication and automating task management to optimizing meetings and improving team engagement, AI tools can revolutionize the way you and your team work together. By leveraging AI-powered solutions, you can overcome language barriers, boost productivity, and create smarter workflows tailored to your needs.

However, integrating AI into your collaboration process requires a thoughtful approach — balancing efficiency with ethical considerations, ensuring data privacy, and maintaining human oversight. This chapter explores how AI can enhance teamwork across various dimensions following the COLLABORATE framework to help you implement AI-driven collaboration strategies effectively. Whether you're looking to improve communication, refine project management, or build trust in AI-assisted workflows, this chapter can guide you through the essential steps to harness AI's power for your team's success.

Integrating AI to Strengthen Team Collaboration

AI is revolutionizing teamwork by streamlining communication, automating routine tasks, and enhancing decision-making. In today's digital workplace, where remote and hybrid teams are common, AI helps bridge gaps, optimize workflows, and reduce administrative burdens. By handling repetitive processes and providing real-time insights, AI allows teams to focus on creativity, problem-solving, and strategic work. However, misconceptions — such as fears of job displacement or concerns about AI functioning without oversight — can create resistance. Understanding AI as a collaborative tool rather than a replacement for human input is key to successful adoption.

The COLLABORATE framework (see Figure 7-1) highlights key areas where AI enhances teamwork, from communication and scheduling to project management and ethical considerations. AI-powered tools can facilitate multilingual conversations, automate knowledge sharing, and improve engagement tracking, helping teams stay aligned and productive. Although AI offers significant benefits, organizations must also address challenges like data privacy, ethical AI use, and employee adaptation. By strategically integrating AI, teams can unlock new levels of efficiency, foster collaboration, and create a future-ready workplace.

 C - Clarifying AI's Role in Team Collaboration

 O - Optimizing Communication with AI Chat Tools

 L - Leveraging AI for Global Team Language Translation

 L - Linking AI to Smarter Scheduling and Planning

 A - Automating Task Management with AI

 B - Boosting Productivity with AI-Enhanced Project Management

 O - Organizing Team Knowledge with AI-Powered Information Sharing

 R - Reimagining Meetings with AI-Driven Optimization

 A - Assessing and Improving Team Engagement with AI

 T - Trusting Ethics and Data Privacy in AI Collaboration

 E - Executing AI-Driven Collaboration Strategies

FIGURE 7-1: The COLLABORATE Framework.

Clarifying AI's Role in Team Collaboration

AI is a powerful tool for enhancing teamwork, but it's not a substitute for human collaboration. Instead, AI acts as a facilitator, streamlining processes, improving communication, and automating routine tasks so teams can focus on strategic thinking and creative problem-solving. Although AI can assist with decision-making and workflow management, it still requires human input to provide context, oversight, and critical thinking. Successful AI integration in collaboration is about using technology to *support*, rather than *replace*, human interactions.

There's a key distinction between AI-assisted collaboration and AI-driven collaboration. AI-assisted collaboration enhances human interactions by automating repetitive tasks, summarizing discussions, and offering real-time insights. Think of tools like ChatGPT providing content suggestions or AI-powered scheduling assistants optimizing meeting times. In contrast, AI-driven collaboration relies more heavily on automation, where AI makes recommendations, prioritizes tasks, or even executes decisions with minimal human input. While AI-driven workflows can increase efficiency, they still require human oversight to ensure accuracy and ethical considerations.

One of AI's most valuable roles in teamwork is reducing communication gaps and fostering seamless workflows. AI-powered language translation tools enable global teams to collaborate more effectively across language barriers. Smart email assistants can draft responses, summarize threads, and highlight urgent messages, ensuring that important information doesn't get lost in an overflowing inbox. AI-driven project management platforms use machine learning to prioritize tasks and suggest deadlines based on past work patterns, which helps keep teams aligned and on track.

Real-world examples of AI improving teamwork are already visible across industries. Companies like Microsoft and Google have integrated AI-driven meeting assistants that transcribe conversations, identify action items, and provide summaries, ensuring that key takeaways are captured and followed up on. AI-powered HR tools analyze team engagement and suggest ways to improve collaboration dynamics. Even in creative fields, AI enhances brainstorming by generating content ideas, analyzing trends, and automating routine design tasks, allowing teams to focus on innovation.

By clarifying AI's role in collaboration, organizations can harness its strengths while maintaining the human connections that drive successful teamwork. Rather than seeing AI as a disruptive force, teams should view it as a valuable partner that enhances productivity, bridges communication gaps, and helps create an efficient and inclusive work environment.

Optimizing Communication with AI Chat Tools

Effective communication is the foundation of successful teamwork, and AI-powered chat tools are transforming how teams interact by making conversations more efficient, accessible, and organized. Platforms like Slack with AI, Microsoft Teams AI Copilot, and ChatGPT are enhancing workplace communication by automating responses, summarizing discussions, and facilitating seamless collaboration. These tools reduce the burden of managing large volumes of messages, ensuring that team members stay informed without being overwhelmed by unnecessary notifications.

AI chatbots play a crucial role in answering queries, summarizing conversations, and managing group discussions. In team chat platforms, AI can quickly provide responses to frequently asked questions, eliminating the need for repetitive explanations. AI-powered summarization tools extract key points from long conversations, allowing team members to catch up without sifting through entire chat threads. Additionally, AI can manage group discussions by recognizing action items, tagging relevant participants, and even scheduling follow-ups based on the conversation's context.

A compelling example of AI-driven communication is a company that implemented AI chatbots to streamline internal communication. A global tech firm integrated an AI-powered chatbot within Slack to handle IT support requests. Instead of employees waiting for human assistance, the chatbot provided instant solutions to common technical issues, guided users through troubleshooting steps, and escalated complex cases to human agents only when necessary. This reduced response times, minimized disruptions, and allowed IT staff to focus on higher-priority issues, ultimately improving overall team efficiency.

To maximize the benefits of AI chat tools without overwhelming team members, organizations should follow best practices for AI integration. First, AI should be introduced gradually, allowing employees time to adapt. Teams should customize AI settings to prioritize relevant notifications while filtering out unnecessary alerts. Additionally, AI chatbots should complement — not replace — human communication, ensuring that important discussions still involve human input. Finally, organizations should continuously monitor AI interactions to improve accuracy and maintain trust in automated systems.

Leveraging AI for Global Team Language Translation

TIP

In today's global workforce, you may find yourself collaborating with team members who speak different languages. Overcoming language barriers is essential for fostering inclusivity, improving productivity, and ensuring clear communication across borders. AI-powered translation tools make this easier by providing real-time language support, allowing you and your team to work seamlessly without fluency in multiple languages.

With tools like Google Translate (https://translate.google.com), DeepL (www.deepl.com), and Microsoft Translator (https://translator.microsoft.com/), you can instantly translate emails, chat messages, and documents, ensuring that language differences don't slow down your workflow. Many workplace communication platforms, such as Slack, Microsoft Teams, and Zoom, now integrate AI-driven translation features, enabling you to understand and respond to messages in your preferred language. This means you can collaborate effectively, regardless of where your teammates are located.

One of the most powerful applications of AI translation is real-time multilingual transcription during virtual meetings. AI-powered features in Zoom and Microsoft Teams can transcribe and translate conversations live, allowing everyone to follow along in their native language. This ensures that you and your colleagues can fully participate in discussions without fear of miscommunication. With AI-generated subtitles and summaries, you can stay engaged and aligned, even in multilingual settings.

REMEMBER

However, AI translation tools have their limitations, and it's important to use them wisely. Although AI can translate text quickly, it may struggle with nuances of language, cultural context, and industry-specific terms. Sometimes, a direct translation won't fully capture the intended meaning, and certain phrases may require human interpretation. Additionally, privacy concerns arise when sensitive conversations are processed through third-party AI services. To mitigate these risks, use AI translations as a support tool rather than relying on them entirely — especially for critical communications that require accuracy.

Linking AI to Smarter Scheduling and Planning

Coordinating schedules across teams can be a time-consuming challenge, especially when dealing with multiple time zones, varying workloads, and conflicting priorities. AI-powered scheduling tools can simplify this process by automatically finding the best times for meetings, optimizing workload distribution, and ensuring that planning remains flexible and efficient. By using AI to handle scheduling logistics, you can reduce time spent on back-and-forth coordination and focus on more meaningful work.

Tools like Google Calendar AI (https://workspace.google.com), Microsoft Scheduler (www.microsoft.com/en-us/microsoft-365/scheduler), and Motion (www.usemotion.com) use machine learning to analyze team availability and propose optimal meeting times. Instead of manually checking calendars, these tools consider time zones, existing commitments, and individual preferences to suggest meeting slots that work for everyone. AI assistants can also reschedule meetings dynamically, adjusting for last-minute conflicts and ensuring minimal disruptions to team productivity.

AI also plays a crucial role in balancing workloads and allocating resources. Intelligent planning tools can analyze ongoing projects, deadlines, and task distribution to recommend the best way to assign work across a team. By identifying potential bottlenecks and preventing burnout, AI-driven workload management helps ensure that no single team member is overwhelmed while others remain underutilized.

To maximize AI's effectiveness in scheduling and planning, you must strike the right balance between automation and flexibility. First, configure AI tools with clear team preferences and guidelines to avoid scheduling conflicts. Encourage team members to provide input on their availability so AI-generated schedules can align with real-world needs.

TIP

Maintain human oversight so that AI scheduling remains a supportive tool rather than a rigid system. It should allow for exceptions, last-minute changes, and personalized adjustments when necessary.

Automating Task Management with AI

Managing tasks efficiently is critical to keeping projects on track and ensuring that teams stay productive. AI-powered task management tools help streamline workflows by automatically prioritizing tasks, organizing workloads, and eliminating repetitive administrative work. By leveraging AI, you can reduce time spent on manual task assignments and focus on high-value activities that drive results.

Tools like Asana (`https://asana.com`), Trello AI (`https://trello.com`), and ClickUp AI (`https://clickup.com/ai`) use artificial intelligence to analyze deadlines, task dependencies, and team workload to determine the most efficient way to organize work. AI prioritization ensures that urgent and high-impact tasks are addressed first, while lower-priority items are scheduled accordingly. These platforms also offer smart notifications and task reminders, helping teams stay on top of their responsibilities without constant manual tracking.

AI also plays a key role in automating repetitive administrative tasks. AI-driven task management systems can automatically assign tasks based on team members' roles and workload, generate progress reports, and even suggest deadlines based on past project timelines. This reduces administrative overhead and allows teams to focus on creative problem-solving and strategic planning rather than spending time on routine task coordination.

However, while automation brings efficiency, it's crucial to balance AI automation with human oversight. AI can help streamline workflows, but it lacks human intuition, contextual understanding, and the ability to navigate complex decision-making scenarios. Teams should regularly review AI-generated task assignments to ensure accuracy, adjust based on real-time priorities, and intervene when human judgment is required. Maintaining this balance ensures that AI enhances productivity without introducing inefficiencies or errors.

Boosting Productivity with AI-Enhanced Project Management

Effective project management is essential for keeping teams aligned, meeting deadlines, and ensuring successful outcomes. AI-powered project management tools enhance productivity by providing intelligent tracking, real-time updates, and predictive insights that help teams work more efficiently. By leveraging AI, you can automate routine project tracking, anticipate potential roadblocks, and gain valuable insights that enable proactive decision-making.

AI-driven platforms like `Monday.com` (`https://monday.com`), Jira AI (`www.atlassian.com/software/jira`), and Smartsheet AI (`www.smartsheet.com`) help teams track project milestones and progress with minimal manual effort. These tools automatically update project timelines based on task completion, adjust schedules when dependencies shift, and provide predictive analytics to keep projects on track. Instead of manually following up on deadlines, AI ensures that all stakeholders stay informed through automated alerts and progress reports.

Beyond tracking, AI enhances progress reporting and real-time updates by analyzing team performance and identifying potential delays. AI-powered dashboards generate insightful summaries that highlight key milestones, bottlenecks, and areas requiring attention. Automated status updates eliminate the need for constant check-ins, allowing teams to focus on execution rather than administrative reporting.

AI also plays a crucial role in risk assessment and delay prediction. Machine learning algorithms analyze historical project data, team workloads, and external factors to predict potential setbacks before they happen. For example, if AI detects that a critical task is behind schedule, it can suggest adjustments, reallocate resources, or notify managers about the risk of a missed deadline. This predictive capability helps teams take corrective actions early, reducing project delays and improving overall efficiency.

TIP

One of the best examples of AI-driven project management in action is its impact on agile methodologies. In agile workflows, AI can analyze sprint performance, recommend backlog prioritization, and optimize task distribution among team members. AI tools in platforms like Jira AI and ClickUp AI help agile teams refine their workflows by identifying trends, automating stand-up meeting summaries, and suggesting workflow improvements. By integrating AI into agile project management, teams can iterate faster, make data-driven decisions, and increase overall productivity.

Organizing Team Knowledge with AI-Powered Information Sharing

Efficient knowledge management is essential for team collaboration because it ensures that important information is accessible, organized, and easy to retrieve. AI-powered knowledge management platforms help structure data, categorize content, and streamline information-sharing processes, reducing the time spent searching for critical documents and insights. By leveraging AI, you can improve institutional knowledge retention and ensure that valuable information is available to the right people at the right time.

Platforms like Notion AI (www.notion.so/product/ai), Confluence AI (www.atlassian.com/software/confluence/ai), and Guru AI (www.getguru.com/

solutions/ai-enterprise-search) use AI to structure and retrieve data efficiently. These tools automatically tag, organize, and summarize documents, making it easier for teams to find relevant information without digging through endless files or outdated records. AI-powered search functions enable users to ask natural language queries and receive precise, context-aware responses, saving time and improving productivity.

AI also enhances institutional knowledge sharing through smart search and categorization. Instead of relying on manually curated knowledge bases, AI continuously updates and refines information repositories by analyzing team interactions, commonly accessed documents, and frequently asked questions. Consequently, critical insights are always up to date, and team members can easily access the knowledge they need without redundancy or miscommunication.

However, as AI expands knowledge accessibility, avoiding information overload becomes a key challenge. To prevent AI from surfacing too much irrelevant data, implement filters, customize AI recommendations, and regularly audit knowledge bases to remove outdated or redundant content. Also, encourage employees to provide feedback on AI-generated knowledge suggestions to help refine search accuracy over time.

TIP

When using AI-powered knowledge management tools, customize filters and tagging systems to ensure the most relevant information surfaces first. Regularly auditing and refining AI-generated content helps prevent knowledge overload and keeps your team's resources accurate and up to date.

Reimagining Meetings with AI-Driven Optimization

Meetings are essential for collaboration, but they can also be time-consuming and inefficient if not managed properly. AI-driven tools are transforming the way teams conduct meetings by automating transcription, note-taking, and follow-ups, ensuring that discussions are more productive and actionable. By leveraging AI, you can streamline meeting workflows, reduce unnecessary gatherings, and keep teams aligned without excessive time spent in discussions.

Platforms like Otter.ai (https://otter.ai), Fireflies.ai (https://fireflies.ai), and Microsoft Teams AI (www.microsoft.com/en-us/microsoft-teams/ai) provide real-time transcription, automated note-taking, and intelligent summarization. These tools capture key discussion points, identify action items, and generate meeting summaries that can be easily shared with attendees and those who couldn't attend. AI-driven summaries help teams focus on outcomes rather than spending time manually documenting conversations.

AI improves action item tracking and follow-ups by automatically recognizing decisions made during meetings and assigning tasks to relevant team members. AI tools can integrate with project management platforms to send reminders and track progress on assigned action items. This ensures accountability and prevents important decisions from being forgotten after the meeting ends.

One of AI's greatest benefits is reducing unnecessary meetings by supporting asynchronous communication. AI-powered tools can generate meeting recaps that allow team members to stay informed without needing to attend every discussion. Instead of holding repetitive status update meetings, teams can rely on AI-generated insights, allowing them to focus on execution rather than excessive discussions.

A great example of AI-driven meeting optimization comes from a tech company that integrated AI note-taking and follow-up tools into their workflow. The company implemented Fireflies.ai to automate the process of capturing key discussion points and action items, reducing the need for additional clarification meetings. Team members who couldn't attend received AI-generated summaries, eliminating redundant recap sessions. As a result, their meetings became more focused, shorter, and more effective, allowing the team to spend more time executing tasks rather than attending unnecessary discussions.

Assessing and Improving Team Engagement with AI

Keeping employees engaged is critical to maintaining productivity, morale, and collaboration, especially in remote and hybrid work environments. AI-powered tools are transforming the way organizations measure and improve team engagement by analyzing sentiment, collecting feedback, and personalizing strategies to keep employees motivated. By leveraging AI, you can gain deeper insights into team dynamics and take proactive steps to enhance workplace satisfaction.

AI can measure employee engagement through sentiment analysis, analyzing communication patterns, feedback, and survey responses to identify trends in team morale. By processing written and verbal interactions, AI can detect shifts in sentiment, helping managers recognize early signs of disengagement or burnout. This allows leadership to address concerns before they escalate, fostering a healthy and productive work environment.

Platforms like Culture Amp AI (www.cultureamp.com) and Peakon (www.peakon.com) use AI-driven feedback collection and analysis to assess engagement levels. These tools automate pulse surveys, analyze open-ended responses, and provide data-driven insights into what factors influence employee satisfaction. AI identifies common themes and trends in employee feedback, helping organizations make informed decisions about culture, leadership, and workplace improvements.

Another way AI can help with engagement is by personalizing engagement strategies for remote and hybrid teams. It can tailor recommendations based on individual and team preferences. AI-driven platforms can suggest ways to improve work-life balance, recommend career development opportunities, and even provide customized recognition programs. By delivering insights customized to each employee's needs, AI helps organizations create a more supportive and engaging work environment.

However, using AI to monitor engagement comes with ethical considerations. Employees may feel uneasy about AI analyzing their communication, which raises concerns about privacy and trust. Organizations must ensure transparency by clearly communicating how they use AI, what data they collect, and how it benefits employees. Only use AI as a supportive tool to enhance engagement, not as a surveillance mechanism that erodes trust.

Trusting Ethics and Data Privacy in AI Collaboration

As AI becomes more integrated into workplace collaboration, concerns about data security, privacy, and ethical usage are more important than ever. Although AI can enhance efficiency and streamline teamwork, it also processes vast amounts of sensitive information, raising questions about how it stores, shares, and protects data. Building trust in AI-driven collaboration requires organizations to prioritize security, comply with privacy regulations, and ensure AI is used responsibly.

REMEMBER

AI tools must adhere to key privacy regulations and compliance standards, such as the General Data Protection Regulation (GDPR) and the Health Insurance Portability and Accountability Act (HIPAA). These regulations dictate how companies collect, store, and process personal data, emphasizing transparency and user control. Organizations using AI for collaboration must ensure that their tools comply with these standards, safeguard employee and customer data, and provide clear policies on how AI interacts with sensitive information.

One of the most debated issues is ethical AI usage in monitoring employee performance and interactions. AI-powered analytics can assess productivity, track engagement, and identify work patterns, but excessive monitoring can create an environment of surveillance and distrust. If employees feel that managers are using AI to micromanage or evaluate them unfairly, it can damage morale and workplace culture. Instead of using AI for invasive tracking, organizations should focus on leveraging AI for supportive purposes, such as identifying workflow inefficiencies, improving collaboration, and enhancing team well-being.

To balance AI efficiency with privacy concerns, organizations should follow best practices for ethical AI implementation. Here are some examples:

>> **Ensure transparency:** Clearly communicate how AI collects and processes data, and allow employees to opt out of non-essential tracking.

>> **Limit data collection:** Only gather necessary information to prevent excessive AI surveillance.

>> **Use anonymization:** De-identify sensitive data to protect individual privacy while still gaining valuable insights.

>> **Implement human oversight:** Ensure AI-driven insights are reviewed by managers or HR personnel to prevent biased or incorrect conclusions.

Executing AI-Driven Collaboration Strategies

Successfully integrating AI into team collaboration requires a strategic approach that goes beyond simply adopting new tools. To maximize the benefits of AI-driven collaboration, organizations must implement AI tools effectively, prepare teams for the transition, measure success, and stay ahead of emerging trends. By following a structured approach, you can ensure AI enhances productivity while fostering a culture of innovation and adaptability.

The first step in implementing AI collaboration tools effectively is identifying the specific challenges AI can solve within your team. Identify whether you want AI to help automate administrative tasks, streamline communication, or improve project management, and then select the right AI-powered tools for a seamless fit with your workflows. Start small, testing AI solutions in controlled environments before scaling implementation across teams. Training and onboarding are also crucial; teams must understand not only how to use AI tools but also how these tools enhance collaboration without replacing human input.

REMEMBER

Change management plays a critical role in preparing teams for AI adoption. Employees may resist AI due to concerns about job security, data privacy, or the complexity of new technologies. To address this, leadership should emphasize AI as a collaborative assistant rather than a replacement, providing clear communication about its role in enhancing — not replacing — human contributions. Encourage an open dialogue, offer hands-on training, and demonstrate quick wins to help ease concerns and drive AI adoption across the organization.

Once AI tools are in place, make sure to measure the success of AI integration in collaboration. Key performance indicators (KPIs) such as time saved on administrative tasks, improved response times in communication, enhanced task completion rates, and employee engagement levels can provide insights into AI's impact. Gathering feedback from team members is equally important. You need to understand their experience with AI tools so you can refine processes and ensure AI is truly supporting collaboration rather than creating additional complexity.

The future of AI in workplace collaboration will continue evolving, bringing new trends and innovations that reshape how teams work. Advances in generative AI, AI-powered decision-making, and deeper personalization will further enhance collaboration. AI is expected to become more intuitive, seamlessly integrating with existing workflows and adapting to individual work styles. As AI tools grow more sophisticated, organizations that embrace these innovations will gain a competitive edge in efficiency, creativity, and team synergy.

Putting AI to Work for You

Integrating AI into your collaboration workflow doesn't have to be overwhelming. By taking practical, intentional steps, both individuals and teams can harness AI to enhance productivity, streamline communication, and improve overall efficiency. The key is to start small, identify the right tools for your needs, and continuously refine your approach as you gain experience.

To begin, follow these practical steps for using AI collaboration tools effectively:

1. **Identify pain points.**

   Determine where AI can provide the most value, such as automating repetitive tasks, improving knowledge sharing, or optimizing scheduling.

2. **Choose the right AI tools.**

   Research AI-powered platforms that align with your team's needs, such as chatbots for communication, project management AI for task tracking, or transcription tools for meetings.

3. **Start with a pilot test.**

   Implement AI tools with a small team or on a trial basis before scaling usage across the organization.

4. **Provide training and support.**

   Ensure team members understand how AI tools work and how they enhance — not replace — collaboration.

5. **Gather feedback and refine.**

   Regularly assess how AI is impacting your workflows and make adjustments based on team input.

When selecting AI tools, consider the following checklist to ensure you choose the best solutions for your team:

» Does the tool integrate with existing workflows?

» Is it user-friendly and easy to adopt?

» Does it enhance productivity without creating unnecessary complexity?

» How does it handle data privacy and security?

» Does it offer automation features that align with your team's needs?

» Can it scale as your team grows?

REMEMBER

AI-driven collaboration is not a one-size-fits-all solution. It requires experimentation, iteration, and refinement. Encourage your team to test different AI applications, track their effectiveness, and adjust as needed. AI should be an adaptable tool that evolves with your team's workflow, not a rigid system that dictates how you work.

REMEMBER

Ultimately, you should consider AI to be a collaborative partner, enhancing human ingenuity rather than replacing it. While AI can automate tasks, streamline decision-making, and provide valuable insights, the human element — creativity, critical thinking, and interpersonal connection — remains irreplaceable. By thoughtfully integrating AI into your collaboration strategy, you can build a more efficient, innovative, and future-ready team.

3

Applying AI in Everyday Project Management

Chapter **8**

Improving Project Planning and Scheduling with AI

Effective project planning and scheduling are critical components of successful project management. Artificial intelligence (AI) is transforming how project managers approach these tasks by offering advanced tools that enhance accuracy, optimize resource allocation, and automate schedule adjustments. This chapter explores how project managers can use AI to improve project timeline accuracy, allocate resources more effectively, map dependencies, and automate schedule updates.

Enhancing Project Timeline Accuracy with AI

Creating an accurate project timeline is essential for ensuring that your project stays on track and meets deadlines. AI has revolutionized how project managers approach timeline creation by providing data-driven insights and predictive capabilities that were previously difficult to achieve with manual planning methods. By leveraging AI, project managers can enhance the precision of their timelines and create more realistic and adaptable project plans. Basically, AI can help you avoid those oh-so-realistic "best-case-scenario" timelines that never seem to work out.

One of AI's most valuable contributions to timeline accuracy is its ability to analyze historical data. AI can examine data from similar past projects to identify patterns, bottlenecks, and common causes of delays. AI's insight into how long specific tasks have taken in the past helps project managers create timelines that better reflect real-world conditions.

When using AI for historical data analysis, be cautious about uploading sensitive or confidential information, especially if the AI model is not secure or explicitly designed for private data handling. Ensure that only nonsensitive data is used to protect privacy and observe compliance.

For example, if a project manager is overseeing a construction project and needs to estimate the time required for a certain phase, AI can analyze data from similar construction projects to provide an estimate based on historical performance. This reduces guesswork and results in more reliable timelines. Tools like Microsoft Project with AI Insights and Smartsheet use AI-driven predictive analytics to help project managers make these kinds of informed decisions, ensuring that timelines are grounded in data rather than intuition.

TIP

AI works best when it has access to data from previous projects. Make sure you're feeding it detailed and relevant information to generate more precise timeline predictions.

AI can help you spot project delays and risks before they become big problems. Instead of scrambling to fix issues at the last minute, AI acts like an extra set of eyes on your project, analyzing real-time data and giving you early warnings when something seems off. It doesn't just point out problems; it suggests solutions to help you stay on track.

Imagine you're managing a product launch, and one key task — like designing the packaging — keeps taking longer than expected. Maybe the design team is waiting on approvals, or they're struggling with supplier delays. Normally, you might not realize there's a problem until it starts affecting other tasks, pushing back deadlines and creating a last-minute rush. But with AI, you get an alert as soon as it detects a pattern of delays. It might show that similar projects in the past had the same issue and suggest an adjustment, like shifting deadlines, adding extra review time, or assigning more resources to speed things up. Instead of reacting after the fact, you have the chance to solve the problem before it snowballs.

When AI flags potential delays or risks, act quickly to address them. Proactively adjusting your timeline based on AI predictions can prevent larger issues from derailing your project.

AI can also help prevent burnout and workload imbalances. If one team member is overloaded with work while others have room in their schedules, AI will notice and flag the imbalance. It may suggest spreading tasks more evenly or adjusting assignments to keep the workload fair. This is especially helpful for large teams or remote workers where you might not always see who's struggling. By keeping tasks distributed efficiently, AI helps your team stay productive without exhausting them, which improves morale and reduces the risk of missed deadlines.

AI-powered tools like Wrike and Oracle Primavera take this a step further by tracking risks, predicting bottlenecks, and offering solutions in real-time. If your project is at risk of going over budget or running late, these tools can provide alternative strategies — maybe shifting resources, reordering task priorities, or even recommending vendors that have worked better in similar situations. The best part? These insights are based on real data, not just guesswork, so you can make informed decisions with confidence.

Wouldn't it be great to have a built-in safety net like this? AI won't replace your judgment, but it gives you the insights you need to stay ahead and avoid surprises. Instead of spending all your time putting out fires, you can focus on strategy, problem-solving, and delivering a successful project — on time and with fewer headaches.

Another area where AI shines is in improving individual task duration estimates, which goes beyond simply analyzing historical data to build an overall project timeline. While AI can use past projects to create high-level schedules, it can also focus on specific tasks and make more detailed predictions based on multiple influencing factors.

For example, in a software development project, estimating how long it will take to implement a new feature isn't as simple as looking at past timelines. AI can analyze how long similar tasks have taken under different circumstances, considering factors such as the experience level of the developers assigned to the task, whether they're working with a familiar or new technology, and whether dependencies — such as waiting for client feedback or integrating third-party tools — are likely to slow progress. If AI identifies that a particular developer typically requires more time to complete similar tasks, it can suggest adjusting future estimates or allocating additional resources to keep the project on track.

Unlike traditional estimation methods that rely on best guesses or static averages, AI continuously refines its predictions by incorporating progress updates. If a task is taking longer than expected, AI can update its projections instead of relying on the original estimate. This helps project managers avoid unrealistic expectations and make data-driven adjustments before delays impact the overall timeline.

Tools like Wrike and Asana use AI-driven insights to provide more precise task level duration estimates, making it easier to create flexible, data-backed project schedules that adapt as work progresses. Instead of static timelines that often become outdated, AI ensures that task durations remain as accurate as possible, improving both short-term planning and long-term forecasting.

AI-powered project management tools take the headache out of constantly adjusting schedules when things don't go as planned. Instead of manually shifting task dates and dependencies every time there's a delay, these tools do the heavy lifting for you. They can integrate with time-tracking software, team collaboration platforms, and even email or chat tools to keep an eye on task progress. When something falls behind schedule, the AI detects the delay, recalculates the timeline, and updates the rest of the project plan automatically. You don't have to spend hours clicking and dragging tasks around.

For example, imagine you're managing a product development project, and a key design task is delayed because the client hasn't provided final approval. If your team logs the delay in Smartsheet, its AI features can instantly adjust the timeline, pushing back dependent tasks while keeping the overall project schedule as realistic as possible. Instead of leaving you to discover the issue later, the system notifies you right away, showing exactly how the delay impacts other tasks. You might get a message like the following: The design phase has been delayed by three days, affecting the production schedule. Would you like to notify the manufacturing team? With just one click, you can keep everyone in the loop.

Other tools, like Motion, take this a step further by dynamically rescheduling individual tasks based on shifting priorities. Say you were planning to start testing a new software feature on Wednesday, but the developers need two extra days to finish coding. Instead of forcing you to find a new time slot, Motion's AI automatically reschedules the testing phase for the earliest available window, ensuring it doesn't overlap with higher-priority work.

The best part? You're not stuck constantly checking for updates or chasing down team members for status reports. AI-driven project tools send notifications when major schedule changes occur, allowing you to approve or tweak adjustments as needed. This way, instead of scrambling to fix timeline issues after they cause chaos, you stay ahead of the curve and ensure your project runs smoothly with less tedious manual work.

TIP Look for AI tools that offer automatic timeline adjustments. This feature ensures your project schedule stays up to date, even when unexpected events occur, reducing manual intervention and the risk of delays.

TIP Check out Chapter 3 for more information about how AI improves project efficiency through automation.

Allocating Resources

Effective resource allocation and precise task dependency mapping are critical for ensuring that projects run smoothly and are completed on time. Traditionally, these processes have relied on manual assessment by project managers, which can be time-consuming and prone to errors. With AI, however, resource allocation and dependency mapping become more efficient and data-driven, leading to better project outcomes.

AI-powered tools can analyze vast amounts of historical data and current project dynamics, offering valuable insights that help project managers optimize resource use, avoid bottlenecks, and ensure that tasks are completed in the correct order. This section covers how AI can revolutionize resource allocation and dependency mapping in your projects.

Optimizing resource allocation with AI

Managing resources in a project can feel like a juggling act — especially when unexpected changes happen. AI can help you keep everything balanced by analyzing both past project data and current workload distribution to ensure your team, equipment, and budget are being used efficiently. If resources aren't allocated correctly, your project can quickly run into bottlenecks, delays, or even failure, but AI helps you stay ahead of these risks.

Imagine this scenario: One of your key team members unexpectedly goes on medical leave in the middle of a high-priority task. Instead of leaving you scrambling to reassign their workload, an AI-powered project management tool analyzes your team's availability, workload distribution, and historical data from similar projects to suggest the best way forward. AI may flag another team member with the right skills who has enough availability to step in. If no one else has the expertise, it could recommend shifting deadlines, adjusting dependencies, or redistributing other tasks to free up capacity.

Even if no emergencies arise, AI monitors resource usage throughout the project and adjusts as needed. If a certain task is consuming more time or materials than expected, AI alerts you early and recommends solutions — whether that means bringing in extra support, adjusting the budget, or reordering priorities.

Tools like Kantata and Resource Guru use AI to dynamically adjust resource allocation, ensuring that teams and projects are adequately resourced without overburdening individuals or under-utilizing assets. These tools also factor in the availability and skills of team members to optimize task assignments, ensuring that resources are not only allocated but also utilized efficiently. This makes it easier for project managers to ensure that resources are used effectively to meet project goals while minimizing waste.

By helping you proactively manage resources, AI helps to prevent burnout, ensures critical tasks get the support they need, and keeps your project moving smoothly — even when unexpected challenges arise.

Balancing workloads across teams

One of the key challenges in project management is ensuring that workloads are distributed evenly across teams. AI can analyze team members' current tasks, skills, and availability, which enables it to intelligently assign new tasks to the most appropriate individuals without overburdening anyone. By doing so, AI helps project managers maintain a balanced workload across the team, preventing burnout and ensuring that all tasks are completed efficiently.

Keeping your team's workload balanced is one of the biggest challenges in project management. You don't want some team members drowning in tasks while others have too little to do. AI-powered tools like Asana and Jira help solve this problem by using machine learning algorithms to analyze work distribution, monitor capacity, and dynamically reassign tasks to keep things running smoothly.

These AI tools aren't just guessing when they make adjustments. They rely on real data about your team's workload history and work patterns. For example, AI can track

>> Average hours worked per week to see if someone is consistently logging overtime.

>> Planned versus actual task completion times to identify who is struggling with their workload.

>> Number of projects completed in the past year to measure experience and efficiency.

>> Paid time off and holiday schedules to anticipate availability gaps before they cause bottlenecks.

>> Task complexity and skills required to ensure assignments go to the right people.

Let's say one of your top developers has been assigned a big task that will require deep focus for the next two weeks. Meanwhile, they're also being given small but time-consuming administrative tasks. AI recognizes this conflict and automatically shifts the smaller tasks to a different developer with similar skills who has more availability. Or, if AI sees that multiple team members are nearing their weekly capacity, it might suggest pushing deadlines slightly, breaking down tasks into smaller parts, or temporarily redistributing work to prevent burnout.

This kind of data-driven workload balancing doesn't just improve productivity; it makes your team happier and healthier by preventing overwork. No one wants to feel like they're carrying an unfair load while others have extra bandwidth. AI ensures that work is spread fairly and efficiently, helping your team maintain a good work-life balance while keeping projects on track.

And the best part? AI does all the heavy lifting, but you get the credit for running a well-balanced, high-performing team.

If you ever feel like you struggle to figure out how to objectively assign tasks based on team members' strengths and past performance, AI can help you with that. For instance, AI can recommend assigning complex coding tasks to developers who have successfully completed similar tasks in the past and assigning routine tasks to less experienced team members to ensure that everyone contributes in line with their capabilities. This nuanced task assignment ensures that work is distributed in a way that maximizes the team's strengths while minimizing inefficiencies.

Mapping Task Dependencies with AI

If you've ever made a peanut butter and jelly sandwich, you know there's a right way — and a very wrong way — to do it. Imagine starting by spreading jelly directly on the plate, then adding a layer of peanut butter on top, and finally placing the bread over everything. That's a messy, inefficient process, and your sandwich is ruined before you even take a bite.

The same thing happens in project planning when task dependencies aren't mapped correctly. Some tasks must be completed before others can start, and if the sequence is wrong, you end up with delays, bottlenecks, and missed deadlines. Traditionally, project managers had to manually figure out dependencies, relying on their experience and judgment to decide which tasks should come first. This worked — sometimes — but it was also prone to human error and oversight.

For example, let's say you're managing a product launch. You wouldn't want the marketing team running ads before the final product design is approved or the packaging is ready. If these steps are out of order, you'll end up promoting a product that doesn't exist yet, leading to customer confusion and wasted ad spend.

Or, if a software development project involves both back-end coding and front-end user interface design, AI can automatically determine that back-end coding must be completed first before the front-end design can proceed.

This is where AI can step in and clean up the mess. Instead of relying solely on intuition, AI analyzes past projects, team workflows, and dependencies to create a logical, optimized sequence. It can even detect potential conflicts, like two teams needing the same resource at the same time, and suggest adjustments before it becomes a problem.

With AI-powered dependency mapping, you don't have to worry about peanut-buttering the jelly. Everything happens in the right order, so your project (and your sandwich) turns out exactly as it should.

TIP

AI does a great job mapping task dependencies, but it doesn't always account for real-world changes like scheduling conflicts or shifting priorities. Reviewing the map regularly ensures everything is in the right order and allows you to make adjustments before small issues turn into big delays.

Tools like Wrike and Trello use AI to automate dependency mapping, significantly reducing the risk of sequencing errors. With AI, dependencies are mapped with precision, ensuring that tasks are linked correctly and that project managers can see a clear, accurate roadmap of the project's execution. This automation also makes it easier to visualize and adjust dependencies as the project progresses, helping to keep everything on track.

TIP

Check out Chapter 10 to understand how mapping dependencies can help with managing your project's budget.

Anticipating resource conflicts and constraints

One of the biggest advantages of using AI in project management is that it monitors resource availability and flags conflicts before they disrupt your project. In a fast-moving project with multiple teams, it's easy for different tasks to compete for the same resources, whether it's a specialized team member, a key piece of equipment, or a limited budget.

Imagine you're overseeing a product launch, and both the marketing team and the product design team need the same creative director's time during the same week. Without AI, you might not realize there's a conflict until deadlines start slipping. But with AI constantly monitoring the project schedule, it detects the overlap immediately and alerts you before it becomes a bottleneck. It might suggest shifting one task to a different time slot, reassigning part of the work to another team member, or adjusting priorities based on deadlines.

Instead of waiting for you to manually review schedules and spot issues, AI acts like an early-warning system, giving you the chance to adjust plans before they cause delays. This keeps your project on track and ensures resources are used as efficiently as possible.

For example, an AI tool might detect that two tasks requiring a key developer are scheduled to take place concurrently. Instead of waiting for the conflict to cause a delay, the tool can alert the project manager and suggest solutions, such as rescheduling one of the tasks or assigning the work to another qualified team member. Tools like Smartsheet and Kantata are particularly adept at identifying these types of resource conflicts and constraints.

TIP

Enable AI-driven alerts to proactively identify resource overlaps, such as two tasks requiring the same person or equipment. This allows you to resolve conflicts before they cause delays or impact productivity.

Because AI can evaluate data from past projects, if the AI tool detects a recurring pattern of overbooked resources, it can recommend additional resources for future projects or suggest a different scheduling strategy to avoid conflicts. This proactive approach helps project managers avoid disruptions and keep the project moving forward smoothly.

Optimizing resources with AI-powered forecasting

AI can optimize future resource use through predictive forecasting, which means it analyzes data from past projects and current conditions to predict how resource needs will change as the project progresses. This helps project managers allocate resources not just for the present but for future phases of the project as well.

For example, AI might analyze past projects and predict that a particular phase of the project will require more resources than initially planned due to its complexity. Armed with this information, the project manager can plan ahead and ensure that additional resources are available when needed. AI tools like Resource Guru and Kantata use this type of forecasting to help project managers optimize resource allocation throughout the entire project lifecycle.

Resource forecasting also helps prevent the problem of overallocation. When resources are overstretched, it can lead to delays, cost overruns, and reduced quality of work. AI helps prevent this by redistributing tasks when workloads become unbalanced, which ensures that no one resource is overused and that tasks are completed efficiently.

Automating Schedule Adjustments and Updates with AI

One of the most transformative applications of AI in project management is its ability to automate schedule adjustments and updates. In traditional project management, updating the project schedule often requires significant manual effort and frequent reviews of every task and milestone. This can be especially challenging when managing complex projects with many moving parts. However, AI alleviates much of this burden by continuously monitoring project progress and making real-time adjustments to the schedule when necessary, ensuring that your project stays on track even when unexpected changes occur.

Projects rarely go exactly according to plan, and minor delays in one task can have ripple effects on dependent tasks and overall project timelines. With AI, project managers no longer need to manually adjust the entire schedule when one task falls behind. Instead, AI tools automatically recalibrate the schedule to reflect real-time changes, ensuring that the project timeline remains as accurate as possible.

For example, imagine you're managing the production of a new pharmaceutical product, and a required regulatory approval is delayed by a week. Without AI, you'd have to manually review the project timeline, figure out which tasks need to be pushed back, adjust dependencies, and communicate the changes to multiple teams. But with AI tools like Microsoft Project with AI Insights and Smartsheet, the system recognizes the delay, updates the schedule accordingly, and notifies the teams affected — all without you having to intervene.

With AI handling these adjustments, you can focus on making sure your team adapts smoothly. Instead of being tied up with administrative updates, you have the time to meet with your compliance team to explore ways to speed up approval, check in with the production staff to adjust workflows, or ensure that unaffected work continues as planned. You're not just reacting to schedule changes; you're actively managing the situation, keeping morale high, and making strategic decisions that keep the project moving forward.

Automating schedule updates

Manually updating schedules is often one of the most tedious aspects of project management, particularly when multiple teams, tasks, and resources are involved. AI simplifies this by automating schedule updates, ensuring that your project schedule reflects the most up-to-date status of each task without the need for manual intervention. AI can automatically track task progress, monitor resource allocation, and adjust timelines based on real-time data.

Tools like Monday.com and Trello excel at automating schedule updates. For instance, as team members complete their tasks or update their progress, these AI-powered tools automatically update the project timeline, recalibrate dependencies, and notify relevant stakeholders about any changes. This process removes the manual work of constantly revising the project plan and ensures that everyone remains aligned with the most current version of the schedule.

The automated process eliminates human error that often arises from manual adjustments. The result is fewer missed updates, more accurate timelines, and better decision-making for both project managers and stakeholders. In addition, automated updates ensure that stakeholders have access to accurate and up-to-date information, which reduces the potential for miscommunication.

Proactively addressing schedule conflicts

The ability to anticipate problems rather than just react to them is a key advantage of using AI in project management. Schedule conflicts — such as overlapping tasks or insufficient resources — are common causes of project delays. AI tools can analyze the project schedule to flag potential conflicts, so project managers can focus on optimizing the overall workflow rather than firefighting resource or scheduling issues at the last minute.

For example, imagine you're managing the launch of a large museum exhibit, and two departments — the exhibit design team and the lighting crew — are both scheduled to use the main gallery space at the same time. Without AI, you may not notice the conflict until the teams show up, leading to confusion, lost time, and potential delays. But AI tools like Wrike and Asana can identify the overlap in advance, recognizing that both teams need the same physical space.

Instead of scrambling at the last minute, AI suggests reallocating tasks — perhaps shifting the lighting installation to a smaller completed exhibit while the design team finishes assembling displays. Or, it might recommend adjusting shifts so the two teams work at different times. By resolving the conflict before it becomes a problem, AI helps you avoid unnecessary downtime, keep workflows running smoothly, and ensure that the exhibit opens on schedule.

Automatically notifying stakeholders of schedule changes

Communication is critical in any project, and keeping stakeholders informed of schedule changes is essential to maintaining alignment and trust. AI helps streamline communication by automatically notifying team members and stakeholders when the schedule is adjusted. This ensures that everyone involved in the project is aware of timeline changes, resource reallocations, or task updates, and can adjust their plans accordingly.

AI-powered tools like Slack and Microsoft Teams integrate seamlessly with project management systems to automate notifications. When the schedule is updated, AI can send real-time notifications to relevant team members, alerting them to changes and prompting action if necessary. For example, if a task is delayed, AI can notify the team that the new deadline has been extended and automatically adjust any dependencies. This immediate communication reduces the risk of miscommunication and ensures that everyone remains aligned with the project's goals and timeline.

Not only do these automated notifications keep teams informed, but they also reduce the time project managers spend on updating and communicating schedule changes. Instead of a project manager manually sending emails or scheduling meetings to discuss every change, AI ensures that the right information reaches the right people instantly, allowing teams to stay focused on execution.

Improving collaboration through AI-driven schedule management

AI-powered schedule adjustments and updates also foster better collaboration within teams. By automating time-consuming scheduling tasks, AI allows team members to focus on higher-value activities, like problem-solving and innovation. AI enables better collaboration by creating visibility across the entire project schedule, making it easier for team members to see how their work impacts other tasks and ensuring that everyone understands their role in keeping the project on track.

Tools like ClickUp and Jira use AI to manage schedules across teams, providing a clear overview of each team member's progress and potential blockers. This transparency fosters more collaboration because team members can proactively coordinate with one another to avoid potential delays and ensure the project is completed efficiently.

TIP

While AI can automate much of the scheduling process, it's important to periodically check the updates to ensure they accurately reflect any changes in scope or priority.

TRANSFORMING PROJECT MANAGEMENT WITH AI

TechWave Solutions, a mid-sized software development company, had been facing challenges with project delays, inefficient resource allocation, and inconsistent scheduling. As their client base grew and project complexity increased, they realized they needed to improve their project management processes. To address these issues, TechWave decided to implement AI-powered tools to enhance planning, scheduling, and resource management.

One of the major problems was frequent delays caused by inaccurate task duration estimates. By using Microsoft Project with AI Insights, TechWave was able to analyze data from previous projects to identify patterns and bottlenecks, allowing the company to create more realistic timelines. This improved the accuracy of their scheduling and reduced delays. Additionally, TechWave integrated Asana's AI-powered task assignment feature to optimize resource allocation. This allowed AI to assess team members' skills, workloads, and availability, ensuring that tasks were distributed efficiently and preventing overloading of individual team members.

To ensure smooth project execution, TechWave also employed Wrike's AI-driven dependency mapping, which automatically mapped the relationships between tasks, ensuring the proper sequence of operations. This automation reduced manual effort and ensured that tasks were completed in the correct order. When tasks did get delayed, Smartsheet's real-time schedule adjustment features automatically updated timelines, helping project managers adapt their schedules dynamically and keeping the project on track.

(continued)

(continued)

Resource conflicts were another issue TechWave struggled with, but Mavenlink's AI-powered resource optimization tools proactively flagged potential resource overlaps. By identifying these conflicts before they became critical, TechWave's project managers were able to make adjustments in advance, avoiding disruptions and ensuring smoother workflows.

As a result of these AI implementations, TechWave Solutions saw a reduction in project delays and improved team productivity by distributing workloads more evenly. The company also completed more projects on time, even when unexpected changes occurred, and experienced fewer resource conflicts, leading to higher client satisfaction and a more efficient internal operation. AI tools transformed TechWave's approach to project management, allowing the company to take on more complex projects and deliver them successfully.

Chapter **9**

Predicting and Managing Risks with AI

Risk management is a critical component of project management, and AI is transforming how project managers identify, predict, and mitigate risks. By using AI to analyze data, predict potential risks, and monitor projects in real time, you can proactively address issues before they escalate, ensuring that your project stays on track. This chapter explores how you can use AI to predict project risks, implement AI-powered risk mitigation strategies, and monitor risks in real time with AI alerts.

Using AI to Predict Project Risks

AI excels at analyzing vast amounts of data, identifying patterns, and making predictions. When applied to risk management, AI provides project managers with powerful tools to foresee potential risks before they become critical issues. This allows project teams to take proactive steps to mitigate risks rather than reactively managing them after they've already occurred. By leveraging AI, project managers can increase their chances of project success by staying ahead of potential challenges. Here's how AI can be used to predict project risks.

Analyzing historical data to identify risk patterns

One of the key strengths of AI is its ability to analyze historical data and identify recurring patterns or trends that may signal potential risks in current projects. Project data such as timeline delays, budget overruns, resource allocation issues, and scope changes are all valuable inputs for AI systems to learn from. AI can compare a project's characteristics — such as its duration, available resources, or the complexity of the work — to past projects with similar profiles. By finding similarities between past and current projects, AI can predict risks like budget overruns or missed deadlines. You can then use those predictions to adjust your plans accordingly.

For example, if a past project experienced frequent delays because of a shortage of skilled team members, AI will likely predict that a similar problem could arise in the current project if the team size or skills are insufficient. With this insight, you can take action by reallocating resources or extending deadlines before the issue escalates.

Tools such as RiskLens and IBM Watson use AI-driven analytics to examine historical data and predict risks based on patterns and trends. These tools allow project managers to anticipate challenges early, giving them ample time to adjust resource allocations, budgets, and timelines to minimize the impact of potential risks. This approach is particularly useful for large, complex projects that have many interrelated tasks, where manual identification of risk patterns would be too time-consuming to undertake and prone to error.

TIP

To accurately predict risks in new projects, AI tools need access to comprehensive past project data, including timelines, budgets, resource allocation, and past risk assessments. If an AI tool is newly implemented, historical data may need to be manually fed in or integrated from existing project management systems to ensure accurate analysis and pattern recognition.

Addressing data inaccuracies and bias in AI-driven risk management

While AI is a powerful tool for risk prediction, it's only as reliable as the data it learns from. If your historical project data contains inaccuracies, incomplete records, or biases — such as underreporting certain types of risks or disproportionately focusing on specific issues — AI will inevitably propagate these flaws in its predictions. This means that if past risk assessments overlooked certain challenges or misclassified risks, your AI system may fail to identify them in future projects.

For example, data collected before the COVID-19 pandemic would not account for the widespread supply chain disruptions, remote work challenges, and labor shortages that emerged during the crisis. If an AI risk assessment tool relied solely on prepandemic data, it might underestimate the likelihood of similar disruptions occurring again, leading to poor risk planning. Conversely, if AI models trained on pandemic-era data are used today, they may overestimate risks such as prolonged material shortages or remote work productivity issues, even though business conditions have largely stabilized. In both cases, outdated or skewed data can lead to flawed risk predictions, making it essential to continuously update AI models and contextualize historical data.

Bias can also creep in when historical data reflects systemic inequalities, such as favoring certain vendors, teams, or decision-making processes over others. If an AI model is trained on biased data, it may reinforce those biases by consistently flagging certain projects or teams as "high risk" based on flawed historical patterns rather than objective factors. To mitigate these risks, you need to regularly audit the data feeding your AI tools, validate AI-generated predictions against real-world project outcomes, and implement checks to ensure that biases do not influence critical decisions. Ensuring data accuracy and fairness isn't just about improving AI performance; it's essential to making informed, responsible project management decisions.

Using predictive analytics to forecast risks

AI-powered predictive analytics tools can go a step further by combining historical data with real-time project data to provide accurate risk forecasts. By analyzing multiple factors — such as project progress, resource utilization, task completion rates, and team performance — AI can forecast risks that are likely to emerge in the future. These risks may include delays due to unexpected scope changes, resource shortages, or technical issues. With predictive analytics, you can take action before these risks become critical and disrupt the project's overall success.

For instance, if AI detects that a project is consistently falling behind schedule or that resource usage is higher than expected, it can predict a future deadline overrun and recommend reallocating resources or adjusting task priorities.

TIP

Set up AI alerts for indicators like schedule delays, resource overloading, or rapid budget usage so you can take proactive corrective action.

Tools such as Oracle Primavera and Microsoft Project with AI Insights provide predictive analytics features that help project managers forecast risks and make informed decisions about how to mitigate them. These tools not only predict when risks might occur, but also suggest the most effective ways to address them, such as rescheduling tasks or reallocating resources. This level of forecasting enables you to maintain control over your projects even as new challenges arise, ultimately reducing the likelihood of costly delays or disruptions.

Identifying early warning signs

In addition to forecasting risks, AI can be used to identify early warning signs of potential issues before they escalate into significant problems. AI systems continuously monitor project data in real time, looking for patterns or anomalies that suggest a risk is developing. For example, AI might detect that a specific task is falling behind schedule, a team member is becoming overloaded, or budget spending is accelerating faster than expected. These early warning signs provide critical insights that enable project managers to take corrective actions before the risk becomes critical.

For example, if AI flags that a particular developer is assigned more tasks than other team members, it can alert you to redistribute the workload or extend deadlines. Similarly, if a task shows no progress for several days, AI may recommend increasing resources to help complete the task on time. These early interventions can prevent minor issues from escalating into larger project bottlenecks or delays.

AI-powered tools such as Smartsheet and Wrike are effective at monitoring project data and providing early warnings of potential risks. These tools can trigger alerts that prompt you to investigate and address issues as soon as they arise, keeping the project on track and minimizing disruptions. By catching risks early in the project lifecycle, you can reduce the likelihood of last-minute firefighting and ensure smoother project execution.

Using AI to assess external risks

In addition to internal project risks, you can use AI to assess external risks that may impact a project. Examples include things like these:

>> Market fluctuations

>> Supply chain disruptions

>> Changes in regulations

AI analyzes external data sources — such as economic trends, supplier reliability, political events, or weather forecasts — to identify potential risks outside the project's immediate control. These external risks are often overlooked in traditional risk management approaches, but they can have significant consequences on project timelines and budgets.

For example, AI can monitor the performance of key suppliers and identify potential supply chain disruptions based on historical patterns or real-time data. If AI predicts that a key supplier is likely to experience delays, you can proactively seek alternative suppliers or adjust the project timeline to account for the delay. Similarly, if AI detects upcoming regulatory changes that could affect a project's scope or budget, you can plan for those changes in advance, reducing the risk of non-compliance or budget overruns.

Tools like RiskSense and Predata specialize in monitoring external factors and using AI to predict how they might impact a project. These tools enable you to take a more comprehensive approach to risk management by factoring in both internal and external risks. This proactive approach helps reduce the uncertainty associated with external risks and ensures that you're prepared to adapt their plans accordingly.

Implementing AI-Powered Risk Mitigation Strategies

Predicting risks is only part of the equation. You also need to effectively manage those risks by implementing proactive strategies to mitigate them. In this section, I talk about how AI can be leveraged to implement effective risk mitigation strategies in your projects.

Automating risk mitigation actions

AI tools have the capability to automate risk mitigation actions, which makes it possible for you to dynamically adjust project plans based on identified risks. Instead of waiting for risks to materialize into actual problems, AI predicts potential issues and takes preemptive action. For example, if AI predicts that a key task is at risk of being delayed, it can automatically adjust the project timeline, reschedule dependent tasks, or reassign resources to keep the project on track.

Automation plays a significant role in reducing manual intervention, as AI systems can update project schedules, assign resources, or even recommend additional buffers for high-risk tasks. This reduces the burden on you to micromanage every aspect of the project while ensuring risks are handled efficiently. AI is a tireless worker, automating tasks so you can focus on the big picture.

AI-powered platforms like Monday.com and Trello offer real-time automation for these adjustments, adapting projects quickly for changing conditions. These automated systems ensure that risks are mitigated promptly without disrupting the project's overall workflow.

AI can automatically adjust timelines, reassign resources, or update schedules when risks arise, reducing the need for manual interventions and keeping the project on track.

Providing data-driven mitigation recommendations

AI technology also excels at providing you with data-driven recommendations for risk mitigation. AI systems analyze vast amounts of project data, assessing the potential impact of risks and proposing solutions based on historical patterns and predictive models. These recommendations allow project managers to address risks with evidence-backed strategies rather than relying on intuition or guess-work. Figure 9-1 illustrates how AI identifies and mitigates risks.

1. Risk Identification
AI scans project data to identify risks before they escalate.

2. Risk Analysis & Prediction
AI assesses risk severity and predicts potential impact.

3. Mitigation Strategy Recommendations
AI suggests mitigation strategies such as adjusting deadlines, reallocating resources, or adding contingency plans.

4. Implementation & Monitoring
Project manager reviews AI recommendations and updates the plan. AI continues monitoring for new risks.

5. Risk Resolved/Project Progressing
AI helps ensure risks are addressed early, keeping the project on track.

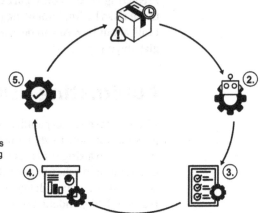

FIGURE 9-1:
How AI identifies and mitigates project risks.

For example, if AI identifies a risk of resource shortages during a critical phase of the project, it might recommend reallocating resources from lower-priority tasks to ensure the high-priority tasks stay on track. Alternatively, if AI detects budget overages, it may suggest reducing the project scope in noncritical areas to maintain financial control. Tools like Microsoft Project with AI Insights and Oracle Primavera use predictive analytics to offer real-time recommendations for mitigating risks based on data analysis. These recommendations might include actions such as increasing the project budget, extending deadlines, or redistributing resources across teams.

By providing these actionable insights, AI empowers project managers to make informed, data-backed decisions that reduce the likelihood of project disruptions. It also ensures that mitigation strategies are grounded in real-time data, ensuring their relevance to the current state of the project.

Optimizing resource allocation to mitigate risks

Resource allocation is a key factor in effective risk mitigation, and AI excels at optimizing how resources are assigned across the project. AI can analyze a project's current status and resource details — availability, team skills, and workload — to identify the optimal way to distribute resources in response to potential risks. By ensuring that the right resources are allocated to the right tasks at the right time, AI helps you minimize the impact of risks.

For example, if AI detects that a critical task is falling behind schedule due to insufficient resources, it can recommend reassigning team members or increasing resource allocation to ensure the task is completed on time. Conversely, if certain tasks are identified as low-risk or less urgent, AI may recommend reallocating those resources to higher-priority areas. AI-powered tools like Wrike and Asana offer resource optimization features that help you allocate resources efficiently, ensuring that project teams can respond to risks without overextending themselves.

TIP

In addition to optimizing internal resources, AI can also provide insights into external resources, such as third-party vendors or suppliers. By analyzing supplier reliability, delivery times, and market conditions, AI can help project managers identify potential supply chain risks and make recommendations or automatic adjustments before they impact the project.

Simulating risk scenarios with AI

AI can also help you simulate different risk scenarios to determine the best course of action for mitigating risks. Risk simulations allow project managers to test different mitigation strategies and see how they would impact the overall project. This helps managers prepare for a variety of potential risks by exploring various "what-if" scenarios and their outcomes.

For instance, AI could simulate what would happen if a key team member became unavailable or the budget is cut significantly. These simulations allow you to explore the effectiveness of different mitigation strategies, such as reallocating tasks, extending deadlines, or increasing resources. You can select the strategy that is most likely to minimize disruptions and keep the project on track.

TIP

Before committing to a mitigation strategy, use AI to simulate various outcomes and choose the solution that minimizes disruption and optimizes project performance. Tools like RiskLens and Oracle Primavera offer scenario-planning features for these simulations.

Enhancing decision-making with AI Insights

AI's ability to provide real-time insights is another powerful tool for improving decision-making around risk mitigation. AI tools can continuously monitor project progress and evaluate the potential impact of different risk mitigation strategies. By analyzing data on task completion rates, resource utilization, and project timelines, AI can recommend which strategies are most likely to succeed and which are less effective.

For example, if AI identifies that extending a project deadline will minimize the impact of a delay but result in higher costs, it can present this data, so you can weigh the trade-offs and make an informed decision. Similarly, if AI predicts that reallocating resources will resolve a potential bottleneck without delaying other tasks, it will highlight this option as the most efficient mitigation strategy.

Tools like Power BI and Tableau provide advanced analytics that help project managers assess the potential impact of different risk mitigation strategies, ensuring that decisions are informed by data rather than intuition. These AI-powered analytics provide you with the confidence to make decisions that are grounded in evidence and likely to result in successful outcomes.

Monitoring Risks in Real Time with AI Alerts

Predicting risks is only the first step. You also need to manage them effectively to keep your project on track. AI helps by continuously monitoring project data, identifying potential risks as they emerge, and sending alerts to ensure you can act before issues become critical. AI-powered tools don't just flag problems; they can also automate mitigation actions and suggest data-driven solutions to help resolve risks proactively.

One of the biggest advantages of AI-driven risk management is its ability to send immediate alerts when a potential issue is detected. These alerts ensure that project managers, stakeholders, and team members are informed without delay, allowing them to take corrective action quickly.

AI alerts can come in different forms, depending on the tools being used and the urgency of the risk:

>> **Email notifications:** Messages can go directly to project managers, executives, or finance teams when budget overruns, resource shortages, or deadline risks are detected.

>> **In-app alerts:** Tools like Microsoft Project, Smartsheet, or Jira display pop-up warnings inside project dashboards, flagging tasks that are delayed or overallocated.

>> **Chat notifications:** AI integrates with communication tools like Slack, Microsoft Teams, and Trello to send direct messages to relevant team members. For example, you might receive a Slack message saying something like the following:

- Task X is running 3 days behind schedule. Would you like to reassign resources?

- Budget allocation for Department Y has exceeded projections by 10%. Suggested action: Adjust spending or request additional funds.

>> **Mobile push notifications:** For project managers on the go, AI tools can send urgent alerts to smartphones, ensuring that time-sensitive risks get immediate attention.

Beyond sending alerts, AI automates risk response by recommending or even initiating mitigation actions. If AI detects that a critical milestone is at risk, it can

>> Suggest resource reallocation to prevent bottlenecks

>> Recommend timeline adjustments based on similar past projects

>> Notify leadership for intervention when high-priority risks arise

By integrating AI-powered alerts with workflow automation, project teams don't just get notified of risks; they also receive actionable insights on how to resolve them. This reduces the burden of constant monitoring, ensuring that you can focus on leading the project instead of chasing down every possible issue.

TIP

Ensure your AI tools send alerts for high-priority risks like delayed tasks or resource shortages, so you can take immediate action to prevent project disruptions.

Tools like Slack and Microsoft Teams integrate with AI-powered risk monitoring systems to deliver real-time alerts directly to project managers and team members. These tools ensure that communication is fast and efficient, allowing project teams to quickly adjust to changing circumstances. Real-time alerts can also be customized based on specific project requirements, ensuring that the most critical risks are prioritized and addressed promptly.

Automating risk response and reporting

AI-powered project management tools not only alert you to risks but can also take action to keep your project on track. When a risk is detected, AI can adjust schedules, reassign resources, or extend deadlines without requiring you to manually intervene. However, how much AI automates depends on how the system is set up. Some tools allow you to predefine responses for certain risks, whereas others analyze the situation and recommend or implement adjustments based on past project data and best practices.

For example, imagine you're overseeing the launch of a large-scale event, such as a trade show or conference. A critical supplier for staging materials suddenly notifies you of a delay. Without AI, you'd have to scramble to find alternative vendors, adjust schedules, and notify multiple teams. But with AI-driven automation, the system detects the delay, updates the production timeline, and suggests alternative suppliers based on past procurement data. If an in-house resource is available, AI might even reallocate internal materials instead of waiting for the supplier to resolve the issue.

This level of risk response automation reduces the time spent managing logistical hiccups, allowing you to focus on higher level decisions — like ensuring keynote speakers are confirmed, promotional materials are finalized, and attendees have a seamless experience. Rather than getting lost in administrative firefighting, AI allows you to stay present and strategically guide your team through unexpected challenges.

Platforms like Wrike and Monday.com offer AI-driven automation features that trigger risk mitigation actions as soon as a risk is detected. These automated triggers help ensure that risks are addressed quickly and efficiently, minimizing the disruption to the project. For instance, if AI detects that a key resource is overallocated, it can automatically reassign tasks to other team members, ensuring that the project timeline is maintained without overburdening the team.

REMEMBER

Use AI-driven automation to handle routine adjustments, such as rescheduling tasks or reallocating resources, allowing you to focus on strategic decision-making.

Not only is AI useful for reacting to risks, but it also helps you stay ahead of them with automated risk reporting. Instead of waiting for issues to escalate, AI can generate detailed reports that track potential risks, their likelihood, and their impact on your project. These reports can be set to run on a daily, weekly, or milestone-based schedule, providing a real-time snapshot of project health.

For example, AI might identify a pattern of delays in a specific department and highlight it in a risk report, allowing you to investigate the root cause before it disrupts the timeline. If your project involves multiple teams or vendors, AI can track supplier reliability, budget deviations, and resource constraints, summarizing them in an easy-to-read dashboard. Some tools even visualize risks with color-coded indicators (for example, red for critical, yellow for moderate, and green for low), making it simple to spot trouble areas at a glance.

By using AI-driven risk reporting, you get a proactive edge, ensuring that no potential issue goes unnoticed. Instead of being caught off guard by unexpected setbacks, you have clear, data-backed insights that allow you to make informed decisions and keep your project moving forward smoothly.

Assessing effectiveness of project adjustments

Monitoring risks in real time is not enough. You also need to assess the effectiveness of their risk mitigation efforts. AI-powered tools can track and report on how well risk mitigation strategies are working, providing valuable insights into whether additional actions are needed. For example, AI can analyze project data to determine whether a delayed task has caught up to the schedule or if further adjustments are required. These reports help project managers make informed decisions about how to continue managing risks throughout the project lifecycle.

TIP

Regularly review AI-generated risk reports to refine mitigation strategies.

Tools like Power BI and Tableau offer AI-driven reporting features that allow project managers to track the success of their risk mitigation strategies. These tools provide visual insights into how risks are being managed and whether the project is back on track after mitigation actions have been taken. By continuously monitoring the effectiveness of risk responses, project managers can ensure that risks are properly addressed and that the project remains on course.

Ensuring stakeholder alignment with AI-driven risk updates

Risk management isn't only about keeping the project on track — it's also about ensuring that stakeholders are informed and aligned with the project's progress. AI can help by automatically generating risk reports and sending updates to stakeholders, ensuring that they are aware of any potential risks and the actions being taken to mitigate them. This transparency helps build trust and ensures that stakeholders remain engaged in the project.

TIP

Tools like Slack and Microsoft Teams provide AI-driven communication features that automatically update stakeholders on risk management efforts. These updates can be scheduled at regular intervals or triggered by specific risk events, ensuring that stakeholders are always kept in the loop. By providing timely updates on risk mitigation efforts, AI helps ensure that stakeholders remain aligned with the project's goals and progress.

HARNESSING AI FOR RISK MANAGEMENT

HorizonTech, a software development company, was struggling with frequent project delays, budget overruns, and missed deadlines due to unforeseen risks. As their projects grew more complex and the pressure to meet tighter deadlines increased, HorizonTech's project managers realized that their existing risk management processes were no longer sufficient. The company decided to implement AI-driven tools to better predict, mitigate, and monitor risks in real time.

Using IBM Watson to analyze historical project data, HorizonTech was able to identify patterns of risks that had led to past delays and cost overruns. This allowed project managers to anticipate similar risks in ongoing projects and adjust their plans accordingly. Microsoft Project with AI Insights provided predictive analytics that helped forecast risks in real time. For instance, when a key development task showed signs of falling behind, the AI tool automatically recommended reallocating resources to prevent delays, reducing the need for manual intervention.

To ensure continuous monitoring, HorizonTech implemented Smartsheet, which provided real-time alerts for issues such as budget overspending or team member overloads, allowing project managers to address potential risks before they escalated. Additionally, Monday . com helped automate the risk response process by adjusting project schedules and reassigning resources when delays were detected. This proactive approach ensured that project timelines stayed on track despite emerging challenges. Power BI was used to track the effectiveness of these risk mitigation efforts, giving HorizonTech insights into which strategies worked best and whether additional measures were needed.

By leveraging AI tools for risk management, HorizonTech saw a reduction in project delays and a decrease in budget overruns. The ability to predict, mitigate, and monitor risks in real time significantly improved their project success rates, increased client satisfaction, and allowed for more efficient use of resources. HorizonTech's adoption of AI-driven risk management tools not only transformed their approach to handling project risks but also set a new standard for efficiency and agility in their operations.

Chapter **10**

Optimizing Budgeting and Cost Control with AI

Managing a project's budget is one of the most critical tasks for any project manager. Cost overruns can derail even the best-planned projects, which is why staying on top of budgeting and cost control is essential. AI is transforming these aspects of project management by helping with accurate budget forecasting, optimizing costs in real time, and preventing budget overruns. This chapter explores how AI can support you in optimizing your budgets and ensuring that costs remain under control throughout the projects' lifecycles.

Helping with Budget Forecasting Using AI

Accurate budget forecasting is essential for project managers to ensure their projects are adequately funded and to avoid unexpected costs that can derail the project. AI plays a crucial role in enhancing the accuracy of these forecasts by leveraging historical data, predictive analytics, and customized scenario planning. This approach allows you to create data-driven and reliable budget forecasts that help keep projects financially on track from start to finish.

Analyzing historical data to inform budget estimates

One of the core budget forecasting strengths of AI is its ability to analyze large datasets, including past project data, to identify patterns and trends in spending. By examining how similar projects were managed in terms of size, scope, resource usage, and timelines, AI can help predict the costs of future projects with a higher degree of accuracy than you could manage by doing it manually.

AI tools like Microsoft Project with AI Insights and Smartsheet analyze historical data and compare it to the current project, taking into account factors such as labor costs, material expenses, and project duration. Then you can generate budget estimates based on the data from previous projects, rather than relying solely on assumptions or best guesses. AI's ability to draw from a larger dataset than a human project manager manually reviewing past projects helps reduce the likelihood of budget surprises later in the project lifecycle.

AI also enhances budget forecasting by using predictive analytics to refine cost estimates. Predictive analytics models use real-time data and market trends to project future costs based on factors like vendor pricing, resource availability, and inflation. By factoring in current conditions, AI can adjust budget forecasts to account for price fluctuations or changes in the availability of critical resources.

AI-powered tools like Oracle Primavera and IBM Watson leverage vendor pricing trends and resource demand data to estimate material and labor costs at various stages of a project. These tools use a combination of historical pricing data, real-time market trends, and predictive analytics to adjust cost forecasts dynamically. Some systems can also interface directly with vendor databases, procurement platforms, or enterprise resource planning (ERP) systems to pull in up-to-date pricing information, ensuring that budget estimates reflect the latest market conditions.

By integrating external cost drivers — such as fluctuations in material prices, labor availability, and supplier lead times — AI enables project managers to create more accurate and data-driven budget forecasts. This proactive approach helps mitigate financial risks, especially in volatile markets, giving teams greater confidence in their cost estimates.

Customizing budget forecasts for different scenarios

Another key feature of AI in budget forecasting is its ability to create customized budget forecasts for various project scenarios. For example, if you're considering expanding the scope of the project or allocating more resources to a critical task, you can have the AI tool simulate how these changes will impact the overall budget.

Tools like RiskLens and Power BI offer scenario planning features that allow project managers to run "what-if" analyses to see how different variables affect costs. These tools can provide forecasts for best-case, worst-case, and most likely budget scenarios, helping project managers prepare for a variety of outcomes. Scenario-based forecasting is particularly useful for large, complex projects where scope changes or unexpected events can have a significant financial impact.

TIP

In addition to helping with short-term budget forecasting, AI can support long-term financial planning by analyzing data from multiple projects over time. This analysis enables AI to identify trends in project spending and provide insights into future financial needs. For example, AI can predict when a company may need additional funding for an ongoing project or when cost-saving measures should be implemented to maintain financial health.

AI tools like Kantata and Wrike help project managers plan for long-term financial sustainability by forecasting future expenses and identifying cost-saving opportunities. By analyzing trends from past and ongoing projects, AI enables project managers to make more informed financial decisions, ensuring that projects remain viable in the long run.

Optimizing Costs in Real Time with AI

A key factor in making sure a project remains on budget is real-time cost optimization. AI provides you with the ability to monitor spending continuously, identify inefficiencies, and make real-time adjustments to optimize costs. This dynamic approach enables you to stay agile and adapt to changes as they occur by helping you ensure that resources are used efficiently. AI is your penny-pinching partner, constantly on the lookout for ways to save money on your project.

Tracking spending in real time

AI-powered tools excel at tracking spending in real time, giving you up-to-date visibility into how funds are being allocated across different project areas. Project managers commonly track project metrics using a dashboard like the one in Figure 10-1.

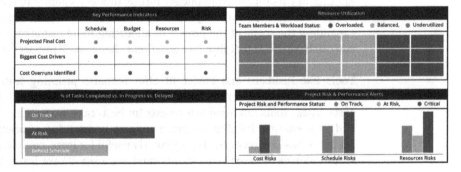

FIGURE 10-1: Dashboard showing real-time project performance metrics.

AI can monitor everything from labor costs to material expenses to equipment rentals and provide a comprehensive view of how closely spending aligns with the approved budget. This constant monitoring allows you to quickly identify discrepancies and make the necessary adjustments before costs spiral out of control.

AI-driven tools like Smartsheet and Asana excel at real-time project spending tracking, ensuring that budgets remain under control. These platforms continuously compare actual spending to the planned budget and automatically flag discrepancies. More importantly, they pinpoint specific areas where costs are exceeding projections — whether it's labor, materials, subcontractor fees, or equipment costs — allowing project managers to take targeted action.

For example, if material costs are 15 percent higher than planned due to supplier price increases, the AI system can notify the project team and suggest alternative vendors or bulk purchasing strategies. This real-time visibility enables managers to intervene early, preventing minor cost overruns from escalating into major financial risks.

This level of insight is particularly critical for large-scale projects, where rapid spending fluctuations can quickly lead to budget overruns. For a deeper dive into real-time budget performance tracking and key performance indicators (KPIs), check out Chapter 11.

Identifying cost-saving opportunities

AI actively helps project managers identify cost-saving opportunities throughout the project lifecycle. By analyzing spending patterns, resource allocation, and vendor pricing, AI can pinpoint inefficiencies and recommend more cost-effective alternatives.

For example, if AI detects that your current supplier is charging more than the industry average for a specific material, it may suggest switching to a lower-cost supplier. Depending on the system's capabilities, this recommendation can be based on two approaches:

>> **Direct supplier cost comparison:** Some AI tools integrate with procurement platforms, supplier databases, or ERP systems to pull in real-time pricing data from multiple vendors. This allows the AI to provide concrete recommendations on switching to a supplier that offers better rates, ensuring cost savings without compromising quality.

>> **Spending pattern analysis:** If the system doesn't have direct supplier cost data, it may identify trends where your spending on a certain category (for example, raw materials, subcontractor fees, or logistics) is higher than expected. In this case, AI flags an anomaly and suggests exploring alternative vendors, negotiating better pricing, or adjusting procurement strategies.

Beyond supplier costs, AI can also recommend resource reallocation, such as shifting labor from lower priority tasks to critical activities, or renegotiating payment terms to improve cash flow. These insights enable proactive cost control, helping you eliminate unnecessary expenses and optimize your project budget.

TIP

AI can highlight inefficiencies, so make it a habit to assess and implement its suggestions, such as switching vendors or optimizing resource allocation.

Tools like Wrike and Trello use AI to highlight areas where costs could be reduced, offering data-driven recommendations for improving budget efficiency. For instance, AI might detect that one vendor is consistently charging more than competitors for the same materials, which could prompt you to explore alternatives. Similarly, AI might identify underutilized team members or equipment, suggesting that resources be reassigned to areas where they can deliver more value. This ability to uncover cost-saving opportunities in real time can have a significant impact on the overall financial success of a project.

Optimizing resource allocation to reduce costs

AI is also highly effective at optimizing resource allocation in real time, which can lead to significant cost reductions. By continuously analyzing how resources — such as labor, materials, and equipment — are being used, AI can identify the most efficient way to allocate them. For example, if AI detects that a particular task is progressing more slowly than expected due to a lack of resources, it can recommend shifting resources from less critical areas to ensure that the higher priority task is completed on time and within budget. This real-time resource optimization prevents overspending and ensures that funds are directed to where they are needed most.

Tools like Kantata and ClickUp are particularly useful for optimizing resource allocation. These platforms analyze resource utilization data and provide actionable insights on how to distribute resources more effectively. For example, if a task is under-budget and has surplus resources, AI may suggest reallocating those resources to a higher priority task that is facing delays. By continually optimizing resource allocation, AI helps you make the most efficient use of their budget, ensuring that project costs remain under control.

Enhancing supplier and vendor negotiations

AI can also play a key role in optimizing costs by enhancing supplier and vendor negotiations. AI can analyze market data, pricing trends, and vendor performance to help identify opportunities to negotiate better deals. For example, AI might recommend switching to a supplier that offers more competitive pricing or suggest renegotiating terms with an existing vendor to secure discounts or extended payment terms. These AI-driven insights you managers with the information they need to optimize procurement costs and make more strategic decisions about supplier relationships.

TIP

AI-driven tools can provide valuable data on market trends and vendor performance, helping you secure better deals and optimize procurement costs.

Tools like GEP SMART and SAP Ariba are designed to enhance supplier and vendor negotiations using AI. These platforms analyze historical purchasing data and market trends to identify opportunities for cost savings. You can use the information AI reports to enter negotiations with a clear understanding of where savings can be achieved. By optimizing vendor relationships through better deals and more favorable terms, AI helps reduce project costs and increase overall budget efficiency.

Automating cost adjustments in real time

AI's role in cost adjustments is less about fully automating financial decisions and more about providing real-time insights that empower project managers to make informed budgetary adjustments. Rather than autonomously reallocating funds, AI tools track spending trends, detect budget imbalances, and generate actionable recommendations for project managers to review and implement.

For example, if AI detects that a specific task is consistently coming in under budget, it might flag the surplus and suggest redirecting those funds to another area where costs are running higher than expected. Conversely, if a task is at risk of exceeding its budget, AI can recommend cost-saving strategies — such as adjusting procurement timing, negotiating better vendor terms, or redistributing non-essential resources — to keep the project on track.

This function is distinct from resource allocation optimization, which focuses on efficiently distributing labor and materials to reduce costs. In contrast, AI-driven cost rebalancing helps manage financial flexibility within a project by ensuring funds are allocated where they're most needed without disrupting the overall budget structure.

Ultimately, AI acts as a financial advisor, continuously analyzing project expenses, identifying potential risks, and providing data-driven suggestions, but the final decision remains in the hands of the project manager.

TIP

Use AI-driven cost insights as a financial early warning system, allowing you to proactively adjust budgets before small overruns become major financial risks.

Tools like Monday.com and Smartsheet use AI-driven automation to help project managers track spending in real time and identify opportunities for cost optimization. These tools continuously analyze budget data and flag potential issues, such as overspending in certain areas or inefficiencies in resource allocation. Although AI can suggest actions — such as reallocating resources, adjusting timelines, or renegotiating vendor contracts — it generally doesn't automatically reallocate funds or make financial decisions without user approval. Instead, it provides data-driven recommendations to help you make informed adjustments while reducing the time spent on manual budget monitoring. This approach ensures that projects remain financially viable without sacrificing managerial oversight.

Using AI to Prevent Budget Overruns

Preventing budget overruns requires more than tracking expenses and making real-time adjustments. It demands a proactive strategy that anticipates financial risks before they escalate. Earlier sections of this chapter explore how AI enhances budget forecasting and optimizes costs as they arise, whereas this section focuses on AI's ability to predict, prevent, and mitigate budget risks before they become major issues.

By leveraging predictive analytics, risk modeling, and automated contingency planning, AI helps you identify early warning signs, assess financial vulnerabilities, and implement preemptive measures to keep your project within budget. Instead of simply reacting to cost overruns after they occur, AI continuously analyzes spending patterns, detects potential disruptions, and recommends proactive solutions to ensure financial stability. This section explores how AI-driven tools can provide early risk detection, contingency budget planning, and strategic decision support, enabling you to stay ahead of budget threats without last-minute scrambles or reactive cost-cutting.

Employing AI-powered early warning systems for budget risks

Even with a well-structured budget, unexpected costs can arise at any stage of a project. Causes may include supply chain disruptions, labor shortages, or scope changes. AI-driven early warning systems help you stay ahead of financial risks by continuously analyzing spending patterns and historical project trends to predict potential overruns before they happen. Rather than reacting to budget issues once they escalate, AI allows you to intervene early, making adjustments before minor cost deviations become major financial problems.

By examining historical project data, AI can detect trends such as

>> Recurring cost spikes at specific project phases, such as labor costs increasing toward the final stages

>> Vendors who frequently exceed estimated costs based on past contracts

>> Tasks or workstreams that consistently require more resources than budgeted

>> Common external cost drivers, such as seasonal price fluctuations in raw materials

By identifying these risk indicators, AI can forecast the likelihood of future budget overruns and provide recommendations to mitigate them before they impact the project.

Instead of relying on manual budget reviews, AI-powered systems continuously monitor spending and trigger automatic alerts when cost trends start deviating from projections. These alerts can be customized based on predefined thresholds, such as

>> Material costs increasing by more than 10 percent compared to the original estimate

>> A specific workstream exceeding 75 percent of its allocated budget too early in the project

>> Labor hours trending higher than planned, indicating a possible resource overload

When a cost deviation is detected, AI notifies you, and it provides insights on why the variance is occurring and suggests corrective actions. For example:

>> If subcontractor expenses are exceeding estimates, AI may suggest renegotiating contracts or reallocating internal resources.

>> If equipment rental costs are unexpectedly high, AI could recommend alternative vendors or adjusting the rental period to optimize expenses.

AI-powered early warning systems give you the ability to foresee budget risks before they become problems. By analyzing past overruns and continuously monitoring spending, AI detects cost deviations early, triggers automated alerts, and provides recommendations to keep your project financially on track. With AI as an intelligent financial watchdog, you can stay in control of your budget instead of being caught off guard by unexpected expenses.

Set up real-time AI alerts for key budget metrics to catch potential overspending before it becomes a major issue.

Using predictive analytics to identify budget threats

Cost overruns often seem sudden, but they usually stem from patterns and inefficiencies that go unnoticed until it's too late. AI-powered predictive analytics helps uncover these hidden spending trends by analyzing historical data, current expenditures, and external market factors. Rather than simply alerting you when costs exceed the budget, predictive analytics allows you to forecast potential overruns before they happen, giving you the opportunity to take corrective action early.

AI-powered predictive analytics identifies budget threats by analyzing vast amounts of historical project data, vendor pricing trends, labor costs, and supply chain disruptions. It looks for patterns that precede cost overruns. Here are some examples:

>> Escalating labor costs when similar projects reached a certain phase

>> Frequent change orders in projects of the same scope, indicating a risk of scope creep

>> Material price volatility in certain industries, predicting future cost spikes

>> Vendor price inconsistencies, where similar suppliers offer lower rates for the same materials

>> Unusual spending trends, such as a department reaching the limits of its budget earlier than expected.

Instead of manually analyzing financial reports, AI automates this process, providing you with data-backed forecasts and recommended actions to avoid cost overruns before they occur.

CASE STUDY: PREDICTIVE ANALYTICS PREVENTS A MAJOR COST OVERRUN

A construction firm was managing a multimillion-dollar infrastructure project when its AI-driven budget tool flagged a risk: Predictive analytics indicated that labor costs were trending higher than expected at the midpoint of the project. The AI system identified this risk based on historical data from past projects, where similar trends resulted in budget overruns in the final phases.

By catching this early, the project team investigated the cause: an overreliance on overtime pay due to inefficient scheduling. With AI's insights, the company adjusted labor shifts, hired additional staff at standard rates, and improved scheduling efficiency. These changes prevented additional labor costs, keeping the project within budget.

Without AI, project teams often realize financial issues too late, when they have fewer corrective options. Predictive analytics shifts budget management from reactive to proactive, giving you the ability to

>> Spot financial risks before they impact the project

>> Adjust spending plans based on historical trends and real-world market conditions

>> Improve vendor selection and negotiation by identifying cost-efficient alternatives

>> Reduce the impact of supply chain disruptions and unexpected cost spikes

Automating financial contingency planning

Even with careful budgeting, unexpected cost fluctuations can threaten a project's financial stability. Traditional contingency planning relies on broad estimates and static reserve funds, but AI introduces a more dynamic, data-driven approach by continuously assessing financial risks and adjusting contingency plans accordingly. Instead of setting aside an arbitrary percentage of the budget for unforeseen costs, AI can analyze project-specific risk factors, market conditions, and historical spending patterns to determine exactly how much contingency funding is needed — and where it should be allocated.

AI can evaluate risk levels continuously by identifying budget threats such as rising material costs, delays that increase labor expenses, or supplier pricing inconsistencies. Based on these risks, AI can suggest precise contingency budgets for different project phases, ensuring that funds are allocated where they're most likely to be needed. If a project has a history of last-minute procurement cost increases, AI may recommend a higher contingency reserve for materials while reducing unnecessary reserves in lower risk areas. This approach prevents over-reserving funds, which can limit cash flow, while also minimizing the risk of a funding shortfall.

Beyond setting contingency budgets, AI also runs what-if simulations to model potential financial scenarios before they happen. By analyzing past projects, industry trends, and current market conditions, AI can predict how certain cost variables — such as fuel prices, labor shortages, or material tariffs — might impact the overall budget. If AI detects a potential risk, such as a 15 percent increase in steel prices within the next six months, it can recommend proactive strategies like securing long-term vendor contracts at fixed rates or adjusting the project timeline to avoid peak pricing periods. These simulations allow project managers to test multiple financial scenarios and implement safeguards before external factors drive up costs.

AI-driven decision support: When to adjust versus when to cut costs

Managing a project budget is a balancing act between spending where it's necessary and cutting costs without sacrificing quality or efficiency. AI-driven decision support systems help you make data-backed financial choices by distinguishing between essential expenses and avoidable overruns. Instead of applying blanket cost-cutting measures that could impact project outcomes, AI analyzes spending patterns, performance metrics, and market conditions to recommend cost-saving actions that maintain project integrity.

AI can evaluate historical project data, vendor pricing, and productivity trends to determine where spending is justified. For example, if a critical phase of the project is running slightly over budget but contributes directly to overall project success, AI may suggest adjusting budget allocations rather than making immediate cuts. Conversely, if AI detects excessive spending in noncritical areas — such as underutilized labor hours, redundant software subscriptions, or inflated supplier costs — it can recommend specific cost-cutting measures that reduce expenses without disrupting operations.

Beyond identifying where cuts can be made, AI also helps you prioritize spending for maximum impact. If multiple areas of a project require funding adjustments, AI can rank them based on factors like return on investment, timeline urgency, and overall project dependencies. This ensures that funds are reallocated strategically rather than indiscriminately. Additionally, AI can analyze alternative cost-saving strategies, such as negotiating better vendor contracts, optimizing resource scheduling, or adjusting procurement timelines to avoid peak pricing periods.

USING AI-DRIVEN BUDGET CONTROL AT NEXATECH

NexaTech, a mid-sized software development firm, was experiencing frequent budget overruns on its projects, leading to delays and strained relationships with clients. To address this issue, the company decided to implement AI-powered tools to help improve budgeting and cost control throughout the project lifecycle.

For one of its high-profile projects — a new mobile app development for a large client — NexaTech used AI-driven budgeting tools to forecast project costs. The AI analyzed historical data from previous projects with similar scope and timelines, giving NexaTech a more accurate and reliable budget estimate. Tools like Microsoft Project with AI Insights allowed the project manager to predict costs for labor, materials, and third-party vendors with greater precision than before.

As the project progressed, AI tools helped NexaTech monitor spending in real time. The project manager used Smartsheet to track labor costs, materials, and equipment expenses, comparing actual spending to the projected budget. When the AI detected that the vendor supplying critical development tools was charging more than anticipated, it flagged this as a potential budget risk. This early warning allowed the project manager to renegotiate the vendor's contract, resulting in a significant cost saving.

Throughout the project, AI-powered tools like Monday . com automated corrective actions whenever spending started to deviate from the budget. For instance, when a particular task was at risk of exceeding its allocated budget, the AI recommended reallocating resources from a lower-priority task, ensuring that costs stayed under control without delaying the project timeline.

To ensure transparency and keep all stakeholders aligned, NexaTech used Microsoft Teams to send automated budget updates. These updates ensured that the client and internal team members were always informed of any changes to the project's financial status, which helped build trust and prevent miscommunications.

By leveraging AI to predict risks, track spending, and automate budget adjustments, NexaTech successfully completed the project on time and within budget. The company saw a reduction in budget overruns and strengthened its relationship with the client, showcasing how AI can be a valuable asset in managing project finances efficiently.

IN THIS CHAPTER

» Automating performance reports
with AI to save time and
reduce errors

» Tracking key performance indicators
in real time

» Monitoring project progress
dynamically to identify bottlenecks

Chapter **11**

Tracking Performance and Reporting with AI

Performance tracking and reporting to assess progress, identify areas for improvement, and ensure that your project stays on track are essential components of project management. AI is transforming these processes by automating project performance reports, tracking key performance indicators (KPIs) in real time, and monitoring progress dynamically. This chapter explores how AI can streamline performance tracking and reporting, helping project managers make informed decisions and keep your projects on course.

Automating Project Performance Reports with AI

Performance reporting is an essential task in project management, but manually creating reports can be time-consuming, prone to errors, and difficult to keep up with as projects grow in complexity. AI offers a solution by automating the entire process of generating performance reports, from data collection to report customization. By leveraging AI-powered tools, project managers can produce accurate, up-to-date reports that keep all stakeholders informed, while saving significant time and effort.

AI-generated reports make it possible for you to say goodbye to the dreaded report-writing marathon! Think of AI as your new sidekick, automating data collection and report generation, so you can spend more time doing what you love instead of paperwork.

Automating data collection for reports

One of the most tedious aspects of creating project performance reports is collecting data from various sources. Traditionally, you would have to gather information from different tools or team members manually, which is both time-consuming and prone to inaccuracies. AI-powered tools can automate this process by seamlessly pulling data from different project management systems that track task progress, resource usage, and budget performance.

Tools like Microsoft Project with AI Insights and Smartsheet are designed to automate the collection of project data, reducing the burden on project managers. The AI that is built into these tools can gather information from multiple project sources and consolidate it into one place, ensuring that the data used in reports is accurate, up to date, and free of manual errors. With AI, you no longer have to worry about missing or outdated information.

Automating data collection makes it possible to generate more timely and reliable reports, ensuring that everyone stays informed about project progress. It also frees you to focus on higher value tasks, such as analysis and decision-making.

Set AI-powered tools to automatically pull data from multiple sources at regular intervals, ensuring that performance reports always reflect the latest project information.

Generating real-time reports with AI

One of AI's most powerful features is its ability to generate up-to date reports with the click of a button. In traditional project reporting, updates are typically created using a lengthy process and they are published at scheduled intervals, such as weekly or monthly. However, this approach can leave project managers and stakeholders in the dark between reporting periods. That model makes it difficult to respond quickly to emerging issues. With AI, project managers can generate up-to-the-minute performance reports at any time, providing continuous visibility into project progress.

Tools like Monday.com and Wrike use AI to monitor project data and generate performance reports on the fly. This enables project managers to assess the status of the project whenever you need to, without waiting for the next reporting cycle. Current reports are especially useful when projects are experiencing rapid changes, as they allow managers to quickly identify bottlenecks, resource shortages, or budget risks as soon as they arise.

To generate a project status report using project management software, start by defining the report's scope: identifying key stakeholders, reporting frequency, and essential metrics like schedule, budget, risks, and accomplishments. Most project management tools such as, Microsoft Project, Jira, Asana, and ClickUp offer built-in reporting features, allowing you to select or customize templates such as milestone, budget, or risk reports. Extract key data, including project progress, task status, financial updates, and upcoming actions, and present it using visual tools like Gantt charts, burndown graphs, and color-coded status indicators. Once formatted, set up automated reports and dynamic dashboards that continuously update with the latest project data.

Customizing reports to meet stakeholder needs

Different stakeholders often require different types of reports, depending on their roles and interests. Executives may prefer high-level summaries that provide an overview of the project's status, whereas team leads may need detailed reports that track the progress of specific tasks. Manually creating customized reports for each stakeholder group can be time-consuming and difficult to manage, but AI simplifies this process by automatically generating tailored reports based on the needs of each audience.

AI-driven tools like Power BI and Tableau enable you to customize performance reports to meet the specific needs of different stakeholders. These tools can create different versions of reports, adjusting the level of detail and the type of data presented depending on the audience. For example, AI may generate a summary report for executives with KPIs and overall progress, but a report for the project team may include task completion rates, budget breakdowns, and resource usage.

Many project management tools provide interactive views that allow stakeholders to monitor progress, track key metrics, and identify risks as they emerge. Instead of relying solely on static reports, stakeholders can then access live updates, filter information based on their exact needs, and drill down into specific tasks or budget details. This approach ensures that project decisions are based on the most current information, improving responsiveness and efficiency.

REMEMBER

Customizing reports with AI ensures that each stakeholder receives the information that is most relevant to them, presented in a format that is easy to understand. This tailored approach improves communication, enhances stakeholder engagement, and reduces the risk of miscommunication or misunderstanding.

Visualizing data with AI-powered dashboards

In addition to generating written reports, AI can also visualize project performance data through dashboards, making it easier for stakeholders to quickly grasp the status of the project. AI-powered dashboards present key metrics, trends, and progress indicators in a visual format, such as graphs, charts, or timelines. These dashboards are dynamic and automatically update as a project progresses, providing an at-a-glance overview of the project's current performance.

Tools like Microsoft Power BI and Tableau offer advanced AI-driven data visualization features that allow project managers to create dashboards tailored to your specific needs. These dashboards can display critical KPIs such as task completion rates, budget utilization, and resource allocation, enabling stakeholders to quickly assess whether the project is on track or if adjustments are needed. Visual data representation is particularly helpful for busy stakeholders who may not have time to sift through detailed reports.

TIP

AI-powered dashboards also provide the flexibility to drill down into specific metrics for more detailed insights, offering both a high-level overview and deeper analysis when necessary. This allows project managers and stakeholders to quickly identify trends, spot potential issues, and take corrective action before problems escalate. Check out Chapter 7 to find out how AI-driven dashboards improve communication between teams and stakeholders.

Figure 11-1 shows an interactive project dashboard built in PowerBI that provides real-time insights into the progress, budget status, missed deliveries, and risk levels associated with each task in a construction project. This dashboard allows project managers and stakeholders to quickly assess overall project health while also diving into specific task details when needed.

One of the things that makes this dashboard dynamic is its interactive filtering capability. Users can click on any task in one chart, and the corresponding data automatically highlights in the other charts. For example, selecting Framing in the Task Progress Chart instantly filters the Budget Utilization, Missed Deliveries, and Risk Level visualizations to show only data related to that task. This enables you to quickly identify dependencies, correlations, and bottlenecks without sifting through static reports.

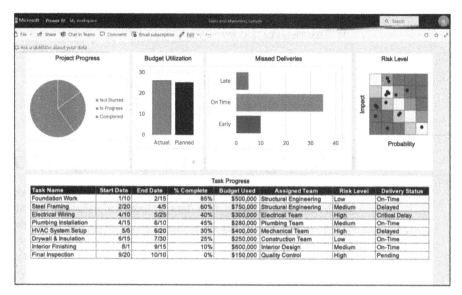

FIGURE 11-1:
Sample
real-time
project
dashboard.

To get up-to-the-minute updates, this report can access data from other systems, such as the purchasing system and the transportation management system. With its AI-enhanced insights, the dashboard can also flag potential schedule risks, cost overruns, and supply chain disruptions, enabling proactive decision-making and ensuring that construction milestones stay on track.

One of the advantages of using AI in project management is the ability to generate customized reports that cater to the specific needs of different stakeholders. Instead of a one-size-fits-all approach, AI can analyze vast amounts of project data and extract the most relevant insights for each audience.

For example, here's how AI can tailor reports based on the needs of various stakeholders to make sure that every stakeholder gets the right level of detail, which improves decision-making and alignment across the organization:

>> Vice president/executive leadership

- High-level project status and overall progress

- Financial impact, including ROI and budget utilization

- Key risks and strategic opportunities

>> Department manager

- Department-specific performance metrics and milestones

- Resource allocation and workload distribution

- Dependencies and potential bottlenecks

>> Team lead/project manager

- Task completion rates and upcoming deadlines

- Individual and team productivity insights

- Issues, blockers, and immediate action items

Reducing errors in reporting with AI

One of the biggest challenges in manual reporting is the risk of human error, which can lead to inaccurate data, missed information, or misreporting. These errors can undermine the reliability of performance reports, leading to misguided decisions and potential project risks. AI can reduce the risk of errors by automating the entire reporting process, from data collection to report generation, ensuring that reports are accurate, complete, and reliable.

There are always risks of data errors when people have to manually enter information, such as updating progress percentages or reporting completion statuses. AI helps mitigate this risk by automating many of these steps, as well as checking the data that is entered to identify inconsistencies. As a result, data that's collected and collated by AI tends to have fewer errors. That said, it's still essential that you remain vigilant and validate the accuracy of reports, ensuring that any anomalies or discrepancies are addressed before they impact decision-making.

Tools like ClickUp and Asana leverage AI to automate key aspects of project reporting, reducing manual effort and minimizing errors. They can automatically collect and enter data by pulling task updates, time logs, and status changes from team inputs. AI-driven features track project progress by updating timelines and completion percentages based on assigned tasks and dependencies. These platforms also generate customized reports, eliminating the need for manual compilation. Additionally, they can prioritize tasks, assign work based on workload balancing, and send automated notifications for overdue tasks or approaching deadlines. AI helps detect errors by identifying inconsistencies, duplicate entries, or missing information, ensuring reports remain accurate. Moreover, these tools create dynamic dashboards and visualizations, such as Gantt charts and workload views, without requiring manual configuration. By automating these processes, ClickUp and Asana help teams produce more accurate, timely, and actionable project reports, improving overall decision-making.

With AI handling data collection and report generation, project managers can be more confident that their reports are accurate and reliable. This reduces the likelihood of making decisions based on faulty data and improves overall project outcomes by ensuring that stakeholders are working with correct information.

Check out Chapter 5 for ways AI can automates routine reporting tasks.

TIP

Tracking Key Performance Indicators with AI

KPIs are essential to project management because they measure progress and success against established goals. Tracking KPIs manually can be time-consuming and prone to errors, but AI simplifies this process by automating data collection, identifying trends, and providing insights. By leveraging AI, project managers can ensure that their projects remain on track and that any deviations from targets are addressed promptly. AI, your project's personal cheerleader (and tough critic), tracks your KPIs, celebrates your successes, and gently nudges you when you need to improve.

Automating KPI tracking and updates

Manually updating KPIs can be tedious and inefficient. Doing it the old-fashioned way often leads to delays or inaccurate data. Fortunately, AI-powered tools streamline this process by automating the tracking and updating of KPIs. With AI, you can rely on continuous monitoring of key metrics such as task completion rates, budget utilization, and resource efficiency. These updates occur automatically, reducing the need for manual data entry and ensuring that you always have access to the most current information.

Tools like Smartsheet and Monday.com enable you to automate KPI tracking, allowing them to focus on higher-level decision-making. These platforms pull data from various sources and update KPIs as changes happen, eliminating the risk of outdated or inaccurate information. This real-time automation ensures that project performance is measured accurately and that any potential issues are identified early.

Identifying trends and patterns in KPI data

In addition to tracking the current status, AI offers the ability to analyze KPI data and identify trends or patterns that may not be immediately obvious. AI can continuously monitor data to detect recurring issues such as delays, inefficiencies, or shifts in resource allocation that may signal a problem. For example, AI might notice that a specific task is consistently delayed or that resource utilization has been declining over time. When AI flags this for you, it prompts you to do further investigation.

Tools like Microsoft Power BI and Tableau use AI to analyze KPI data and present trends in a clear and actionable way. This enables project managers to identify patterns that could affect the project's success, allowing them to take corrective action before small issues become major setbacks. AI-driven trend analysis is particularly valuable for long-term projects where changes in performance may occur gradually over time.

The task complexity versus completion time scatter plot shown in Figure 11-2 visually represents how the time required to complete a task varies with its complexity. At first glance, the data points may appear scattered without a clear pattern, making it difficult for a project manager to draw immediate conclusions. However, AI-powered analysis can identify underlying trends that may not be obvious, such as whether higher complexity tasks consistently take longer or certain complexity levels have unpredictable completion times due to external factors. By detecting these patterns, AI can help project managers predict delays, optimize resource allocation, and adjust schedules proactively. For example, if AI identifies that tasks rated seven or higher in complexity tend to experience significant delays, the project manager can assign additional resources, break down complex tasks into smaller components, or adjust deadlines accordingly. This data-driven decision-making approach reduces inefficiencies, improves forecasting accuracy, and ensures that projects stay on track.

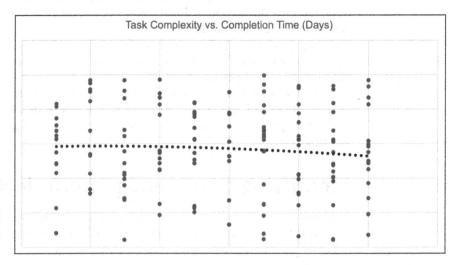

FIGURE 11-2: Graph showing how AI can identify trends in data.

Customizing KPI dashboards with AI

Determining which KPIs to track can be just as important as monitoring them. AI helps project managers and stakeholders identify the most relevant metrics by analyzing historical data, project goals, and industry best practices. AI-driven systems can prompt users with intelligent recommendations tailored to their specific role and project type, so project managers don't have to decide which KPIs to use. For example, an LLM (large language model) can ask targeted questions about the project's scope, industry, and primary objectives and then suggest KPIs that align with those factors. A project manager working on a construction site might be advised to track schedule variance, subcontractor efficiency, and safety incidents, whereas an executive overseeing multiple projects could receive recommendations for portfolio performance, budget adherence, and overall risk exposure.

AI-powered tools like Power BI and Tableau further refine KPI selection by continuously analyzing project data and suggesting adjustments based on emerging patterns. If a recurring issue is detected — such as delays in a critical task or cost overruns — AI might recommend adding new KPIs, like lead time for material deliveries or change order frequency, to improve visibility into problem areas. By leveraging AI to dynamically determine which metrics to track, your project team can ensure you're focusing on the most actionable insights rather than drowning in irrelevant data.

Customize AI-driven dashboards to provide relevant KPI insights to different stakeholders, ensuring everyone receives the information they need in real time.

REMEMBER

Setting and adjusting KPI targets with AI

Setting realistic KPI targets can be challenging, particularly when project conditions are constantly evolving. AI simplifies this process by using historical data and predictive analytics to set achievable targets based on past performance and current conditions. AI can also adjust KPI targets dynamically as the project progresses, helping project managers stay flexible and respond to changes as they occur.

With tools like Wrike and Smartsheet, you can set and adjust KPI targets with AI. These platforms analyze project data to recommend targets that align with both historical trends and real-time performance metrics. When you set data-driven targets, you can ensure that goals remain attainable and relevant throughout the project lifecycle.

Providing alerts when KPIs deviate from targets

One of the most valuable aspects of AI in KPI tracking is its ability to provide real-time alerts when performance deviates from established targets. If a key metric starts trending in the wrong direction, AI-powered tools can send immediate notifications to project managers, allowing them to address the issue before it escalates. For example, if task completion rates begin to drop or budget utilization exceeds projections, AI will trigger an alert, prompting corrective action.

Here are some examples of KPIs that would trigger alerts when something is off track:

>> **Task completion rate:** Alerts when task progress falls below a set threshold or when critical milestones are missed

>> **Budget utilization:** Triggers a notification if spending exceeds projections or if cost overruns occur in a specific phase

>> **Schedule variance:** Sends an alert like the one shown in Figure 11-3 when actual progress deviates significantly from the planned timeline

>> **Resource allocation efficiency:** Flags when certain team members are over- or underutilized, leading to inefficiencies

>> **Risk exposure score:** Issues warnings when the overall project risk level increases due to emerging threats or unresolved issues

>> **Material delivery delays:** Notifies teams when supplier shipments are late, potentially impacting the project schedule

>> **Change order frequency:** Alerts when excessive change orders are submitted, indicating scope creep or misalignment with the project plan

>> **Quality defect rate:** Triggers a warning if the number of defects or rework requests rise beyond acceptable limits

>> **Customer or stakeholder satisfaction scores:** Sends alerts when stakeholder feedback trends negatively, signaling potential project dissatisfaction

Tools like Asana and ClickUp offer AI-driven alerts that monitor KPIs in real time, ensuring that project managers stay informed about potential risks. These alerts enable quick responses to deviations, helping you take proactive steps to keep the project on track.

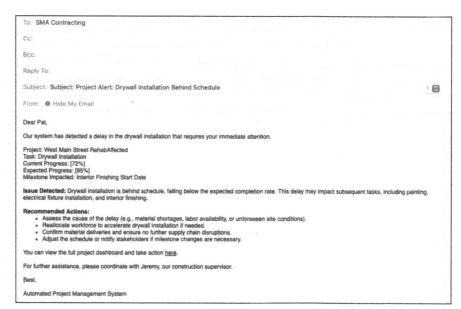

To: SMA Contracting

Cc:

Bcc:

Reply To:

Subject: **Subject: Project Alert: Drywall Installation Behind Schedule**

From: ● Hide My Email

Dear Pat,

Our system has detected a delay in the drywall installation that requires your immediate attention.

Project: West Main Street RehabAffected
Task: Drywall Installation
Current Progress: [72%]
Expected Progress: [95%]
Milestone Impacted: Interior Finishing Start Date

Issue Detected: Drywall installation is behind schedule, falling below the expected completion rate. This delay may impact subsequent tasks, including painting, electrical fixture installation, and interior finishing.

Recommended Actions:
- Assess the cause of the delay (e.g., material shortages, labor availability, or unforeseen site conditions).
- Reallocate workforce to accelerate drywall installation if needed.
- Confirm material deliveries and ensure no further supply chain disruptions.
- Adjust the schedule or notify stakeholders if milestone changes are necessary.

You can view the full project dashboard and take action here.

For further assistance, please coordinate with Jeremy, our construction supervisor.

Best,

Automated Project Management System

FIGURE 11-3: Project alert email generated by AI.

Monitoring Progress and Making Adjustments with AI

In project management, real-time monitoring is critical for ensuring that tasks stay on schedule and resources are used efficiently. Without up-to-date insights, project managers risk missing early warning signs of delays or inefficiencies, which can lead to larger problems down the road. AI simplifies monitoring by continuously tracking project data, providing instant updates, and recommending adjustments when needed. By leveraging AI, project managers can proactively manage progress and make real-time adjustments to keep their projects on track.

Before the widespread use of project management software, real-time monitoring was nearly impossible. Project managers relied on manual status updates, in-person meetings, and paper-based reports to track progress, often receiving out-dated information by the time it reached them. For example, in a large construction project, a project manager might not find out about a supplier delay until a weekly meeting, at which point the team had already lost valuable time. Similarly, in manufacturing, production bottlenecks might only become evident at the end of a reporting cycle, making it difficult to respond quickly. Even after digital project management tools became available, early systems still required manual data entry, meaning real-time monitoring depended on how frequently team members updated their progress. AI can eliminate many of these delays by automating data collection, identifying patterns, and alerting managers to issues as soon as they arise, enabling proactive decision-making instead of reactive problem-solving.

Figure 11-4 compares how tasks were handled before AI and how they can now be managed with AI.

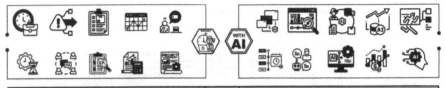

Project Management Without AI		Project Management With AI
Manual task assignment and scheduling, leading to inefficiencies.	→	AI automates task assignment, optimizing workloads and efficiency.
Project managers rely on past experience and intuition to predict risks.	→	AI analyzes real-time data to predict potential risks and recommend mitigations.
Progress updates are gathered through status meetings and manual reports.	→	AI continuously tracks progress and provides alerts when delays occur.
Decisions are made based on historical data and static reports.	→	AI-driven insights recommend the best course of action based on trends and predictive analytics.
Managers manually adjust workloads, often leading to burnout or inefficiencies.	→	AI detects overworked team members and redistributes tasks for balanced workloads.
Schedules are adjusted reactively when delays are noticed.	→	AI dynamically adjusts project timelines based on evolving conditions.
Stakeholder communication is handled through emails and manual reports.	→	AI-powered dashboards and chatbots provide instant project updates to stakeholders.
KPIs are tracked manually, often leading to delays in detecting issues.	→	AI tracks KPIs in real time and sends alerts when performance deviates from targets.
Budget planning relies on static financial projections.	→	AI-driven cost forecasting predicts future expenses and prevents budget overruns.
Project documentation is updated manually, making knowledge retrieval slow.	→	AI automates documentation, categorizing and retrieving project knowledge instantly.

FIGURE 11-4: Project management with and without AI.

Real-time monitoring of task progress

Tracking task progress manually can be overwhelming, especially on large projects with multiple moving parts. It's easy for delays to go unnoticed until they start to affect other areas of the project. AI-powered tools solve this issue by monitoring task progress as it happens and providing you with up-to-date information on the status of each task. This continuous monitoring ensures that managers are always aware of which tasks are on schedule, which are falling behind, and which are ahead of schedule.

Tools like Smartsheet and Monday.com use AI to track task progress by automatically gathering and analyzing project data from multiple sources. These platforms can integrate with team workflows, pulling updates from task assignments, time logs, and communication channels to ensure that status information is always current.

For example, when a team member marks a task as complete, logs work hours, or changes a task status (for example, from In Progress to Completed), the AI within these tools instantly detects the update. It then processes the new information and reflects the change across all dashboards and reports. This means that project managers and stakeholders always have access to the most current data without having to wait for manual reports or status meetings. The AI also ensures that dependent tasks and schedules are automatically adjusted, keeping the entire project aligned as updates are made.

If a task is delayed, AI can flag it instantly, allowing project managers to address the issue before it escalates. This automated visibility into task progress makes it easier for managers to stay informed and make timely decisions.

Analyzing progress data to identify bottlenecks

Even when tasks are progressing smoothly, unexpected disruptions can create bottlenecks that slow down an entire project. For example, if a key team member takes an unexpected extended leave, tasks assigned to them — such as drywall installation in a construction project — may stall due to a lack of available personnel. AI can quickly identify this issue by analyzing progress data, detecting that work has not advanced as expected, and flagging the risk of cascading delays. To prevent further setbacks, AI can recommend reassigning crew members, adjusting schedules, or bringing in additional labor to fill the gap.

Delays in one task can have a ripple effect across the entire project. In this scenario, if drywall installation falls behind, dependent tasks like painting, electrical fixture installation, and flooring may also be delayed. This not only pushes back the overall project timeline but can also affect other construction projects that rely on the same labor force or subcontractors. By spotting these risks early, AI enables project managers to reallocate resources efficiently, keep stakeholders informed, and mitigate delays before they spiral into larger disruptions.

Tools like Wrike and Asana provide AI-driven insights into progress data, identifying the root causes of bottlenecks and offering solutions. AI's ability to analyze data and identify bottlenecks gives project managers a clear view of where to focus their efforts to keep the project running smoothly.

TIP

Let AI analyze progress data to spot bottlenecks early, allowing you to reallocate resources or adjust deadlines before small delays become major roadblocks.

Recommending adjustments to project plans

One of the most powerful features of AI in project management is its ability to recommend real-time adjustments based on current progress data. When AI detects a deviation from the project plan — such as a task falling behind or a resource being underutilized — it can provide suggestions for how to course-correct. These recommendations might include reassigning tasks, adjusting timelines, or reallocating resources to ensure that the project stays on track.

TIP

Tools like Trello and ClickUp use AI to continuously analyze project data and suggest adjustments as needed. For example, if a task is at risk of missing its deadline, AI might recommend extending the deadline or assigning additional team members to speed up completion. Similarly, if AI detects that certain resources are underused, it might suggest shifting them to a more critical area of the project. By following these recommendations, project managers can make informed decisions that optimize resource allocation and minimize delays.

Manually adjusting project schedules or reassigning tasks can be time-consuming and tedious, especially when quick changes are needed. While most AI systems do not fully automate dynamic task reassignments (yet), tools like Monday.com and Smartsheet allow project managers to set up automated workflows that assist with tracking task progress and notifying team members when adjustments are necessary. These platforms can trigger alerts when a task is overdue, a milestone is missed, or a team member is overloaded, prompting project managers to act. Additionally, they allow teams to create rules-based automations, such as reassigning tasks when a project status changes or adjusting deadlines based on dependencies.

For example, if a software development team is working on a new feature and the lead engineer falls behind due to an urgent bug fix, an automation could notify the project manager of the delay. Based on preset rules, a task like documentation or code reviews could be flagged for reassignment. The project manager would then manually update the task assignment, prompting an automatic notification to the new developer via their dashboard or email.

Tools like Monday.com and Smartsheet can also ensure that these AI-driven adjustments are clearly communicated. When AI reassigns a task or modifies the schedule, both the project manager and affected team members receive automated notifications. This ensures that the project manager remains informed and can override changes if needed. Team members also receive direct alerts about their new assignments.

For example, if a software development team is working on a new feature and the lead engineer is overloaded, AI may reassign some of their upcoming tasks — such as documentation or minor code reviews — to another available developer. The project manager gets a notification summarizing the changes, and the reassigned developer receives an alert in their dashboard or inbox about their new tasks. By handling these adjustments in real time, AI minimizes disruptions, ensures workload balance, and keeps the project on track without requiring constant manual intervention.

Providing real-time progress alerts

Another function AI can perform is providing real-time alerts that reflect actual work happening on the ground. Unlike KPI alerts, which flag deviations from predefined benchmarks, progress alerts focus on tracking task execution and milestone completion as they unfold.

For instance, if a task is at risk of being delayed due to slow execution or if a team member is suddenly overloaded with additional responsibilities, AI detects these bottlenecks as they occur and sends immediate notifications to the project manager. These alerts allow managers to respond proactively, whether by reassigning tasks, allocating additional resources, or adjusting timelines before a minor issue escalates into a major delay.

TIP

Tools like Slack and Microsoft Teams integrate with AI-powered project management systems to deliver real-time alerts directly to project teams. These alerts ensure that project managers stay informed about evolving issues, not just high-level KPI deviations. Whether it's an unexpected delay, a resource bottleneck, or a critical milestone approaching, AI-generated alerts help project managers maintain control of fast-moving projects by enabling immediate intervention.

In large, complex projects, staying on top of key milestones is challenging. AI continuously tracks progress toward major deliverables, sending automatic milestone updates when a phase is completed or when a milestone is at risk of delay.

For example, tools like Wrike and Asana monitor milestone progress and trigger alerts when deadlines are in jeopardy. If AI detects that a foundation pour is behind schedule, it can suggest corrective actions, such as increasing shift coverage or expediting material deliveries, keeping the project aligned with its overall objectives.

Set up AI-driven real-time alerts to notify you of any deviations from the project plan, allowing you to take quick action to address issues before they escalate.

Enhancing stakeholder communication with real-time updates

Keeping stakeholders informed is crucial for maintaining transparency and ensuring that everyone is aligned on the project's status. AI makes stakeholder communication easier by automating the process of generating real-time updates. You can set AI tools to automatically send progress reports, milestone updates, and KPI summaries to stakeholders, ensuring that they receive timely information without having to request it.

Tools like Slack and Microsoft Teams offer AI-driven communication features that keep stakeholders updated on project progress. These tools can generate reports and send them directly to stakeholders, providing a clear overview of the project's current status. By automating stakeholder communication, AI ensures that everyone is informed and aligned, reducing the risk of miscommunication or confusion.

TRACKING PROJECT PERFORMANCE WITH AI AT ALPHABUILD

AlphaBuild, a mid-sized construction company, was facing challenges in tracking the performance of its projects. With multiple tasks running simultaneously and many stakeholders to keep informed, project managers found it difficult to maintain accurate, up-to-date performance reports. Additionally, delays in tracking KPIs such as task completion rates and resource utilization were leading to bottlenecks and budget overruns. To address these issues, AlphaBuild decided to implement AI-powered tools for performance tracking and reporting.

For a major new project — building a high-rise office complex — AlphaBuild used AI-driven tools like Smartsheet and Power BI to automate the collection of project data and generate real-time performance reports. Instead of relying on manual data entry, AI automatically gathered information on task progress, resource usage, and budget spending, allowing project managers to generate reports instantly. This automation reduced errors and saved AlphaBuild's project managers *hours* of work each week.

The company also utilized AI to track KPIs in real time. Tools like Monday.com helped the project manager monitor task completion rates, resource efficiency, and budget utilization continuously. When AI detected a consistent delay in a specific task, it flagged the issue early, allowing the project team to reassign resources and prevent further delays. This real-time monitoring helped AlphaBuild address potential problems before they became major setbacks.

For example, AI detected a consistent delay in the drywall installation phase, which was falling behind schedule due to a shortage of available subcontractors. Since drywall installation is a critical path task that must be completed before painting, electrical fixture installation, and interior finishing, the delay threatened to push the entire project timeline back. The system flagged the issue early and recommended reallocating additional crew members from less time-sensitive tasks to assist with drywall work. Additionally, AI suggested adjusting material deliveries to align with the new pace, preventing excess inventory from piling up on site. By taking proactive measures based on AI-driven insights, AlphaBuild was able to mitigate delays, optimize labor use, and keep the project on track.

Similarly, when concrete pouring for the foundation was consistently delayed due to uncooperative weather conditions, AI provided alternative scheduling recommendations. It suggested shifting work hours to early mornings when temperatures were more stable and rescheduling other dependent tasks, such as framing and plumbing rough-ins, to ensure that productivity remained high despite the setbacks. These adjustments, facilitated by AI-powered dashboards and tools like Monday . com, enabled AlphaBuild to maintain efficiency and reduce costly downtime while keeping all stakeholders informed through customized reports.

AI-powered dashboards also allowed AlphaBuild to customize reports for different stakeholders. Executives received high-level reports summarizing overall progress, while project team members had access to detailed, task-specific dashboards. This tailored reporting ensured that everyone was informed and aligned on the project's status.

During the project, AI continuously monitored progress and detected a bottleneck when steel deliveries for the foundation were delayed due to supply chain disruptions. The system issued an alert as the delay began to impact the overall project timeline, flagging potential risks to subsequent tasks like framing and electrical work. AI recommended reallocating available labor to other tasks, such as site preparation and plumbing installation, to keep the team productive while waiting for materials. Additionally, it suggested adjusting the project schedule to extend deadlines for affected tasks while ensuring minimal disruption to the overall timeline. By automating these adjustments through tools like Monday . com, the project team was able to quickly adapt, preventing costly downtime and keeping progress aligned with strategic goals.

By integrating AI into its performance tracking and reporting processes, AlphaBuild reduced reporting errors, optimized resource allocation, and improved communication with stakeholders. The project was completed on time and within budget, demonstrating the power of AI in ensuring project success.

4

Ensuring Ethical and Secure AI Adoption

Chapter **12**

Ensuring Ethical Use of AI in Project Management

As artificial intelligence (AI) continues to play a transformative role in project management, ensuring its ethical use has become a critical responsibility for project managers. The integration of AI into project management processes presents new ethical challenges, including fairness, transparency, and the potential for unintended consequences. This chapter explores the key ethical considerations project managers must address when using AI, including understanding AI ethics, promoting fairness and transparency in AI-driven decisions, and navigating ethical dilemmas in AI-powered projects.

Understanding AI Ethics for Project Managers

As AI becomes increasingly integrated into project management, understanding AI ethics is essential so you can ensure that AI systems are used responsibly and appropriately. AI ethics refers to the principles and guidelines that govern the fair, ethical, and accountable use of AI technologies. By understanding these ethical principles, you can avoid potential pitfalls, such as bias and lack of transparency, and ensure that AI serves the best interests of all stakeholders involved.

The importance of ethical AI use

AI has the power to significantly influence decision-making processes within projects, from resource allocation to hiring decisions. Therefore, it's critical for project managers to ensure that AI is used ethically, with a strong emphasis on fairness, privacy, and accountability. When AI systems are not properly designed or monitored, they can reinforce biases, violate privacy, or operate without clear oversight, leading to unintended and potentially harmful consequences.

For example, an AI system optimized purely for cost savings might inadvertently result in unfair outcomes. If a hiring algorithm is trained on historical data that favors lower salaries, it might systematically prioritize candidates from certain demographics over others, reinforcing existing disparities. Similarly, an AI-powered vendor selection tool that prioritizes the lowest bid might disproportionately exclude smaller or minority-owned businesses that cannot compete on cost alone but offer high-quality services.

As a project manager, your role is to ensure that AI-driven decisions align with ethical standards and do not unintentionally disadvantage certain groups. This requires continuous monitoring of AI's outputs, questioning underlying data assumptions, and intervening when necessary to address biases. For instance, a PM might notice a disconnect when project outcomes consistently fail to meet diversity or inclusion goals, or when complaints arise about unfair treatment from workers or vendors.

Ethical AI use is not just about compliance; it's about fostering trust and ensuring that AI contributes to positive and equitable project outcomes. By actively evaluating AI-driven decisions and maintaining openness, project managers can help create systems that benefit all stakeholders.

TIP

Regularly review AI decisions to ensure that they align with ethical standards, and take immediate corrective action if you identify any unfair outcomes.

You need to be familiar with several key principles of AI ethics when overseeing AI-powered projects — fairness, transparency, accountability, privacy, and security:

» Fairness refers to ensuring that AI-driven decisions treat all individuals equitably, without favoring one group over another.

>> Transparency means making AI systems and their decision-making processes understandable to stakeholders, so they can see how decisions are made.

>> Accountability ensures that organizations and individuals take responsibility for the outcomes of AI-driven decisions. This means having clear oversight mechanisms, defining who is responsible for AI-related mistakes or biases, and providing ways to challenge AI-driven decisions when they negatively impact individuals. For instance, if an AI system in hiring disproportionately excludes certain candidates due to biased training data, the organization must have a process to identify the issue, address the bias, and make corrections rather than deflecting blame onto the technology.

>> Privacy ensures that sensitive personal information is protected.

>> Security ensures that AI systems are resilient to unauthorized access or cyberattacks.

Check out Chapter 16 for more insights on avoiding mistakes related to ethical AI use.

Implement a checklist of AI ethical principles — fairness, transparency, accountability, privacy, and security — and use it to evaluate AI decisions throughout the project. You can start with the sample checklist later in this chapter.

Recognizing bias in AI algorithms

One of the most significant ethical challenges with AI is the potential for bias. AI systems are trained on data, and if that data contains biases — related to gender, race, socioeconomic status, or other factors — the AI may perpetuate those biases in its decision-making processes. For example, an AI system used for hiring might inadvertently favor candidates from certain backgrounds if its training data is biased in that direction. Bias can have serious implications for project fairness and stakeholder trust.

You must be vigilant about the potential for bias in AI systems. This involves ensuring that the data used to train AI models is diverse and representative of all relevant groups.

Additionally, you should regularly audit AI-driven decisions to identify patterns of bias or unfair treatment. If you identify biases, you may need to have the AI model retrained with more inclusive data to ensure fair outcomes. Check out Chapter 9 for information regarding how AI-driven risk assessments can sometimes inherit biases from data.

Balancing efficiency and ethics

Using AI in project management is a lot like relying on a GPS for navigation. It can be incredibly helpful, but if you follow it blindly without thinking critically, you might end up in a metaphorical (or literal) ditch. Just as some drivers have landed in lakes or caused accidents by obeying their GPS without assessing real-world conditions, project managers who unquestioningly follow AI-driven recommendations risk making poor or even harmful decisions.

For instance, an AI system might suggest drastic cost-cutting measures to improve efficiency, but if you implement these without scrutiny, you might unknowingly eliminate essential resources, overburden employees, or disproportionately impact certain groups. Much like your GPS telling you to turn right when you're in the wrong lane — causing a dangerous maneuver — you need to pause and assess whether AI-generated recommendations truly make sense within the broader project context.

Always balance efficiency with ethics when using AI. This means critically evaluating whether AI-driven decisions align with organizational values and considering their impact on stakeholders. While AI can optimize workflows and improve productivity, these benefits should never come at the cost of fairness, accountability, or well-being. Just as a responsible driver checks their surroundings before making a turn, a responsible project manager assesses AI recommendations before taking action.

Creating an ethical AI framework for your projects

One way you can ensure the ethical use of AI is by developing an ethical AI framework. This framework should outline the principles and guidelines that will govern the use of AI in the project. It should address issues like fairness, transparency, accountability, and privacy, providing clear standards for how AI will be used and how ethical dilemmas will be handled. The framework can also establish procedures for monitoring AI decisions, auditing outcomes, and addressing any unintended consequences.

Having an ethical AI framework in place provides you with a solid foundation for managing the ethical aspects of AI-powered projects. It ensures that all team members and stakeholders understand the ethical expectations and outlines clear processes for resolving ethical issues as they arise. The framework also fosters trust by demonstrating a commitment to responsible AI use and ethical project management.

Here's an example of a framework that ensures AI is used responsibly in project management by prioritizing fairness, transparency, accountability, privacy, security, and bias mitigation while establishing governance structures for ethical oversight:

1. Fairness: Ensure AI systems make decisions that treat all individuals equitably.

   Guidelines:

      Use diverse, representative data to train AI models.

      Audit AI decisions regularly for bias or discrimination.

   Processes:

      Conduct fairness audits quarterly.

      Retrain models if bias is detected.

2. Transparency: Ensure AI decision-making processes are clear and understandable to stakeholders.

   Guidelines:

      Provide explanations for AI-driven decisions.

      Use explainability features in AI tools.

   Processes:

      Include decision rationales in reports.

      Hold review meetings with stakeholders.

3. Accountability: Hold the team responsible for AI-driven decisions and their outcomes.

   Guidelines:

      Assign accountability for monitoring AI decisions.

      Implement a process for resolving ethical issues.

   Processes:

      Set up an AI ethics task force.

      Submit monthly reports on AI decision impacts.

4. Privacy: Protect individuals' data and ensure compliance with privacy regulations.

Guidelines:

Anonymize data used for AI training.

Ensure AI complies with General Data Protection Regulation (GDPR), Health Insurance Portability and Accountability Act (HIPAA), and so on.

Processes:

Conduct Privacy Impact Assessments (PIAs) for AI systems.

Implement consent and data minimization policies to protect privacy.

5. Security: Ensure AI systems are resilient to unauthorized access and data breaches.

Guidelines:

Update AI systems regularly for security patches.

Encrypt sensitive data processed by AI.

Processes:

Schedule quarterly security audits.

Use multifactor authentication for AI access.

6. Bias mitigation: Ensure AI models avoid perpetuating or amplifying bias.

Guidelines:

Test models for bias before deployment.

Retrain AI models if biased outcomes are identified.

Processes:

Use fairness monitoring tools for demographic performance tracking.

Conduct ongoing bias training for the team.

7. Ethical AI governance: Implement a governance structure for ethical oversight of AI use.

Guidelines:

Establish an AI ethics committee.

Review AI decisions regularly for ethical concerns.

Processes:

Create an internal AI ethics policy.

Conduct quarterly ethical audits of AI systems.

Promoting Fairness and Transparency in AI-Driven Decisions

As AI becomes a vital part of decision-making processes in project management, promoting fairness and transparency is essential to maintaining trust and ensuring ethical outcomes. Fairness ensures that AI systems treat all individuals and groups equitably, whereas transparency allows stakeholders to understand how and why decisions are made. Project managers have a responsibility to ensure that AI-driven decisions adhere to these principles, fostering a project environment that is both equitable and transparent.

Ensuring fairness in AI decision-making

To ensure fairness in AI-driven decision-making, you need a structured approach to evaluating and auditing the data your AI system relies on. This begins with assessing whether the training data is diverse, representative, and free from historical biases. One way to do this is by performing statistical checks on the dataset — looking for imbalances in demographics, such as underrepresentation of certain groups in hiring or resource allocation data. Additionally, conducting bias detection tests can help identify whether AI-generated recommendations disproportionately benefit or disadvantage specific groups.

Tools like Fiddler AI help project managers audit AI systems for fairness by continuously monitoring AI-driven decisions, detecting biased patterns, and providing insights into how AI models reach their conclusions. These tools allow for transparency by surfacing hidden biases and suggesting corrective actions, such as reweighting certain inputs or adjusting the algorithm to mitigate unfair outcomes.

If biases are detected, retraining the AI model is necessary to improve fairness. Retraining involves feeding the AI new, more balanced data that better represents the diversity of the stakeholders affected by its decisions. This might include incorporating additional historical data from underrepresented groups, adjusting weighting mechanisms to correct for bias, or even refining the AI's decision-making criteria to focus on more equitable outcomes. Regularly auditing and updating the AI model ensures that fairness remains a priority throughout the lifecycle of the project.

TIP

Conduct regular fairness audits and use diverse training data to ensure that AI systems treat all stakeholders equitably.

Ensuring transparency

Transparency in AI ensures that the decision-making process is clear and understandable to all stakeholders. AI decisions can sometimes seem opaque, especially when the algorithms involved are complex and difficult to interpret. However, when stakeholders understand how decisions are made, they're more likely to trust the outcomes and feel confident that the AI system operates fairly. Therefore, it's worthwhile for you to prioritize transparency by making the inner workings of AI systems accessible and comprehensible.

To implement transparency, you should require AI systems to provide explanations for the decisions they make. These explanations can detail the factors the AI considered and the weight given to each factor, allowing stakeholders to understand the reasoning behind decisions. Transparent AI systems also help project managers identify any hidden biases or flaws in the algorithm that could lead to unfair outcomes.

Use AI systems with explainability features, such as Google's Explainable AI (XAI), to provide stakeholders with clear insights into how decisions are made.

TIP

Involving stakeholders in AI-driven decisions

One effective way to ensure fairness and transparency in AI-driven decisions is to involve stakeholders in the decision-making process. Project managers can create opportunities for stakeholders to review and provide feedback on AI decisions, ensuring that their perspectives and concerns are considered. This collaborative approach not only fosters trust but also helps identify potential biases or unfair outcomes that may have gone unnoticed.

You can facilitate stakeholder involvement through regular meetings or feedback sessions where you present AI-driven decisions and explain the reasoning behind them. Stakeholders include anyone affected by AI-driven decisions, such as employees, project team members, clients, vendors, and even end-users who rely on the project's outcomes. They should have the opportunity to ask questions, raise concerns, and suggest adjustments where needed. By involving stakeholders in the process, you can promote a more democratic and inclusive approach to AI-driven decision-making, ensuring that all voices are heard and considered.

Schedule regular stakeholder feedback sessions to review AI decisions and gather input.

TIP

AI decisions can sometimes seem confusing or difficult to understand, especially when complex algorithms are involved. You must ensure that AI systems provide clear, comprehensible explanations for their decisions to avoid misunderstandings and build stakeholder trust. You can use tools like LIME (Local Interpretable Model-Agnostic Explanations), which help break down complex AI models into simpler, more understandable components to avoid misinterpretations and ensure that all stakeholders align on how the AI operates.

REMEMBER

Transparency is crucial for fostering trust and ensuring that all parties accept AI-driven decisions. When stakeholders understand how decisions are reached, they are more likely to accept the outcomes and feel confident in the fairness and transparency of the process.

TIP

Check out Chapter 14 to read more about overcoming challenges in AI adoption.

Addressing Ethical Dilemmas in AI-Powered Projects

AI-powered projects can present unique ethical challenges, particularly when it comes to balancing competing priorities, managing unintended consequences, and ensuring responsible AI use. Project managers are often faced with difficult decisions that involve navigating these ethical dilemmas while maintaining project goals. In this section, I talk about how a project manager can understand and address these dilemmas to ensuring the ethical integration of AI into project management processes.

Balancing competing priorities

In AI-powered projects, one of the most common ethical dilemmas involves balancing efficiency, cost savings, and fairness. AI systems are often designed to optimize outcomes, but this optimization can sometimes conflict with other important considerations.

Consider an AI-driven employee performance evaluation system that ranks workers based on productivity metrics, such as the number of tasks completed or hours logged. While this system may optimize efficiency by identifying high-performing employees, it could unintentionally disadvantage workers who take parental leave, need disability accommodations, or perform valuable but less quantifiable tasks like mentoring colleagues. If management follows the AI's recommendations without critical review, employees with extenuating circumstances may be unfairly overlooked for promotions, raises, or job security.

You must weigh these competing priorities carefully to ensure that you aren't compromising ethical principles in the pursuit of efficiency or cost reduction.

One way you can address this dilemma is by adopting a more holistic approach to decision-making. Instead of focusing solely on efficiency or cost, you should also consider the potential ethical implications of AI-driven recommendations. In some cases, you may need to sacrifice a degree of efficiency to ensure that decisions remain fair and equitable. By balancing these priorities, you can ensure that AI systems contribute to both project success and ethical outcomes.

TIP

Use a decision matrix like the one in Figure 12-1 to weigh efficiency, cost, and fairness when evaluating AI recommendations.

FIGURE 12-1: Decision matrix comparing project options.

AI Recommendation	Efficiency (40%)	Cost (30%)	Fairness (30%)	Total Score
Option A	$4 \times 0.40 = 1.6$	$5 \times 0.30 = 1.5$	$2 \times 0.30 = 0.6$	3.7
Option B	$3 \times 0.40 = 1.2$	$4 \times 0.30 = 1.2$	$5 \times 0.30 = 1.5$	3.9
Option C	$5 \times 0.40 = 2.0$	$3 \times 0.30 = 0.9$	$3 \times 0.30 = 0.9$	3.8

To effectively balance competing priorities when an AI tool suggests a course of action that conflicts with project goals or ethical standards, you should establish mechanisms for reporting and addressing any negative consequences that arise, ensuring that affected stakeholders are heard and that corrective actions are taken. By managing these risks, you can minimize harm and ensure that AI systems are used responsibly.

One key mechanism is a review committee or escalation protocol that allows stakeholders to flag AI-generated recommendations that may lead to unfair, impractical, or unethical outcomes. For example, if an AI system suggests a cost-cutting measure that disproportionately affects a particular vendor or employee group, the project manager should have a formal process for raising concerns, such as through stakeholder meetings, an ethics review board, or a designated AI oversight team.

Additionally, project managers should implement decision validation checkpoints, where AI recommendations undergo human review before implementation. This could involve running what-if scenarios to simulate potential outcomes, conducting bias assessments to detect unintended disparities, or comparing AI-driven suggestions against historical project data to ensure feasibility. If the AI-generated decision does not align with the project's broader objectives, you can adjust — for example, by incorporating additional fairness constraints into the AI model or overriding its recommendations based on human judgment.

Finally, maintaining transparent documentation is essential. Whenever you modify or override an AI recommendation, record the rationale to ensure accountability and continuous learning. This helps refine AI systems over time, enabling them to better align with organizational values and project priorities while still leveraging their efficiency and analytical strengths.

Ensuring informed consent

In AI-powered projects that involve the use of personal or sensitive data, ensuring informed consent is a critical ethical consideration. Stakeholders and project participants must be fully informed about how their data will be used, who will have access to it, and the potential implications of AI-driven decisions. Informed consent is especially important in areas such as hiring, performance evaluation, and customer data analysis, where AI-driven decisions can have a direct impact on individuals.

You should implement clear processes for obtaining informed consent, providing stakeholders with transparent information about the use of AI in the project. Your process for doing so should ensure that participants are truly providing informed consent by explaining the risks and limitations of AI systems and helping them understand how AI will influence decision-making in the project.

Ensuring informed consent is crucial in AI-powered projects that involve personal or sensitive data. To assist you in developing appropriate consent forms, here are some resources that provide sample templates:

>> **Medical Group Management Association (MGMA):** Offers a sample patient consent form for using artificial intelligence in dictation and transcription. This template can be adapted to inform participants about AI usage in data processing and to obtain their consent.

>> **Chartnote:** Provides a sample consent form for the use of their AI Scribe during medical encounters. While specific to their application, it can serve as a reference for creating consent forms that explain AI involvement in data handling.

>> **TheraPro:** Offers a sample informed consent form detailing the use of their HIPAA-compliant AI technology platform in therapy sessions. This example emphasizes transparency in AI data usage and patient rights.

When crafting your consent forms, ensure they clearly explain how AI will be used, the type of data collected, who will have access, and the potential implications of AI-driven decisions. It's also important to inform participants of their rights, including the ability to withdraw consent at any time. Consult with legal counsel or an ethics board for additional guidance tailored to your specific project needs.

Make sure to obtain consent before collecting any personal data, and give participants a way to opt out if they're uncomfortable with the AI system's use.

Use tools like DocuSign or OneTrust to streamline the informed consent process by digitizing forms, managing signatures, and ensuring compliance with privacy regulations. These platforms allow you to securely collect, track, and store consent agreements while providing participants with clear information about AI data usage.

Addressing ethical concerns in AI development

Developing AI tools presents unique ethical challenges that go beyond standard technology development. Unlike traditional software, AI systems learn from data, meaning that biases or inaccuracies in training datasets can directly shape decision-making outcomes in ways that are difficult to detect and correct later. Additionally, AI models often function as black boxes, making it hard to explain or justify their decisions, especially when they involve high-stakes applications like hiring, lending, or medical diagnoses.

You can address these risks by collaborating with AI developers to integrate explainability and accountability into the system from the start. One way to improve transparency is by using model interpretability techniques such as SHAP (Shapley Additive Explanations) and LIME (Local Interpretable Model-Agnostic Explanations). SHAP assigns an importance value to each feature in an AI model, showing how much each input contributes to the final decision, which is crucial for identifying potential biases. LIME, on the other hand, creates simplified, interpretable models that approximate the AI's decision-making for individual predictions, helping to pinpoint specific factors that influence outcomes. By applying these techniques, you can better assess whether AI-driven decisions align with ethical standards and intervene when necessary.

Because AI systems continuously evolve as they process new data, ethical considerations don't stop at deployment. You must establish ongoing monitoring mechanisms to track the system's long-term impact, conduct periodic audits using SHAP or LIME to detect changes in decision patterns, and retrain models when biases or unintended consequences emerge. Ensuring that AI remains fair and accountable requires continuous oversight, not just ethical considerations during initial development.

TIP

You can more effectively manage ethical dilemmas in AI development when you have a clear governance structure in place to oversee AI design, training, and deployment. Establishing ethical AI governance involves creating oversight bodies or committees that review AI-driven decisions, assess their impact, and consistently apply ethical standards throughout the development process. This governance structure helps prevent ethical issues from being addressed too late — after deployment — and instead ensures they are considered at every stage, from data collection to real-world use.

An AI oversight committee should include representatives from diverse areas to provide balanced perspectives and expertise, including the following:

>> **Project managers:** To ensure AI aligns with business objectives and project goals

>> **AI developers and data scientists:** To explain technical aspects, address model performance issues, and refine algorithms

>> **Ethics and compliance officers:** To evaluate ethical implications, ensure regulatory compliance, and prevent bias

>> **Legal experts:** To provide guidance on data privacy laws, intellectual property, and liability concerns

>> **End-user representatives:** To advocate for those directly affected by AI decisions, ensuring fairness and usability

>> **Diversity and inclusion specialists:** To help mitigate biases and promote equity in AI-driven outcomes

By assembling a well-rounded oversight committee, you create a governance structure that enables proactive identification and resolution of ethical dilemmas. This ensures that AI development remains aligned with organizational values and societal expectations, rather than being guided solely by efficiency or cost considerations. (See the "Creating an ethical AI framework for your projects" section earlier in this chapter for information on how to establish the guidelines an oversight committee would use.)

The governance framework should be embedded into your project's overall management plan because ethical considerations will be part of the project's daily operations. Additionally, the governance structure should be flexible enough to adapt to new ethical challenges as AI systems evolve.

TIP

Set up an AI ethics committee to oversee AI use in your projects and develop governance guidelines to ensure that AI decisions align with ethical standards.

Fostering a Culture of Ethical AI Use

Creating a culture of ethical AI use within the project team is essential for ensuring that ethical considerations are integrated into decision-making processes. This involves educating team members about AI ethics, promoting open discussions about potential ethical dilemmas, and encouraging a commitment to fairness and transparency in AI-driven decisions. As a project manager, you play a key role in fostering this culture by setting an example and encouraging team members to prioritize ethical principles in their work.

REMEMBER

A culture of ethical AI use not only ensures responsible decision-making but also strengthens trust between the project team and its stakeholders.

Following are some ways you can foster a culture of ethical AI use:

>> Providing training on AI ethics

>> Creating opportunities for team members to discuss ethical concerns by having regular team meetings focus on ethics

>> Developing resources such as ethical guidelines

>> Sharing case studies that illustrate how AI ethics can be applied in real-life scenarios

>> Embedding ethical considerations into the project's daily workflow

ETHICAL AI IMPLEMENTATION AT INNOVATETECH

InnovateTech, a mid-sized technology consulting firm, recently integrated AI-powered systems into their project management processes to optimize resource allocation, improve decision-making, and enhance overall project efficiency. The company's leadership recognized the potential benefits of AI but was also aware of the ethical challenges that could arise. To ensure the responsible use of AI, InnovateTech implemented an ethical AI framework, addressing key areas such as fairness, transparency, and accountability.

One of the first challenges InnovateTech faced was balancing efficiency and fairness. Their AI system recommended cost-saving measures that could have negatively impacted certain employees by prioritizing automated processes over human input.

The project management team decided to sacrifice some efficiency to ensure that these decisions were fair, opting to maintain human oversight in critical areas to protect the interests of all employees. This decision exemplified InnovateTech's commitment to ethical AI use, ensuring that efficiency gains did not come at the expense of fairness.

To prevent unintended consequences, InnovateTech established a regular audit process for AI-driven decisions. Early audits revealed that the AI system was unintentionally favoring certain project teams based on historical data that lacked diversity. The company immediately retrained the AI model using more representative data, ensuring that all teams were treated equitably. By proactively identifying and addressing biases, InnovateTech maintained fairness in its AI-powered decisions and prevented potential harm to marginalized groups within the company.

Ensuring informed consent was another priority for InnovateTech. The company implemented transparent data collection processes, informing employees how their data would be used by the AI systems and allowing them to opt out if they preferred. This approach built trust between the management and employees, with stakeholders feeling reassured that their privacy was respected and their participation in AI-driven processes was voluntary.

To maintain ongoing ethical oversight, InnovateTech created an AI ethics committee, which regularly reviewed the company's AI use and made recommendations for improvement. This governance structure allowed the company to address ethical concerns promptly and keep AI operations aligned with their values. In addition, InnovateTech fostered a culture of ethical AI use by providing training on AI ethics for all employees, encouraging open discussions about potential ethical dilemmas, and ensuring that ethical principles were integrated into the company's day-to-day operations.

By establishing a comprehensive ethical AI framework, InnovateTech successfully navigated the challenges of integrating AI into project management. Through a focus on fairness, transparency, accountability, and ongoing ethical oversight, the company was able to use AI responsibly while maintaining the trust and confidence of its employees and stakeholders. This approach not only optimized project efficiency but also ensured that AI was used in a way that aligned with the company's values and ethical standards.

Chapter **13**

Protecting Data and Ensuring Security with AI

As AI becomes an integral part of project management, safeguarding data and ensuring security are critical responsibilities for project managers. AI tools can help enhance data protection, manage security risks, and ensure that data privacy is maintained throughout AI-driven projects. This chapter explores how to protect data using AI tools, help ensure data privacy in AI-driven projects, and manage security risks with AI technologies.

Safeguarding Your Data Using AI Tools

Data has become one of the most valuable assets in today's digital landscape, and protecting it is essential when you're overseeing AI-driven projects. AI tools can significantly enhance data security by automating processes, detecting threats in real time, and protecting sensitive information from unauthorized access. Leveraging AI for data security ensures that you can address potential vulnerabilities proactively and that sensitive data remains protected throughout the project lifecycle.

Using AI for real-time threat detection

AI-powered tools have transformed the way organizations detect and respond to security threats. By continuously monitoring network activity and analyzing vast amounts of data, AI systems can identify suspicious behaviors and anomalies that may indicate a potential breach. For example, an AI system might detect unusual patterns in data transfers, unauthorized access attempts, or sudden spikes in network activity, all of which could signal an ongoing cyberattack. The advantage of real-time monitoring is that it gives you immediate insight so you can respond quickly to security issues before they escalate.

Real-time threat detection is especially valuable in today's environment where cyberthreats are becoming more sophisticated. AI can detect new forms of malware or phishing attacks that may not have been previously identified by traditional security measures. Additionally, AI can assess the context of the threat, providing insights into whether the activity is genuinely malicious or simply an unusual but benign event. You can use this information to prioritize your responses and allocate resources more effectively. Because of AI, you may have fewer false alarms.

AI's ability to provide 24/7 monitoring helps catch potential security breaches as soon as they occur, even outside of regular business hours. This continuous protection is crucial for organizations that manage sensitive or highly confidential information, where any delay in detecting a breach could result in significant data loss or damage. By integrating AI-powered threat detection tools, project managers can bolster their defenses against cyberattacks and keep their data secure. Check out Chapter 14 for guidance on how to navigate organizational concerns about data security.

TIP

Use tools like Darktrace (https://darktrace.com) or CrowdStrike (www.crowdstrike.com) to continuously monitor network activity and detect real-time security threats, ensuring early intervention before damage occurs.

Automating data security measures

One of the most significant advantages of using AI for data protection is its ability to automate routine security tasks, reducing human error and improving response times. Many security processes, such as applying patches, updating firewalls, and managing user access controls, require constant attention. AI-powered security tools like Darktrace and Artic Wolf (https://arcticwolf.com) continuously scan for anomalies and potential threats, ensuring these tasks are performed consistently and on time without manual intervention. CrowdStrike Falcon automates malware detection and threat intelligence, and Tenable.io (www.tenable.com) identifies and mitigates vulnerabilities before they can be exploited. By integrating AI-driven security solutions, you can strengthen your defenses while reducing the workload for security teams.

AI can also automate more complex security processes, such as incident response and threat detection. For example, AI-powered tools like IBM QRadar (www.ibm.com/qradar) and Azure Security Center (https://azure.microsoft.com) can detect potential breaches, trigger predefined security protocols, and even isolate affected systems to prevent the spread of an attack. AI-driven identity verification solutions, such as Okta Identity Cloud (https://www.okta.com/), continuously assess user behaviors and adjust access permissions in real time, reducing the risk of unauthorized access. In the event of a detected threat, AI can block malicious traffic, alert the security team, or take immediate remediation steps to contain the issue. This ability to detect, respond, and adapt to threats autonomously not only minimizes response times but also significantly reduces the potential damage from cyberattacks. However, AI automation should not replace human oversight entirely. Regularly reviewing AI-generated alerts and refining algorithms ensures that AI security measures remain effective and adaptive to emerging threats.

Leverage AI tools like Symantec by Broadcom (www.broadcom.com/products/cybersecurity) or McAfee (www.mcafee.com) to automate routine security tasks and ensure your systems remain protected at all times.

Encrypting data with AI

Data encryption is a fundamental component of any security strategy, and AI can enhance this process by automating encryption and ensuring that data remains secure throughout its lifecycle. Encryption is designed to make data unreadable to anyone without the proper decryption keys, protecting it from unauthorized access even if the data is intercepted or stolen. AI can manage encryption processes efficiently by automatically encrypting data as it is created, transferred, or stored.

AI-driven encryption tools can also monitor the encryption status of data across the entire organization, ensuring that no sensitive information is left unprotected. If an encryption vulnerability is detected, AI can immediately apply the necessary updates or encryption protocols to secure the data. In addition, AI can adjust encryption standards based on the sensitivity of the data, providing stronger encryption for more critical information.

By automating data encryption, AI helps organizations reduce the risks associated with manual encryption processes, such as forgotten steps or inconsistent application of encryption policies. This ensures that sensitive information, including personally identifiable information (PII) and financial data, is always protected, whether it is in transit or at rest.

TIP

Use AI-driven encryption tools like Bitdefender GravityZone (https://gravityzone.bitdefender.com) or Sophos Intercept X (www.sophos.com/en-us/products/endpoint-antivirus) to automatically encrypt sensitive data and ensure that it is secure throughout its entire lifecycle.

Identifying and mitigating insider threats

While external cyberthreats often receive the most media attention, insider threats — where employees or trusted individuals misuse their access to data — can be just as dangerous. Remember the old saying, "the enemy within?" AI can help you identify any rogue agent within your organization and prevent them from compromising your data. Insider threats can arise from malicious actions, such as employees intentionally stealing sensitive data, or from negligence, where an employee accidentally exposes confidential information. AI tools can help you identify and mitigate these risks by monitoring user behavior for anomalies that may indicate a potential insider threat.

AI-powered systems can track user access patterns and flag any unusual activity that deviates from an employee's normal behavior. For example, if an employee who typically accesses only a few files per day suddenly begins downloading large volumes of sensitive data, the AI system can alert the security team to investigate further. Similarly, AI can detect when an employee attempts to access data or systems that are outside their usual scope of work, which could be a sign of unauthorized activity.

Mitigating insider threats also involves preventing accidental data exposure. AI can help by enforcing security policies that limit access to sensitive information based on an employee's role or responsibilities. If an employee inadvertently tries to share or access sensitive data, the AI system can block the action and alert the relevant team. This proactive approach helps prevent accidental data breaches and ensures that sensitive information is only accessible to those with the appropriate permissions.

TIP

Utilize AI tools like Varonis (www.varonis.com) or Forcepoint Insider Threat (www.forcepoint.com/security/insider-threat) to monitor user behavior and detect potential insider threats before they cause damage.

Providing continuous security monitoring

AI's ability to provide continuous security monitoring is one of its most valuable contributions to data protection. Unlike traditional security measures that may rely on periodic checks or manual oversight, AI systems can monitor networks, systems, and data in real time to detect potential threats immediately. Continuous monitoring is particularly important for large organizations or projects that involve sensitive data because any security gap, no matter how brief, could result in a breach.

AI-driven monitoring tools are capable of scanning for vulnerabilities, identifying potential threats, and even taking immediate action to prevent security incidents. For instance, if AI detects unusual traffic patterns that may indicate a distributed denial of service (DDoS) attack, it can automatically block the malicious traffic and scale system resources to mitigate the impact. This ensures that the organization remains protected around the clock, even during periods when the security team is unavailable.

Continuous monitoring also enables you to always stay informed about the security posture of your projects. AI can generate real-time reports on potential risks, system vulnerabilities, and security events, so you have the insights you need to make informed decisions about data protection. By ensuring that data is constantly monitored, AI helps organizations maintain a strong security posture in an increasingly complex digital environment.

TIP

Implement AI tools like Splunk (www.splunk.com) or Exabeam, formerly Log-Rhythm (www.exabeam.com) for continuous security monitoring to help protect your data around the clock.

Protecting Data Privacy in AI-Driven Projects

In AI-driven projects, data privacy is not just a legal obligation but a critical responsibility for maintaining trust with stakeholders and users. As AI systems often rely on large amounts of personal and sensitive data, project managers must ensure that privacy is protected throughout the entire lifecycle of the project. By implementing AI-driven privacy protocols, anonymizing data, managing consent, and ensuring compliance with regulations, you can effectively safeguard data privacy and reduce the risk of breaches or misuse.

Implementing data privacy protocols

One of the first steps to ensuring data privacy in AI-driven projects is establishing strong privacy protocols that define how data will be collected, stored, processed, and shared. These protocols act as a framework for ensuring that personal and sensitive information is handled responsibly at every stage of the project. AI tools can help automate these protocols, reducing the likelihood of human error and ensuring consistency across the organization. For example, AI systems can automatically enforce data privacy policies, restrict access to sensitive information, and notify you of any potential privacy violations.

Privacy protocols should cover both internal and external data handling practices. This includes protecting data from unauthorized access by employees and ensuring that any third-party partners who have access to the data adhere to the same stringent privacy standards. By automating the enforcement of these policies through AI tools, you can provide continuous protection for personal information without requiring constant manual oversight.

TIP

Make sure to review and update protocols regularly to reflect any changes in regulations or advances in AI technology. AI tools can assist in identifying gaps in current privacy policies and recommend updates that will strengthen data protection. By making privacy an integral part of the project's foundation, you can ensure that sensitive data is handled ethically and securely throughout the AI project's lifecycle.

TIP

Use AI-driven privacy management tools like OneTrust (www.onetrust.com) or BigID (https://bigid.com) to automate the enforcement of privacy protocols and ensure that sensitive data is handled securely.

Anonymizing data with AI

Anonymizing data is one of the most effective ways to protect personal information in AI-driven projects. When data is anonymized, identifying details such as names, addresses, or Social Security numbers are removed or masked, making it impossible to trace the information back to a specific individual. This ensures that personal information is protected, even if the data is shared with third parties or used in AI analysis. AI tools can automate the anonymization process to mask personal data appropriately before it's used for analysis or shared with other teams.

In many AI-driven projects, anonymized data is still highly valuable because it allows organizations to generate insights and predictions without compromising individual privacy. AI can effectively anonymize large datasets in real time, so you can analyze the data without violating privacy regulations. For example, AI might anonymize customer data before someone uses it for market analysis or anonymize employee data before a performance evaluation system is implemented.

An important aspect of anonymization is ensuring that it's done correctly. If the anonymization process leaves certain data points exposed or fails to mask enough details, there's a risk of "reidentification," where it becomes possible to trace the data back to an individual. AI tools can help prevent this by using advanced anonymization techniques, such as differential privacy, which ensures that even when combined with other datasets, the anonymized data cannot be reidentified.

Utilize AI tools like Informatica (www.informatica.com) or Truata (www.truata.com) to automate the anonymization process and protect personal data from reidentification.

Managing consent and data usage with AI

Obtaining informed consent for the collection and use of personal data is a critical part of data privacy in AI-driven projects. Ensuring that individuals understand how their data will be used and explicitly agree to that usage is essential for compliance with privacy regulations such as the General Data Protection Regulation (GDPR) and Health Insurance Portability and Accountability Act (HIPAA). AI can assist project managers by tracking who has provided consent, what data they've consented to share, and how that data is being used within the project.

AI-driven tools can manage consent by creating a centralized system that logs all data usage permissions, making it easier for you to ensure that data is only used in ways that individuals have agreed to. If a user withdraws consent or wants to know how their data is being used, AI systems can quickly retrieve this information and take action, such as halting the use of their data or deleting it altogether. Automating this process ensures that data privacy is maintained throughout the project and that the organization remains compliant with legal requirements.

Additionally, AI tools can help manage consent on an ongoing basis, ensuring that when new data is collected or new uses for data are identified, updated consent is obtained from the data subjects. This ensures transparency and gives individuals control over how their personal information is used. Using AI to track and manage consent helps you reduce the risk of noncompliance and build trust with stakeholders who expect their data privacy to be respected.

Use AI-driven consent management tools like DocuSign (www.docusign.com) or OneTrust (www.onetrust.com) to ensure that data usage is compliant with privacy laws and that individuals' preferences are respected.

Complying with data privacy regulations

Compliance with data privacy regulations is essential in any AI-driven project, especially when dealing with large amounts of personal or sensitive information. Regulations such as the GDPR in Europe or HIPAA in the U.S. set strict guidelines on how personal data should be handled, and noncompliance can result in significant fines or legal action. AI tools can help you ensure that your projects remain compliant with these regulations by automating data protection processes and monitoring for potential privacy violations.

AI can assist in compliance by generating detailed reports on data usage, identifying any areas where data privacy rules may have been violated, and providing recommendations for corrective actions. These tools can also ensure that data is processed in accordance with the law, such as automatically deleting data after a certain period or flagging data transfers that may require additional consent. This level of automation helps you stay ahead of evolving privacy regulations and ensures that all data-handling activities are conducted within legal frameworks.

Furthermore, AI tools can provide real-time alerts when a potential privacy violation is detected, which enables you to take immediate action. This proactive approach to compliance helps prevent legal issues before they escalate and keeps the organization protected from regulatory penalties by ensuring that privacy best practices are consistently followed. AI tools also make it easier to provide proof of compliance in the event that regulatory authorities request audits or reports on data-handling practices.

TIP

Leverage AI-driven compliance management tools like TrustArc (https://trustarc.com) or BigID to ensure that your project adheres to privacy regulations and can generate real-time reports for audits.

Building a culture of privacy in AI-driven projects

While AI tools can provide significant technical safeguards for data privacy, fostering a culture of privacy within the project team is equally important. A strong culture of privacy ensures that all team members understand the importance of data protection and are committed to handling data ethically and responsibly. You can promote this culture by providing privacy training, encouraging open discussions about potential privacy concerns, and integrating privacy considerations into every stage of the project.

Privacy training can help team members stay informed about the latest data protection regulations and best practices. It equips them to handle sensitive information responsibly. AI-driven training platforms can personalize the training based on individual roles within the team, which helps ensure that everyone understands how privacy applies to their specific tasks. Additionally, by creating a space for open discussions, you can identify and address potential privacy risks before they become issues, fostering a proactive approach to data protection.

In addition to training and discussions, you can integrate privacy into every stage of the AI project by embedding privacy-by-design principles into the workflow. This means considering privacy implications from the earliest stages of the project rather than treating it as an afterthought. By prioritizing privacy at every step, your team can build solutions that respect user privacy while still achieving any data-driven goals.

TIP

Implement AI-driven training tools like Navex (www.navex.com) to provide team members with up-to-date privacy training and promote a culture of data protection.

Managing Security Risks with AI Technologies

As organizations increasingly adopt AI-driven solutions in their projects, managing security risks becomes a critical priority. AI itself can be a powerful tool in addressing these risks by helping you identify vulnerabilities, predict threats, and automate responses. By leveraging AI to protect systems, data, and users, you can ensure that your projects are resilient to ever-evolving cyberthreats. From predicting potential security risks to managing endpoint security and automating incident response, AI technologies offer significant advantages in maintaining security in today's digital environment.

REMEMBER

It's not unlike a doctor conducting regular checkups for your health; continuous monitoring with AI is like giving your data a constant health check. It helps identify and address any emerging issues before they become serious problems.

Predicting security threats with AI

One of AI's most valuable contributions to managing security risks is its ability to predict potential threats. AI tools can analyze historical data, real-time activity, and trends and forecast when and where security risks are likely to occur. This predictive capability enables you to take proactive steps to prevent attacks before they happen. For example, AI can analyze patterns in previous cyberattacks to identify indicators of an impending threat, such as unusual network activity or attempted breaches at specific times. By giving you an early alert that there are indicators of a possible security threat, the AI tool gives your team time to implement safeguards before any real damage is done.

Predictive analytics extend beyond external threats. AI can identify internal vulnerabilities, such as outdated software, improperly configured systems, or gaps in access controls that may lead to future breaches. By highlighting these vulnerabilities in advance, AI helps you prioritize their security efforts to address the most critical risks first. AI can even forecast the likelihood of specific types of attacks — such as phishing or ransomware — based on current trends, which helps you allocate resources more efficiently to protect your most vulnerable assets.

AI tools can continuously monitor global cyberactivity and provide early warning signals for potential widespread attacks, such as distributed denial of service (DDoS) attacks targeting certain industries or regions. This allows project managers to strengthen defenses in anticipation of a broader cyber event, reducing the potential for disruption.

TECHNICAL STUFF

Use AI-driven tools like Darktrace or IBM AI Cybersecurity (www.ibm.com/ai-cybersecurity) to predict potential threats based on past data and real-time monitoring, allowing your team to act before a breach occurs.

Automating security risk assessments

Security risk assessments are an essential part of managing cyber risks, but they can be time-consuming and complex to conduct manually. AI simplifies this process by automating security risk assessments, continuously scanning systems for vulnerabilities and assessing the potential impact of those vulnerabilities. AI-driven tools can analyze data across all layers of a project's infrastructure, identifying weaknesses in software, hardware, and network configurations that may leave the system exposed to attacks.

AI monitoring not only saves time but also ensures that security risk assessments are comprehensive and consistent. Rather than relying on periodic manual assessments, AI can perform continuous risk evaluations to look for vulnerabilities that may go unnoticed between check-ins. AI can prioritize risks based on their likelihood of exploitation and the potential damage they could cause. That gives you the opportunity to focus on the most critical security issues first.

Automating risk assessments also ensures that emerging threats are addressed quickly. As new vulnerabilities are discovered or new attack methods emerge, AI tools can immediately evaluate their potential impact on the project and recommend actions to mitigate the risk. This level of responsiveness is especially important in dynamic environments where new vulnerabilities can emerge rapidly, and manual assessments may struggle to keep up.

Implement AI-powered tools like Qualys (`www.qualys.com`) or Rapid7 (`www.rapid7.com`) to automate continuous security risk assessments and prioritize vulnerabilities based on their potential impact.

Managing endpoint security with AI

Endpoints — such as computers, mobile devices, and internet of things (IOT) devices — are often the most vulnerable points in a project's security infrastructure. These devices can serve as entry points for attackers seeking to access sensitive information or disrupt systems. AI-driven solutions can enhance endpoint security by monitoring these devices for threats, enforcing security policies, and automatically taking action to prevent unauthorized access or data breaches.

AI can continuously monitor endpoints for signs of compromise, such as unusual behavior, unauthorized access attempts, or malware activity. When an anomaly is detected, AI systems can automatically quarantine the affected device, revoke access privileges, or block network connections until the issue is resolved. This prevents security threats from spreading across the network and minimizes the damage caused by compromised endpoints.

AI can also help enforce endpoint security policies by ensuring that all devices meet the required security standards. For example, AI can detect when a device is running outdated software or has inadequate encryption settings and prompt the user to update or strengthen their security configuration. This ensures that all devices connected to the network comply with the organization's security policies and reduces the risk of breaches caused by poorly secured endpoints.

Use AI-powered tools like CrowdStrike or Carbon Black (`www.broadcom.com/products/carbon-black`) to continuously monitor endpoint devices and automatically respond to security threats, ensuring that compromised devices are quickly isolated.

Mitigating distributed denial of service (DDoS) attacks with AI

Distributed denial of service (DDoS) attacks are a common and highly disruptive form of cyberattack in which attackers flood a system with excessive traffic to overwhelm its resources and render it unavailable to legitimate users. AI technologies play a critical role in mitigating these attacks by detecting unusual traffic patterns, filtering out malicious traffic, and automatically scaling system resources to absorb the excess load. This ensures that the system remains operational, even under attack.

AI-powered DDoS mitigation tools are particularly effective because they can analyze traffic in real time, identifying the difference between legitimate and malicious traffic. For example, if AI detects a sudden spike in traffic from a particular region or a large number of requests from unknown sources, it can block or redirect that traffic before it overwhelms the system. AI can also adapt to new DDoS attack methods, learning from past attacks to improve its ability to detect and respond to future threats.

Aside from traffic filtering, AI can automatically allocate additional resources — such as server capacity or bandwidth — to absorb the impact of the attack without affecting legitimate users. This dynamic scaling helps ensure that services remain available to customers, even while the system is under attack. Once the attack subsides, AI systems can automatically return resources to normal levels to maintain system efficiency.

TIP

Use AI-driven DDoS protection tools like Cloudflare or Akamai to filter malicious traffic and automatically scale resources during a DDoS attack, ensuring minimal disruption to services.

Automating incident response with AI

When a security incident occurs, the speed and effectiveness of the response are critical in minimizing the damage. AI can automate many aspects of incident response to contain threats quickly and efficiently. AI-powered systems can identify the source of the breach, isolate affected systems, and take immediate action to mitigate the threat. For example, if AI detects that a device has been compromised, it can automatically revoke the user's access, block further network communication from that device, and alert the security team for further investigation.

Automating incident response also reduces the risk of human error during high-pressure situations. Instead of relying on manual processes to identify and address security breaches, AI can follow protocols that have been established to ensure that incidents are handled consistently and effectively. This includes automating routine tasks such as generating reports, notifying stakeholders, and coordinating recovery efforts. In more complex incidents, AI can assist security teams by providing real-time recommendations based on the type of threat and the best course of action.

TIP

Incident response automation is especially valuable in large-scale incidents or when multiple systems are affected simultaneously.

TIP

Use AI-powered incident response tools like Palo Alto Networks Cortex XSOAR or Splunk to automate containment and recovery processes, ensuring that security incidents are addressed quickly and effectively.

DATAGUARD SOLUTIONS SECURES DATA WITH AI

DataGuard Solutions, an IT consulting firm, faced escalating challenges in safeguarding client data and managing sophisticated cyberthreats. Recognizing the limitations of traditional security measures, the company embarked on a comprehensive strategy to integrate AI-driven tools into their project management processes, aiming to enhance data protection, ensure regulatory compliance, and proactively mitigate security risks.

To achieve real-time threat detection, DataGuard implemented Darktrace's AI-powered platform, which continuously monitors network traffic to establish a baseline of normal activity. Upon detecting deviations indicative of potential threats, such as unusual data transfers or unauthorized access attempts, Darktrace alerts the security team, enabling immediate investigation and response. For automated data encryption, DataGuard deployed Bitdefender GravityZone, ensuring that data at rest and in transit remains encrypted, thereby reducing the risk of unauthorized access. This integration with KnowBe4's SecurityCoach further enhances security by providing real-time coaching to employees, reinforcing best practices in data handling.

Navigating the complexities of data protection regulations, DataGuard adopted OneTrust to manage client consent and meticulously track data usage. The platform automates compliance workflows, maintains records of data processing activities, and

(continued)

(continued)

enforces privacy protocols, thereby minimizing the risk of regulatory breaches. To address potential internal security risks, DataGuard integrated Varonis into its infrastructure. Varonis monitors user behavior analytics, identifying anomalies such as unauthorized access to sensitive files or unusual file activity patterns, enabling the security team to promptly detect and respond to insider threats.

Recognizing the critical role of human factors in cybersecurity, DataGuard implemented KnowBe4's AI-driven security awareness training program. The platform delivers simulated phishing attacks and interactive modules to educate employees on effectively identifying and responding to security threats, thereby fostering a security-conscious culture within the organization.

By strategically integrating these AI-driven tools, DataGuard Solutions not only fortified its cybersecurity framework but also cultivated a proactive security culture. This comprehensive approach ensured robust data protection, regulatory compliance, and effective management of security risks, thereby enhancing the firm's reputation for delivering secure and reliable IT consulting services to its clients.

Chapter **14**

Managing AI Adoption and Change in Your Organization

ntroducing AI into your organization is not just about implementing new technologies; it's about managing change effectively. AI adoption often requires a shift in how teams operate, collaborate, and make decisions. As a project manager, you play a key role in leading AI adoption and managing change within your organization. In this chapter, I share how to lead AI adoption efforts, train your team on AI tools and best practices, and overcome resistance to AI adoption.

Leading AI Adoption and Change Management Efforts

A successful AI adoption begins with a well-thought-out strategy that aligns with your organization's overall goals. Developing this strategy requires a clear understanding of how AI will support business objectives, improve operations, and deliver measurable value. Start by outlining the reasons for AI adoption and the expected benefits. Consider how AI will enhance current processes, where it can add value, and how it will address existing pain points in your operations. This strategic foundation will guide your adoption efforts and keep everyone focused on common goals.

Your AI adoption strategy should also address potential challenges, such as employee resistance, skill gaps, and budgetary constraints. Identify these hurdles early on and plan how you will mitigate them. For instance, if your team lacks AI expertise, you might plan for training or hiring AI specialists. If there are concerns about job displacement, include strategies for reskilling or role redefinition in your plan. The more comprehensive and realistic your strategy, the smoother your AI adoption will be.

Another critical aspect of developing an AI adoption strategy is timeline management. Implementing AI is a complex process that requires phased execution, including pilot programs, feedback loops, and eventual scaling. Define key milestones for your AI integration, including short-term objectives that keep the project moving forward and long-term goals that align with your organization's strategic vision. Flexibility is important, so be prepared to adjust your timeline as challenges arise.

TIP

Regularly revisit and update your AI adoption strategy to adapt to changing organizational needs and technological advancements.

Identifying key stakeholders and champions for AI adoption

Engaging the right stakeholders is essential for the successful integration of AI into your organization. Identifying key decision-makers, department heads, and subject matter experts from various areas of the business will ensure that AI adoption has broad support. These stakeholders will provide valuable insights into how AI can impact different functions, allowing for a more holistic adoption strategy. From finance to operations and HR, ensure every relevant department is represented in your AI planning process.

TIP

Identifying champions who are enthusiastic about AI is crucial for driving adoption. These champions should be influential within their teams and have a strong understanding of how AI will benefit their departments. AI champions can act as advocates, helping build excitement and acceptance for AI across the organization. These individuals should be involved from the beginning, participating in pilot programs and providing feedback on AI implementation.

Empower champions and stakeholders to communicate the advantages of AI to their peers. Their role is to address concerns, answer questions, and provide support as AI is rolled out. By ensuring that champions are actively involved in the AI adoption process, you can build internal momentum and increase buy-in across the organization. These champions will also play a key role in navigating resistance by showcasing early wins and advocating for AI's value. Check out Chapter 15 for practical advice on promoting AI adoption within your team.

TIP

Regularly check in with AI champions to ensure they feel supported and equipped to promote AI adoption within their departments.

Communicating the benefits of AI adoption

Clear, transparent, and consistent communication is one of the most critical aspects of managing change. To gain widespread support for AI adoption, you must articulate the benefits of AI in a way that resonates with employees at all levels. Begin by outlining how AI can improve daily workflows, automate mundane tasks, and enhance decision-making capabilities. Highlight specific use cases that relate directly to your team's responsibilities to demonstrate how AI adoption will directly benefit them.

It's equally important to address concerns and potential misconceptions about AI upfront. Employees may fear job displacement or feel uncertain about learning new technologies. As part of your communication strategy, acknowledge these concerns and provide a realistic perspective on how AI will impact the organization. Emphasize that the intent for AI is to support employees, making their roles more strategic rather than replacing them. By being transparent about both the opportunities and challenges of AI adoption, you build trust and create a more open dialogue.

Using multiple communication channels is essential to ensure that your message reaches all employees. Consider using newsletters, town hall meetings, and departmental briefings to communicate the progress and benefits of AI adoption. This will help keep everyone informed and aligned with the organizational goals. Additionally, encourage two-way communication, where employees can ask questions, share concerns, and offer feedback on AI-related changes.

TIP

Set up regular Q&A sessions where employees can raise concerns about AI adoption and ensure these sessions are open and accessible to all staff.

Aligning AI adoption with organizational culture

Successfully implementing AI requires aligning its adoption with the existing culture and values of your organization. If your organization values innovation, you can emphasize how AI can fuel creativity by generating new product ideas, automating repetitive tasks to free up time for strategic thinking, or providing predictive analytics to inspire data-driven decision-making. For example, AI-powered design tools like Adobe Sensei (https://business.adobe.com/products/sensei/adobe-sensei.html) can help creative teams generate concepts faster, while AI-driven market trend analysis can uncover opportunities for new offerings.

For organizations that prioritize customer satisfaction, highlight how AI can enhance the customer experience by providing personalized recommendations, faster response times, and proactive service solutions. AI-powered chatbots like Zendesk AI (www.zendesk.com/service/ai) can improve customer support by handling common inquiries efficiently, whereas AI-driven sentiment analysis can help businesses gauge customer satisfaction and address issues before they escalate. The goal is to make AI adoption feel like a natural extension of the organization's existing values, reinforcing its commitment to excellence rather than introducing a disruptive change.

One effective way to align AI with company culture is to demonstrate how AI will enhance collaborative efforts across teams. For example, you could showcase how AI-driven tools facilitate better cross-department communication or enable faster decision-making. By framing AI adoption in ways that complement your organization's strengths, you create a smoother transition and increase the likelihood of successful adoption.

Also, keep in mind that fostering a culture of continuous learning is essential for long-term AI success. AI technologies are constantly evolving, so it's crucial to promote an organizational mindset that embraces change and innovation. Encourage employees to see AI adoption as an opportunity for growth, providing access to learning resources and creating an environment where experimentation is valued. This cultural alignment makes employees feel more comfortable with the changes AI brings.

TIP

Align AI adoption with your company's key values by integrating AI tools that support collaboration, innovation, and customer satisfaction.

Creating a roadmap for AI adoption

An AI adoption roadmap provides the structure and clarity needed to ensure a smooth integration of AI technologies into your organization. This roadmap should detail every step of the process, from the initial assessment and pilot projects to full-scale deployment. By breaking the adoption process into manageable phases, you can track progress, address roadblocks, and make data-driven decisions along the way. The roadmap also provides transparency for employees, helping them understand the overall timeline and what to expect as AI is integrated into their work.

Here are six steps you can follow to create your AI roadmap:

1. Define your AI adoption goals.

   Identify key objectives (for example, efficiency, cost savings, improved decision-making) and establish success metrics.

2. Assess readiness and identify use cases.

   Evaluate current technology, workforce skills, and infrastructure while determining where AI can provide the most value.

3. Outline phases of AI adoption.

   Break the process into stages (exploration and planning, pilot testing, evaluation and refinement, full-scale deployment, and continuous improvement).

4. Create a timeline for implementation.

   Assign time limits to each phase and set milestones such as employee training, system testing, and performance reviews.

5. Develop a communication and training plan.

   Establish a strategy for educating employees, addressing concerns, and keeping teams informed about AI progress.

6. Monitor progress and adapt.

   Set up a feedback loop, track AI performance, and refine implementation strategies based on real-world results and employee input.

The roadmap should also include clear metrics for success, such as productivity improvements, cost savings, or customer satisfaction gains. These metrics will help you measure the effectiveness of AI adoption at each stage and provide a basis for continuous improvement. In addition, the roadmap should be flexible enough to accommodate feedback and adapt to unforeseen challenges. As you move through each phase, gather input from employees and stakeholders and adjust as needed.

Regularly communicating milestones and progress as you move along the roadmap is essential for maintaining engagement. Celebrate each phase of successful AI integration, whether it's completing training programs, launching pilot projects, or achieving efficiency gains. This helps keep the team motivated and reinforces that the organization is committed to AI adoption as a long-term strategy.

TIP

Use visual tools, such as Gantt charts or dashboards, to clearly display the roadmap and progress, making it easier for all stakeholders to track the journey.

Understanding Different Models for Change and Transition

Successfully integrating AI into your organization requires more than just adopting new technology. It demands a structured approach to managing change. As a project manager, you play a critical role in guiding your team through this transformation, ensuring that both technical and human factors are addressed. To help you navigate this process, this section explores three widely recognized change management models: ADKAR, William Bridges' Model of Change and Transition, and the DIRECT Project Leadership framework. By understanding and applying these frameworks, you can create a smoother, more effective AI adoption strategy that minimizes resistance and maximizes long-term success.

Using the ADKAR model for change management

The ADKAR (awareness, desire, knowledge, ability, and reinforcement) model is a change management framework developed by Prosci (www.prosci.com) that focuses on guiding individuals through the process of change. The model is widely used across industries for managing organizational transformations, including the adoption of new technologies like AI.

ADKAR represents the five essential steps that individuals must go through for successful change. Unlike other models that focus primarily on processes, ADKAR emphasizes the human side of change by addressing the emotional and psychological aspects that can often be barriers to successful adoption. By using this model, project managers can systematically lead teams through the stages of awareness, motivation, training, practical application, and continuous reinforcement, ensuring that change is both sustainable and impactful.

Awareness: Helping employees understand the need for AI adoption

The first step in the ADKAR model is building awareness about the need for AI adoption. Employees need to understand why AI is being introduced and how it will benefit both the organization and their individual roles. Without this understanding, it is difficult for employees to fully support the transition. Begin by clearly explaining the business challenges AI can solve and the opportunities it opens for innovation, efficiency, and productivity. Emphasize how adopting AI is necessary to stay competitive in a rapidly evolving digital landscape.

It's also essential to communicate the risks of not adopting AI, such as falling behind competitors or missing out on efficiency gains. Employees must see AI adoption not as a threat but as an opportunity to grow and succeed in a more advanced, data-driven work environment. Providing real-world examples or case studies from other organizations can help illustrate the tangible benefits of AI and why the shift is necessary.

REMEMBER

The goal at this stage is to create a sense of urgency while ensuring that employees feel informed and included in the process. Consider holding town hall meetings, sending out informational materials, and allowing employees to ask questions and voice concerns. By fostering an open dialogue, you can ensure that everyone is on the same page and feels comfortable with the change.

TIP

Regularly communicate updates on AI adoption to maintain awareness and provide employees with ongoing insights into why AI is essential for the organization's growth.

Desire: Motivating employees to support AI adoption

Once employees are aware of the need for AI, the next step is fostering a genuine desire to participate in the change. Without personal motivation, employees may resist AI adoption or disengage from the process altogether. To build this desire, it's important to address any fears or concerns employees may have. Common concerns include job security, the fear of being replaced by AI, or the anxiety of learning new technologies. Be transparent about these concerns and emphasize that AI is meant to complement human skills rather than replace them.

Help employees understand how AI can make their work more meaningful by automating repetitive tasks and allowing them to focus on more strategic, creative, or value-adding activities. Highlight how AI can streamline workflows, reduce inefficiencies, and support better decision-making. By framing AI as a tool that empowers them, you can create excitement about its potential.

You can also build motivation by involving employees in the AI adoption process. Invite them to participate in pilot programs, provide feedback on AI tools, and contribute ideas for how AI can enhance their roles. When employees feel a sense of ownership over the changes, they are more likely to embrace the transition.

Share early wins and success stories from pilot AI projects to motivate employees and demonstrate the positive impact of AI adoption.

Knowledge: Equipping employees with the skills to use AI effectively

After establishing desire, the next step is providing employees with the knowledge they need to use AI tools effectively. Training is crucial at this stage because employees need to feel confident in their ability to work with AI technologies. Begin by assessing your team's current knowledge level and identifying gaps to address. Different roles may require different levels of training; for instance, some employees may need basic knowledge of how AI works, whereas others may require more advanced technical training.

Develop a comprehensive training program that covers both the technical aspects of using AI tools and the strategic understanding of how employees can apply AI in their work. Consider offering a variety of training formats, such as workshops, online courses, and hands-on practice sessions, to accommodate different learning styles. This helps ensure that all employees are equipped with the skills they need to confidently engage with AI technologies.

Continuous learning is also critical. AI technologies are constantly evolving, and employees need to stay up to date with the latest advancements. Encourage employees to take advantage of ongoing upskilling opportunities and provide access to resources such as online learning platforms or AI certifications. This ensures that your team continues to grow their AI capabilities long after the initial training.

Ability: Ensuring employees can apply AI in their daily work

Providing knowledge is only half of the equation: Employees must also develop the ability to apply AI effectively in their daily work. This stage is about moving beyond theoretical understanding and ensuring that employees have the practical skills to integrate AI into their workflows. Begin by setting up pilot projects or sandbox environments where employees can experiment with AI tools in a low-risk setting. Hands-on practice is essential for helping employees gain confidence and see the direct application of AI in their specific roles.

One of the key challenges at this stage is bridging the gap between knowledge and real-world application. Employees may understand how AI works conceptually, but they need the ability to adapt those concepts to their everyday tasks. For instance, a marketing team may need to learn how to use AI for customer segmentation, and a logistics team might focus on using AI to optimize supply chain operations. Tailoring the learning experience to specific use cases will make the transition smoother.

Ongoing support is crucial to helping employees build their abilities. Encourage a culture of collaboration where employees can share insights, tips, and best practices for using AI tools. Mentorship programs, peer learning groups, or AI champions within teams can provide additional support, ensuring that employees feel confident and capable as they begin applying AI in their work.

TIP

Regularly review employees' progress and provide additional training or resources for those who need further support in developing AI-related skills.

Reinforcement: Sustaining AI adoption through ongoing support and feedback

The final stage of the ADKAR model focuses on reinforcement — ensuring that the changes made through AI adoption are sustained over time. Even after employees have gained the knowledge and ability to use AI tools, continuous reinforcement is needed to prevent regression to old ways of working. Reinforcement comes in the form of ongoing feedback, progress recognition, and continuous improvement support. Providing regular check-ins with employees to discuss their experience with AI tools can help identify any challenges or areas where further assistance is needed.

Recognition is another powerful tool for reinforcing AI adoption. Celebrate successes and acknowledge employees or teams that have effectively integrated AI into their workflows. Public recognition of AI-related achievements not only motivates those individuals but also encourages others to embrace AI adoption. Regularly sharing stories of how AI is driving positive outcomes for the business can help keep momentum going.

Additionally, it's important to keep employees informed about future developments in AI technology. As AI continues to evolve, there may be new tools, features, or processes that could benefit your team. Reinforcing a culture of continuous learning and improvement will help ensure that AI adoption is not seen as a one-time event but rather as an ongoing journey of growth and innovation.

TIP

Create AI champions within teams who can provide ongoing support and help reinforce the long-term adoption of AI tools across the organization.

William Bridges' model for change and transition

The Bridges Transition Model emphasizes the psychological and emotional aspects of change. Bridges argues that successful change doesn't just depend on external processes and systems, but also on how people transition through it internally. The model identifies three key stages of transition:

>> **Endings:** This is the first stage, where employees may experience resistance, anxiety, or fear as they let go of old ways of working. During AI adoption, it's essential to acknowledge these feelings and provide support to help employees move past them. Clear communication and reassurance can help ease this process.

>> **Neutral zone:** This is a period of uncertainty and adjustment. Employees are learning to adapt to new AI tools and workflows, but the old ways of working are not yet entirely behind them. This phase can feel chaotic and confusing, but it's also where innovation and creativity can flourish. Providing continuous training and support during this stage is crucial.

>> **New beginnings:** In this final stage, employees start embracing the new AI-driven processes. They begin to see the benefits of AI, and their confidence in using these tools grows. Celebrating successes and reinforcing positive behaviors help solidify this new beginning.

By understanding and addressing the emotional side of change, Bridges's model helps you manage the human transitions that accompany AI adoption. With it, you can guide your team through the process of letting go of the old, navigating the uncertainty of the transition, and ultimately embracing the new.

Introducing the DIRECT Model for Project Leadership

Leading a project can sometimes feel overwhelming, but the DIRECT model simplifies project leadership into six key responsibilities. By using the acronym *DIRECT*, you can easily remember the six pillars of effective project leadership: define, investigate, resolve, execute, change, and transition.

- **Define the vision:** The first pillar is all about defining a vision for your project. Your responsibility as the project leader is to ensure that everyone understands the project's objectives and that there's ongoing support to achieve those goals. A well-defined vision aligns your team and sets the foundation for success.

- **Investigate the options:** Before making any decisions, you must explore alternatives. Investigate the ways you could approach the project, weighing the pros and cons of each option. How much will each choice cost? How long will it take? How well does it solve the problem? By thoroughly investigating options, you ensure that your team has the information needed to make informed decisions.

- **Resolve to a course of action:** At some point, a decision needs to be made. After investigating your options, resolve to a clear course of action and commit to a plan. This pillar is about deciding on the best approach and ensuring that your team is aligned and ready to move forward.

- **Execute the plan:** Execution is where the plan comes to life. This stage involves coordinating your team to get the work done and tracking their progress. Your role as a leader is to monitor performance, remove obstacles, and ensure that the project stays on track. Execution requires focus, coordination, and adaptability.

- **Change the system:** Every project leads to change, whether it's a new software implementation or a new business process. This pillar emphasizes the importance of leading that change. For many people, the go-live phase of a project may be their first direct interaction with the work you've been doing, so it's essential to guide them through the change to ensure acceptance and success.

- **Transition the people:** Transitioning is about ensuring that people adapt to the new solution once the project is complete. While change focuses on the tangible aspects of the project, transition is about the human side: how people react and respond. Successful transition is crucial for ensuring that the improvements you've made truly take root and deliver long-term value.

By following the DIRECT model, you'll have a clear framework to lead any project effectively. This simple but powerful approach ensures that both the technical and human elements of project leadership are covered, setting you and your team up for lasting success.

Overcoming Resistance to AI Adoption

Resistance to AI adoption is common, particularly when employees feel uncertain about the impact of AI on their roles or fear that AI could replace them. Addressing these concerns and overcoming resistance is essential for ensuring that everyone in the organization embraces AI adoption. Here's how to overcome resistance to AI adoption.

Understanding the root causes of resistance

Resistance to AI adoption often stems from multiple underlying concerns, including fear of job displacement, uncertainty about new technologies, and concerns over the need to develop new skills. To effectively address these concerns, it's critical to first understand why employees may be hesitant. Engage in open conversations with your team and gather feedback through surveys, focus groups, or one-on-one meetings. Understanding their perspective allows you to pinpoint the exact causes of their resistance and develop strategies to address them.

Fear is a common driver of resistance, particularly if employees believe AI will replace their roles. It's important to clarify that AI is not meant to replace them but to enhance their ability to work more efficiently. Addressing this early in the process can ease some of the anxiety surrounding AI adoption. Additionally, you may discover that employees are concerned about the steep learning curve associated with new AI tools. In such cases, offering ample training and support can help to alleviate these concerns.

Another factor to consider is organizational culture. If your organization has historically been slow to adopt new technologies, the resistance may stem from a general aversion to change. In these cases, resistance can be a symptom of larger cultural challenges, and AI adoption must be positioned as a positive shift that aligns with the company's goals and values.

TIP

Use anonymous feedback tools to gather honest insights into the specific concerns employees have about AI adoption. This helps to ensure you address the right issues from the start.

Addressing fears about job displacement

One of the most significant barriers to AI adoption is the fear of job displacement. Employees may worry that AI will automate their tasks and make their roles redundant, leading to layoffs or reduced job security. To address these concerns, clearly communicate the intent of AI within the organization. AI is most effective when used to complement human skills by automating repetitive, low-value tasks, freeing employees to focus on more strategic, creative, or customer-focused responsibilities.

Provide examples of how AI has been successfully implemented in other organizations without resulting in widespread job cuts. Frame AI adoption as an opportunity for employees to upskill and take on more meaningful roles within the organization. If possible, create pathways for career growth that are tied to AI adoption. For example, employees who learn to use AI tools might transition into higher-level roles where they oversee AI systems or use AI to improve processes.

TIP

Reassure your team that AI is not a threat but a tool to enhance productivity and innovation. Demonstrating how AI can reduce mundane tasks and create more time for complex problem-solving or customer engagement will help employees see the value of AI in their daily work.

Building trust through transparency

Trust is essential for overcoming resistance to AI adoption, and building that trust requires transparency at every stage of the process. Employees want to know why the organization is adopting AI, how they will use it, and what impact it will have on their roles and the overall organization. Be clear about the organization's goals for AI adoption, whether it's to increase efficiency, reduce costs, or improve decision-making. Open communication about the benefits and challenges of AI helps to reduce the sense of uncertainty that often accompanies change.

Transparency should extend to the AI technologies themselves. Many employees may be concerned about how AI will make decisions or whether those decisions will be fair and unbiased. Take the time to explain how AI systems work, the data they rely on, and the safeguards in place to ensure ethical use. Providing information on the potential risks and how they will be managed shows that the organization is committed to using AI responsibly.

Regular updates on the progress of AI adoption and success stories from early pilot projects can help sustain trust throughout the transition. Use various communication channels, such as internal newsletters, team meetings, or dedicated AI discussion forums, to keep employees informed and allow them to ask questions or raise concerns.

Create a dedicated AI adoption FAQ page that addresses common employee concerns and provides up-to-date information on the progress of the implementation.

Involving employees in the AI adoption process

Engaging employees in the AI adoption process can transform resistance into enthusiasm. Employees are more likely to embrace AI if they feel like active participants in the journey, rather than passive recipients of top-down decisions. Involving them early in the process and giving them a sense of ownership will reduce anxiety and promote buy-in.

Start by identifying employees who are particularly interested in or excited about AI and make them champions of the initiative. These champions can help spread positive messages about AI adoption and act as a resource for their peers. Invite employees to participate in pilot projects, giving them hands-on experience with AI tools before they are fully rolled out across the organization. This involvement helps demystify AI and shows employees how the technology can be integrated into their workflows.

Employee feedback is also crucial during the early stages of AI implementation. Encourage teams to share their experiences, offer suggestions for improvement, and highlight any challenges they encounter. By incorporating employee input into the AI adoption strategy, you demonstrate that their voices are valued and that the organization is committed to making the transition as smooth as possible for everyone. Check out Chapter 16 for insights on overcoming common challenges during AI integration.

Host regular feedback sessions or focus groups to allow employees to voice their opinions on the AI adoption process and suggest ways to improve integration.

Providing support and resources for the transition

Adopting AI requires employees to learn new skills and adapt to new ways of working, which can be overwhelming without proper support. Providing a robust support system, including training, mentorship, and access to AI experts, will ease the transition and reduce resistance. Ensure that employees feel equipped with the knowledge and tools they need to use AI technologies effectively.

Offer tailored training sessions that address the specific needs of different teams or roles within the organization. For instance, a data analytics team may require in-depth technical training on AI algorithms, while a marketing team might need training on how AI can help improve customer segmentation. In addition to formal training, consider setting up peer-to-peer learning networks where employees can collaborate and share their experiences using AI tools.

Mentorship programs can also play a valuable role in supporting employees during the transition. Pair employees who are confident in using AI with those who are less experienced to foster knowledge-sharing and build confidence. Providing access to AI experts, either internally or externally, ensures that employees have a resource to turn to when they encounter challenges or have questions.

TIP

Set up a dedicated AI support hub with resources, guides, and a help desk to address any technical or workflow challenges employees face during the adoption process.

Celebrating success stories

One of the most effective ways to overcome resistance to AI adoption is to celebrate early successes. Sharing success stories from teams or individuals who have successfully integrated AI into their workflows demonstrates the tangible benefits of the technology. Highlight the positive outcomes, such as increased productivity, improved decision-making, reduced workload, and even enhanced work-life balance. For example, AI-powered automation can streamline repetitive administrative tasks, allowing employees to focus on more meaningful, strategic work while reducing burnout and overtime.

These success stories help shift the narrative around AI from one of fear and uncertainty to one of opportunity and growth. They can also serve as motivation for other employees who may still be hesitant about adopting AI. Be sure to recognize and reward employees or teams that have embraced AI and seen positive results. This recognition not only reinforces their commitment to AI adoption but also encourages others to follow suit.

Share success through internal newsletters, presentations at team meetings, or case studies that highlight specific use cases of AI within the organization. By celebrating these wins, you create a positive feedback loop that helps build momentum for continued AI adoption.

TIP

Consider creating an internal AI Champion award to recognize employees who are excelling in their use of AI tools, inspiring others to do the same.

By addressing the root causes of resistance, providing support and resources, and celebrating early successes, project managers can overcome employee hesitance and foster widespread acceptance of AI adoption.

INNOVATETECH'S AI ADOPTION SUCCESS

InnovateTech, a rapidly expanding tech company, encountered significant employee resistance when it introduced AI-powered tools across its departments. Employees expressed concerns ranging from job displacement due to automation to anxieties about mastering new, complex technologies. Maria, a seasoned project manager, was tasked with spearheading the AI adoption initiative and knew a top-down mandate wouldn't suffice. She understood that addressing the root causes of this resistance was paramount.

Maria's strategy began with clear and consistent communication. Instead of vague pronouncements about "digital transformation," she provided concrete examples of how AI would be used within InnovateTech. For instance, she explained how AI-powered tools could automate the tedious data entry previously handled by the marketing team, freeing them up to focus on more strategic campaign development. She also demonstrated how AI could streamline the software testing process, allowing developers to concentrate on more creative coding tasks. Crucially, Maria emphasized that AI was being implemented to augment employee capabilities, not replace them. She framed it as a tool that would empower employees to be more efficient and effective, ultimately enhancing their roles.

Recognizing that trust was essential, Maria prioritized transparency. She established an internal AI progress tracker accessible to all employees, detailing the rollout plan, pilot project results, and even addressing any setbacks the team encountered. Regular company-wide meetings were held where she answered employee questions directly and honestly. To further build buy-in, Maria actively involved employees in the implementation process. She recruited "AI Champions" from different teams — early adopters who were enthusiastic about the technology and could act as advocates within their respective departments. These champions played a key role in engaging their colleagues in pilot projects, providing valuable feedback and fostering a sense of ownership.

Maria also understood that training and support were critical for successful adoption. She implemented tailored training programs for each team, focusing on the specific

AI tools relevant to their work. For example, the sales team received training on using an AI-powered CRM to personalize customer interactions, while the customer support team learned how to leverage AI chatbots to handle routine inquiries, allowing them to focus on more complex customer issues. Recognizing that employees might struggle even after formal training, Maria established an AI help desk staffed with experts who could provide ongoing support and answer questions as they arose.

As a result of Maria's thoughtful and comprehensive approach, InnovateTech successfully integrated AI into its operations. The company saw a significant boost in productivity across multiple departments. For example, the marketing team was able to launch more campaigns in the same timeframe, and the software development team reduced the time required to complete their testing cycle. Beyond the tangible improvements, Maria's leadership fostered a culture of innovation and a positive attitude toward technology, positioning InnovateTech for continued success in the rapidly evolving tech landscape.

5

The Part of Tens

Chapter **15**

Ten Tips for Getting Started with AI as a Project Manager

As a project manager, the thought of incorporating AI into your projects can be both exciting and overwhelming. To help you get started on the right foot, here are ten actionable tips that will set you up for success. Whether you're just beginning your AI journey or looking to expand your use of AI tools, these tips will guide you toward integrating AI into your project management processes effectively and efficiently.

Start Small

When it comes to adopting AI in project management, it's important to start small and gradually integrate AI tools into your processes. Rather than attempting a full-scale implementation, begin by identifying a specific area where AI can provide immediate value, such as automating task assignments, managing notifications, or enhancing schedule forecasting. By focusing on a well-defined task or workflow, you can test how AI fits into your project management environment without overwhelming your team. This targeted approach allows you to measure the effectiveness of AI in that particular area and adjust before expanding its use.

Starting with a limited scope also minimizes the risk of disrupting existing workflows or creating unnecessary complexity. As your team becomes more comfortable with AI tools and their capabilities, you can gradually expand their application to other areas of project management, such as resource optimization or risk assessment. This incremental approach not only allows for smoother integration but also helps your team build confidence in AI-driven processes. By refining your AI implementation one step at a time, you can ensure that your team benefits from the technology while maintaining operational efficiency and continuity. Check out Chapter 4 to explore options for small-scale AI tool adoption.

TIP

Choose a pilot project where the benefits of AI are clear, such as improving task prioritization or resource allocation. This will allow you to gauge AI's impact before expanding its use.

Leverage Predictive Analytics

One of the most valuable ways AI can support you as a project manager is by analyzing historical data and offering predictive insights tailored to your specific needs. By tapping into the power of predictive analytics, you can anticipate challenges, spot trends, and make smarter, data-driven decisions that improve the success of your projects. Imagine being able to forecast timelines, understand your resource needs, and pinpoint potential risks before they become an issue. With AI-powered tools, this becomes a reality, allowing you to proactively manage your projects and stay one step ahead.

Instead of reacting to problems as they come, predictive analytics empowers you to plan with precision, giving you the ability to anticipate roadblocks and address them before they cause delays. This shift from reactive to proactive project management enables you to optimize your strategies and keep your projects running smoothly. With AI at your side, you'll have the insights you need to confidently allocate resources, refine schedules, and stay in control of your project's success from start to finish. Check out Chapter 6 for more details on how you can use predictive analytics effectively in project management.

TIP

Implement AI tools like Microsoft Project AI or Smartsheet's predictive analytics features to forecast project timelines, identify potential bottlenecks, and adjust plans accordingly.

Automate Repetitive Tasks

One of the biggest advantages of AI is its ability to automate repetitive and time-consuming tasks, allowing your team to focus on more strategic, high-value work. By automating tasks like data entry, status updates, and report generation, AI-powered tools can save you countless hours that you'd otherwise spend on manual processes. With AI managing the routine aspects of your projects, you can ensure that resources are allocated where they matter most. Furthermore, it also significantly reduces the risk of human error, ensuring that tasks are completed accurately and efficiently.

In addition to saving time, automation helps streamline your workflow, simplifying complex processes and making project management more efficient. AI-driven automation improves the speed and consistency of routine tasks, allowing your team to operate more smoothly and with fewer interruptions. Whether it's automatically updating stakeholders on project progress, generating reports, or assigning tasks based on team availability, automation enhances overall productivity.

TIP

Use AI tools like Asana, Monday.com, or Trello to automate routine tasks like updating task statuses or generating progress reports, allowing your team to focus on higher-value activities.

Focus on Data Quality

AI is only as powerful as the data it relies on, meaning that the quality of your data directly impacts the accuracy and value of the insights your AI-powered tools provide. To get the most out of AI, it's essential to focus on collecting clean, accurate, and relevant data. This involves not only ensuring that the data is well-organized and error-free but also comes from regularly updated and well-maintained datasets that reflect the most current information. If you don't make a consistent effort to manage data quality, AI tools may produce incorrect predictions or generate unreliable outcomes, which can lead to poor decision-making and project setbacks. Simply put, if your data isn't trustworthy, the insights drawn from it won't be either.

By prioritizing data quality, you lay the foundation for more accurate and actionable AI-driven recommendations. Whether you're forecasting timelines, optimizing resource allocation, or identifying potential risks, having reliable data ensures that the AI's suggestions are more likely to be effective and impactful. Ultimately, investing time in data management and quality assurance helps maximize the value of your AI tools, allowing you to run smoother, more successful projects.

Implement data governance policies to ensure that your data is consistently clean, accurate, and up to date. Use AI tools that can identify and rectify data inconsistencies.

Integrate AI with Existing Tools

To truly maximize the value of AI in project management, it's crucial to integrate AI tools with your existing project management software. This integration allows AI to enhance your current workflows without adding unnecessary complexity or disrupting your team's familiar processes. Rather than forcing your team to learn a completely new system, AI tools are designed to work seamlessly with popular platforms like Asana, Jira, Microsoft Project, and Trello, ensuring that you can incorporate AI-driven features such as automation, predictive analytics, and task prioritization into your existing operations. This smooth integration empowers your team to enjoy the benefits of AI while maintaining continuity in their workflow, which is essential for minimizing disruptions and improving adoption rates.

Integrating AI with your existing project management tools leads to a smoother adoption process for your team, ensuring they can make the most of AI without needing a full system overhaul. This approach also allows you to gradually introduce AI features — such as task automation, resource optimization, or data-driven insights — while maintaining the structure of your current processes. When AI enhances rather than replaces your established workflows, you can elevate efficiency, improve decision-making, and optimize project outcomes without overwhelming your team. The key is to let AI *complement* your current tools, resulting in better performance and smoother transitions as AI becomes a natural part of your project management ecosystem.

Explore AI-powered integrations for tools like Microsoft Project, Jira, and Trello that allow you to enhance your existing workflows with AI capabilities.

Prioritize User-Friendly Solutions

Not all AI tools are created equal, and some can be more complex and challenging to implement than others. When introducing AI into your project management process, it's crucial to start with user-friendly solutions that your team can quickly learn and integrate into their daily workflows. After all, no one wants to spend more time deciphering AI tools than actually using them.

AI tools with intuitive interfaces, easy navigation, and clear instructions make the adoption process more seamless than investing significant time and resources in training and troubleshooting complex AI tools. Additionally, opting for tools that provide robust support — such as tutorials, user guides, and responsive customer service — ensures that your team feels supported as they navigate new technologies. Choosing AI solutions that are easy to understand and use will empower your team to embrace the technology without feeling overwhelmed by a steep learning curve.

Prioritizing user-friendly AI solutions ensures a faster, more effective rollout of AI technology, allowing your organization to quickly reap the benefits of automation and data-driven decision-making. By focusing on tools that are accessible and easy to use, you build confidence in AI's potential, leading to greater productivity and more successful project outcomes.

TIP

Look for AI tools that offer onboarding tutorials, easy-to-navigate interfaces, and responsive customer support. Tools like Wrike and Monday.com are known for their user-friendly AI features.

Incorporate AI in Risk Management

AI can significantly enhance your risk management efforts by proactively identifying potential risks early in the project lifecycle, analyzing their potential impact, and recommending effective mitigation strategies. Traditional risk management often relies on manual processes and reactive measures, but AI-powered tools can transform this into a proactive endeavor by continuously monitoring project data in real-time. These tools can detect patterns and anomalies that might indicate emerging risks, such as missed deadlines, overallocated resources, or budget overruns. By analyzing vast amounts of project data, AI can provide you with predictive insights, allowing you to address potential issues long before they escalate into major problems. This not only helps you stay ahead of risks but also allows for more informed decision-making throughout the project.

Incorporating AI into your risk management processes offers a more efficient and proactive approach to keeping your projects on track. AI tools can automatically send alerts when they detect risks, providing real-time updates that allow you to act swiftly and minimize disruptions. These alerts might flag issues such as resource shortages, scope creep, or delays, enabling your team to quickly implement mitigation strategies to keep the project moving smoothly. By automating risk detection and analysis, AI empowers project managers to manage risks with greater accuracy and foresight, ultimately ensuring that your team is well-prepared to address challenges as they arise. With AI-driven risk management, you can ensure a more resilient and adaptable approach to project delivery, leading to more successful outcomes.

TIP

Use AI-driven risk management tools like RiskWatch to monitor for potential risks and develop AI-driven strategies for mitigating those risks.

Build an AI-Friendly Team Culture

Successful AI adoption goes beyond simply implementing new tools. It requires creating a team culture that embraces innovation, continuous learning, and collaboration.

To foster an AI-friendly culture, encourage your team to experiment with AI tools in their day-to-day workflows, allowing them to discover new ways to streamline tasks and optimize project management processes. Promote an open environment where team members can share their experiences, successes, and challenges with AI, creating a space for learning and growth. This collaborative approach not only helps your team learn from one another but also builds excitement around AI because individuals feel more empowered to explore its potential in a supportive setting.

To ensure your team feels confident using AI, provide ongoing training and upskilling opportunities. Offering workshops, tutorials, and hands-on training will help bridge any knowledge gaps and equip your team with the skills they need to effectively leverage AI. Continuous learning should be a priority because AI technology is constantly evolving, and staying updated on new features and capabilities is key to maximizing its impact. By fostering a culture that supports AI adoption through education and collaboration, you'll empower your team to embrace AI as a valuable tool in project management, leading to greater efficiency, innovation, and overall success. This cultural shift can transform how your team approaches problem-solving and project execution, unlocking the full potential of AI across your organization.

TIP

Organize regular training sessions, workshops, and team discussions to help your team become more comfortable with AI. Celebrate successes and encourage a growth mindset when it comes to learning new technologies.

Measure AI Impact Regularly

As you integrate AI into your project management processes, it's essential to regularly measure the impact of these tools on your project outcomes. Tracking key metrics, such as productivity, efficiency, project timelines, and success rates, is crucial for assessing whether AI is providing tangible value to your team. Monitoring how AI-powered features — like task automation, predictive analytics, and resource management — affect project performance allows you to identify what's working well and what may need improvement. By evaluating these metrics consistently, you can gain a clear understanding of how AI is transforming your workflows and where it might be falling short.

This data-driven approach enables you to refine your AI strategy over time, making necessary adjustments to ensure that your AI initiatives are delivering the desired results. For example, if AI is improving task automation but not significantly impacting overall project efficiency, you may explore ways to enhance how AI handles more complex tasks or better integrate it into your project management tools. Continuously optimizing your approach based on real-time feedback helps you make informed decisions, ensuring that AI remains a valuable asset in achieving your project goals. Ultimately, regularly measuring the impact of AI empowers you to adapt your processes, maximize the benefits of AI, and drive ongoing improvements in project success rates.

TIP

Implement AI-powered analytics tools to track the impact of AI on your projects. Regularly review performance data to identify areas where AI is adding value and areas where further improvements are needed.

Stay Informed

AI is an ever-evolving field, with new tools, techniques, and best practices emerging regularly. To make the most of AI in project management, it's crucial to stay informed about these developments and continuously update your knowledge. One way to do this is by reading industry publications, blogs, and research papers that cover advancements in AI and its applications in project management. Engaging in webinars, online courses, and conferences dedicated to AI can also help you stay ahead of the curve, giving you insights into how industry leaders are leveraging AI to optimize their processes. This ongoing learning will ensure that you and your team are familiar with the most recent innovations, enabling you to take full advantage of AI's capabilities.

In addition to individual learning, networking with other project managers who are already using AI can provide valuable insights and shared experiences. Connecting with peers who are integrating AI into their projects allows you to exchange tips, learn about potential challenges, and discover tools or strategies you might not have considered. By fostering relationships with other AI-savvy professionals, you'll be better equipped to lead AI adoption within your organization, ensuring that your projects remain competitive and benefit from cutting-edge technologies. Staying informed about the latest AI advancements helps position you as a forward-thinking project leader who can drive successful AI integration and deliver more efficient, data-driven project outcomes.

TIP

Subscribe to industry newsletters, follow AI thought leaders on social media, and participate in online communities focused on AI in project management. Consider joining professional organizations like the Project Management Institute (PMI) to stay connected with industry trends.

Chapter **16**

Ten Common Mistakes to Avoid When Using AI in Projects

While AI can offer incredible benefits for project management, it's essential to avoid common pitfalls that can undermine your efforts. Implementing AI requires careful planning, training, and ongoing oversight to ensure that it delivers the intended results. This chapter explores ten common mistakes to avoid when using AI in projects and how you can steer clear of these issues to maximize AI's potential.

Avoiding these common mistakes will help you integrate AI into your project management processes more effectively. By understanding AI's limitations, maintaining human oversight, prioritizing training and data security, and aligning AI with your business goals, you can maximize the benefits of AI and drive successful project outcomes.

Overestimating AI Capabilities

One of the most common mistakes when integrating AI into project management is overestimating what AI can do. It's easy to get carried away by the hype surrounding AI. AI is a powerful tool, but remember, it's not a magic wand that can solve all your problems.

AI excels at processing large amounts of data and identifying patterns, but it still requires human input to function effectively. In addition, while AI can forecast potential delays or suggest resource reallocation based on data, it cannot consider the nuances of team dynamics, project culture, or sudden shifts in project priorities. As a result, relying too heavily on AI without human oversight can lead to misguided decisions or overlooked risks.

It's essential to understand the limitations of the AI tools you're using and set realistic expectations about what they can and cannot achieve. You should view AI as a tool that enhances your decision-making process, not as a replacement for it. This means project managers should be prepared to complement AI's capabilities with their expertise, critical thinking, and intuition. For instance, AI can generate insights, but it's up to the project manager to interpret those insights within the broader project context and make informed decisions. By recognizing the limitations of AI and striking a balance between automation and human oversight, you can harness AI as a powerful tool that boosts productivity and efficiency while ensuring that complex, nuanced decisions remain firmly in human hands.

REMEMBER

Understand the limitations of the AI tools you're using. Set realistic expectations about what AI can and cannot achieve and be prepared to complement AI's capabilities with human expertise.

Neglecting Human Oversight

Although AI can automate many processes and enhance decision-making, human oversight is crucial to ensure that AI-driven decisions align with project goals and ethical standards. AI, though highly capable of analyzing data and making predictions, can sometimes produce results that are biased or misaligned with the broader objectives of a project. This happens because AI relies on the data it has been trained on, which may carry biases, incomplete information, or hidden errors. Without human intervention, these flawed outcomes can lead to unintended consequences, such as skewed recommendations, incorrect predictions, or overlooked risks. For example, an AI tool may prioritize resources based on historical data without accounting for changes in team dynamics or project requirements, leading to inefficiencies or missed opportunities.

To prevent these issues, it's essential to involve humans in the AI decision-making loop. Regularly reviewing AI-generated insights, predictions, and recommendations is key to ensuring they are accurate, relevant, and contextually appropriate. Human oversight helps to catch errors that AI may miss and provides the necessary judgment to make adjustments based on the specific needs and circumstances of the project. By maintaining a balance between automation and human input, you can ensure that your organization uses AI responsibly, aligning with both its technical and ethical standards. This approach not only enhances the quality of AI-driven decisions but also ensures that you address any issues or anomalies promptly, maintaining the integrity and success of the project.

REMEMBER

Always involve humans in the decision-making loop when using AI. Regularly review AI-generated insights, predictions, and recommendations to ensure they are accurate and appropriate.

Skipping Training

AI tools often require a certain level of specialized knowledge to be used effectively, and skipping training can have significant negative consequences. Throwing your team into the AI deep end without any training is like expecting them to fly a plane without knowing how to start the engine. Without proper training, team members may not fully understand the capabilities of AI tools, which can lead to underutilization or misinterpretation of the data and insights they provide. This can result in mistakes in implementation, missed opportunities to improve efficiency, or even project delays due to misaligned AI-driven decisions. For example, team members unfamiliar with AI automation might continue handling tasks manually, defeating the purpose of introducing AI in the first place. Without a clear understanding of how AI can enhance processes, your team may struggle to integrate it meaningfully into their workflows.

To avoid these pitfalls, invest in comprehensive training for your team, covering both the technical aspects of using AI tools and the strategic ways you can apply AI in project management. Providing in-depth training ensures that your team feels comfortable and confident navigating AI-powered platforms, enabling them to leverage AI's full potential. This should include not only how to operate the tools but also how to interpret AI-generated insights and apply them to real-world project scenarios. When your team is well-equipped with the knowledge they need, they can fully harness the benefits of AI, such as improving decision-making, optimizing workflows, and ultimately enhancing project outcomes. Training ensures that AI becomes an integral part of your project management strategy rather than an underused or misunderstood tool.

Invest in comprehensive training for your team, covering both the technical aspects of using AI tools and the strategic application of AI in project management.

Ignoring Data Security

AI relies heavily on data to function, making protecting that data a critical priority. Ignoring data security can have serious consequences, such as breaches, unauthorized access, or even data loss, which can disrupt projects and harm the organization's reputation. AI systems, while powerful, can also introduce new security vulnerabilities, especially if they aren't properly managed or kept up to date. For instance, AI tools that handle sensitive information — such as customer data or proprietary business insights — are prime targets for cyberattacks if appropriate security measures are not in place. Furthermore, without strong data security protocols, there's a risk that data could be mishandled or exposed to unauthorized users, leading to compliance violations and legal repercussions.

To safeguard your AI-driven projects, you must implement robust data security protocols. This includes measures like encryption to protect data in transit and at rest, access controls to limit who can view or manipulate data, and regular audits to ensure compliance with data protection regulations such as the General Data Protection Regulation (GDPR) or the California Consumer Privacy Act (CCPA). Additionally, you need to regularly update AI tools to address emerging security threats and vulnerabilities because outdated software can become an easy entry point for hackers. Ensuring that your AI systems adhere to these security protocols not only protects your organization from potential breaches but also ensures that your AI initiatives remain compliant with privacy laws. Prioritizing data security gives you peace of mind that your AI tools are functioning safely and responsibly, minimizing risks and maintaining the integrity of your projects.

Implement strong data security protocols, including encryption, access controls, and regular audits. Ensure that AI tools are compliant with data protection regulations and that you regularly update them to address emerging security risks.

Not Aligning AI with Business Goals

AI should be a strategic asset, not a random experiment. Ensure that your AI initiatives are directly linked to your business objectives, or you may find yourself chasing shiny objects instead of achieving meaningful results. When AI initiatives are not directly connected to your company's objectives, they can easily become disjointed from the core mission, leading to wasted resources, misaligned priorities, and missed opportunities for true value creation. For instance, deploying AI without a clear understanding of how it supports project goals or business outcomes can result in automating the wrong processes or focusing on areas that don't contribute to business growth. It's essential to consider how AI can enhance areas such as efficiency, customer satisfaction, or innovation while staying aligned with the company's strategic direction.

To ensure the success of your AI implementation, clearly define how AI will support your project's goals and contribute to the overall success of the organization. Integrating AI initiatives into your strategic planning process allows you to focus on AI use cases that provide measurable benefits. For example, if your business goal is to improve customer satisfaction, you can use AI to streamline customer support operations or provide predictive insights into customer behavior. By making AI a part of your overall strategy, you ensure that your investments in AI deliver tangible, impactful results, helping your organization achieve long-term success and competitiveness in the market.

REMEMBER

Clearly define how AI will support your project's goals and contribute to the overall success of your organization. Ensure that you integrate AI initiatives into your strategic planning process.

Underestimating the Importance of Data Quality

AI's effectiveness is directly tied to the quality of the data it processes, making data the foundation of any successful AI-driven initiative. Poor data quality can lead to inaccurate predictions, faulty insights, and suboptimal decision-making. For example, if your AI system is processing incomplete or outdated data, it may generate flawed recommendations that could steer your project off course. Inaccurate data could mislead AI algorithms into making incorrect forecasts, skew resource allocations, or overlook critical risks. Underestimating the importance of data quality not only undermines the value of AI but also increases the risk of wasted time and resources and missed opportunities.

To avoid these pitfalls, prioritize data quality by implementing robust data governance policies. This includes regularly cleaning, validating, and updating your datasets to ensure that the data feeding into your AI systems is accurate, relevant, and up to date. Developing a strong data governance framework ensures that all data sources are reliable, and data is appropriately managed throughout its lifecycle. This attention to data quality helps ensure that the insights generated by your AI tools are meaningful and actionable, driving better decision-making and improving overall project outcomes. By focusing on the integrity and accuracy of your data, you set your AI projects up for success and maximize the value of your AI investments.

Prioritize data quality by implementing robust data governance policies. Regularly clean, validate, and update your datasets to ensure that the data feeding into your AI systems is accurate and reliable.

Failing to Adapt AI Over Time

You need to monitor AI systems continuously and adapt them as your projects and business needs evolve. AI models, algorithms, and data inputs can become outdated over time if left unchecked, leading to stale insights that no longer align with the current state of your projects or the external environment. For example, an AI model designed to predict customer demand based on past behaviors may become less effective if market conditions shift or new product lines are introduced. Failing to update AI tools regularly can result in missed opportunities to optimize processes, adapt to new trends, or stay ahead of potential risks. AI is a dynamic tool that requires ongoing attention and refinement to maintain its effectiveness.

Keep your AI systems aligned with project goals and evolving market conditions by implementing a process for regular reviews and updates. This means periodically checking that the AI tools you're using reflect the latest data, trends, and project requirements. As your project progresses or shifts in scope, recalibrate AI models to ensure they remain accurate and relevant. Continuously refining and adapting AI tools helps them keep pace with changing project dynamics, ensuring they provide up-to-date and actionable insights that support the project's success. By treating AI as an evolving asset rather than a set-it-and-forget-it solution, you maximize its value and ensure it continues to drive meaningful impact over the long term.

Regularly review and update your AI systems to ensure they are still aligned with your project's goals and that they reflect the latest data and trends. Continuously refine and adapt your AI tools to keep pace with changing project dynamics.

Misinterpreting AI Insights

AI can offer valuable insights by analyzing vast amounts of data and identifying trends or making predictions that would be difficult for humans to process manually. However, remember that misinterpreting AI-generated insights can lead to poor decision-making, potentially steering a project in the wrong direction. AI's predictions and recommendations, while powerful, are often based on historical data and patterns, which may not fully capture the nuances or changing dynamics of a project. As a result, being overly reliant on AI without considering other external factors — such as team feedback, market conditions, or unique project complexities — can lead to suboptimal outcomes. Remember that AI insights are one piece of the puzzle rather than the sole basis for decision-making.

To effectively use AI insights, combine them with human judgment and domain expertise. You need to interpret AI outputs within the context of the specific project, and project managers should ensure that their team understands how to interpret these results. Training teams on how to critically analyze AI-generated data and use it to inform decision-making, rather than allowing AI to dictate decisions outright, is key. This balance between AI-driven insights and human expertise ensures that decisions are grounded in both data and contextual understanding, allowing for better alignment with the project's goals. Interpreting AI outputs correctly and with care will help you make more informed, strategic choices that drive project success.

REMEMBER

Combine AI-generated insights with human judgment and domain expertise. Ensure that your team understands how to interpret AI outputs and how to use them to inform rather than dictate decision-making.

Neglecting Ethical Considerations

AI systems have the potential to introduce significant ethical challenges, particularly in areas such as bias in decision-making, privacy concerns, and unintended consequences for stakeholders. Since AI models are built on data, they can inherit and even amplify biases present in the datasets, leading to discriminatory or unfair outcomes. For example, if historical hiring data used in an AI recruitment tool contains biases against certain demographics, the AI may perpetuate these biases in hiring recommendations. Additionally, AI systems often process large amounts of personal data, raising concerns about data privacy and how this information is used. Failing to address these ethical concerns can not only harm individuals but also expose your organization to legal issues and reputational damage, eroding stakeholder trust.

To ensure responsible AI use, it's crucial to incorporate ethical guidelines into your AI adoption process from the very beginning. This means regularly reviewing AI systems for potential biases and continuously monitoring them to identify and correct unintended effects. Safeguarding data privacy should also be a priority, with strict protocols in place to protect sensitive information and ensure compliance with privacy regulations like GDPR or CCPA. Moreover, consider the broader ethical implications of AI-driven decisions: How will they impact your customers, employees, or the communities you serve? By taking a proactive approach to ethics, you help ensure that AI tools are used responsibly, positively contributing to both your organization and society as a whole. This commitment to ethical AI fosters long-term trust, reduces risks, and ensures that AI delivers sustainable benefits.

Incorporate ethical guidelines into your AI adoption process. Regularly review AI systems for potential biases, ensure that data privacy is protected, and consider the broader ethical implications of AI-driven decisions.

Skipping Pilot Testing

Implementing AI on a large scale without pilot testing can expose your organization to significant risks, including costly mistakes, operational disruptions, and wasted resources. Skipping the pilot testing phase means that potential issues, such as compatibility problems, workflow bottlenecks, or inaccurate data interpretations, may not be identified until after the AI system is fully implemented. At that point, it's much more difficult and expensive to fix them. Additionally, rolling out AI tools without first understanding how they integrate with your current systems or how your team will adapt to using them can result in suboptimal outcomes. The initial investment in AI can quickly become a drain on resources if unforeseen challenges aren't addressed early on.

To avoid these pitfalls, it's crucial to conduct pilot tests before fully implementing AI solutions across your organization. Pilot testing enables you to experiment with AI tools and processes in a controlled environment, giving you the opportunity to gather valuable feedback, observe how the AI performs in real-world scenarios, and identify any challenges that may arise. It also enables your team to get familiar with the new technology and provides a space to refine your approach based on actual results rather than assumptions. By using pilot tests to fine-tune the AI system, you can ensure you address potential issues early and that your AI initiatives are well-thought-out and aligned with your goals before scaling up. This reduces the risk of failure, maximizes the value of your AI investment, and ensures a smoother, more successful full-scale implementation.

Always conduct pilot tests of AI tools and processes before rolling them out across your organization. Use pilot testing to gather feedback, identify challenges, and refine your approach before scaling up.

Chapter **17**

Ten AI Tools Every Project Manager Should Know

The world of AI-powered project management tools is exploding, with new platforms and applications constantly emerging. It can feel overwhelming to navigate this landscape and determine which tools are truly valuable. While there's no single "best" AI tool for every project manager, this chapter focuses on ten key tools that every project manager should be at least somewhat familiar with. These ten represent a cross-section of the most impactful AI capabilities currently available, from automating routine tasks and providing predictive analytics to offering intelligent insights. Understanding the functionalities and potential applications of these specific tools will give you a solid foundation for evaluating and selecting the right AI solutions for your unique project needs, even as the AI landscape continues to evolve. By becoming familiar with these core tools, you'll be better equipped to leverage the power of AI to streamline workflows, optimize resources, and ultimately achieve greater project success.

Asana with AI-Powered Workflows

Asana is a powerful project management platform designed to help teams collaborate, track tasks, and manage projects of varying complexities. One of Asana's key differentiators is its AI-powered tools, which enable teams to automate routine tasks and optimize workflows across different departments. With Asana's AI capabilities, project managers can streamline processes by automating repetitive activities such as task assignments, status updates, and deadline reminders. The platform's AI can intelligently assign tasks based on team members' workloads, skills, and availability, ensuring that work is distributed fairly and efficiently. This automation reduces the manual effort required to keep the project on track, allowing teams to focus on higher-priority tasks that require strategic decision-making and collaboration.

Beyond automating routine tasks, Asana's AI enhances productivity by prioritizing tasks based on their impact on the overall project. By analyzing project data, Asana provides actionable insights that help teams identify critical tasks and adjust resources to meet project goals more effectively. For complex projects that involve multiple teams and require cross-functional collaboration, Asana's AI-driven insights ensure that teams stay aligned, identify potential bottlenecks early, and adjust workflows as needed. Additionally, Asana integrates seamlessly with other AI tools and popular platforms such as Slack, Google Workspace, and Microsoft Teams, making it a flexible and scalable solution for organizations managing intricate, multifaceted projects. With its ability to automate workflows, prioritize tasks, and provide valuable data-driven insights, Asana empowers teams to work smarter and more efficiently, leading to better project outcomes.

Key features:

>> Automates task assignments and prioritization

>> Provides workflow optimization across teams

>> Integrates with other AI tools for enhanced functionality

ClickUp

ClickUp is a highly versatile project management platform that integrates AI-driven features to automate task management, streamline workflows, and provide intelligent insights that enhance project planning and execution. By leveraging AI, ClickUp helps teams automate routine tasks such as updating statuses, assigning priorities, and tracking progress in real time. This automation reduces the burden of manual task management, allowing teams to focus on more critical, strategic activities. Whether it's automating status updates across boards or prioritizing tasks based on deadlines and resource availability, ClickUp ensures that the project management process is efficient and seamless.

In addition to task automation, ClickUp offers AI-powered insights that provide project managers with real-time data to make more informed decisions. These insights help identify potential bottlenecks, such as delays in task completion or resource shortages, before they impact the overall project timeline. With predictive analytics and data-driven recommendations, project managers can proactively adjust schedules, reallocate resources, or implement workflow changes to prevent issues from escalating. This combination of automation and AI insights ensures that projects stay on track, boosting productivity and enabling teams to deliver results more effectively.

Key features:

>> Automates task management and progress tracking

>> Provides intelligent insights for project planning

>> Streamlines workflows for better efficiency

Jira with AI-Powered Automation

Jira is a highly popular project management tool widely used by agile teams to track tasks, manage sprints, and ensure timely project delivery. Designed to support agile methodologies like Scrum and Kanban, Jira offers an intuitive interface that enables teams to break down large projects into manageable tasks, assign them to team members, and monitor progress in real time. A standout feature of Jira is its AI-powered automation, which plays a critical role in streamlining workflows and reducing the need for manual intervention. This automation capability allows teams to set predefined rules that trigger actions based on specific conditions, such as moving tasks between boards, updating statuses, or notifying stakeholders when milestones are reached. With Jira, agile teams can eliminate much of the manual work that typically accompanies project management, leading to faster, more efficient execution.

Jira's AI-driven automation goes beyond simple task management by enabling teams to automate more complex workflows, such as creating new issues when certain criteria are met or escalating tasks when deadlines are approaching. For instance, when a developer completes a task, Jira can automatically update the status, notify the relevant team members, and even create follow-up tasks without the need for manual input. This not only enhances team productivity but also ensures that nothing falls through the cracks. These automation capabilities allow agile teams to remain focused on delivering value, addressing high-priority items, and improving sprint efficiency, while routine tasks and administrative overhead are handled seamlessly in the background. By integrating AI into its platform, Jira empowers teams to maintain momentum and ensures that project workflows remain efficient and optimized at every stage.

Key features:

>> Automates repetitive tasks and workflows

>> Supports agile project management

>> Reduces manual work and improves productivity

Microsoft Project with AI Insights

Microsoft Project is a widely recognized project management tool that has long been a staple for managing projects of all sizes and complexities. One of its key strengths is the integration of AI-powered features that provide project managers with predictive analytics to improve decision-making and planning. These AI-driven insights allow project managers to forecast project timelines, resource requirements, and budgets with greater accuracy. By analyzing historical data from past projects, Microsoft Project can automatically suggest realistic timelines, identify potential bottlenecks, and optimize resource allocation. This reduces the risk of delays and helps ensure that you use resources efficiently, enabling project teams to meet deadlines and stay within budget.

The AI-driven predictive capabilities of Microsoft Project are particularly valuable for complex, multiphase projects where minor delays can cascade into major setbacks. The platform's ability to anticipate challenges before they occur allows project managers to proactively address risks and adjust plans accordingly. By forecasting potential issues, such as resource shortages or scheduling conflicts, Microsoft Project empowers teams to make more informed decisions and adjust project strategies as they happen. This not only improves overall project efficiency but also increases the likelihood of delivering successful outcomes. With its AI-enhanced functionality, Microsoft Project helps project managers stay ahead of challenges and ensures that projects are completed on time, within scope, and with optimal resource usage.

Key features:

>> Provides predictive analytics for timelines and resource planning

>> Analyzes historical data for better forecasting

>> Helps identify potential risks early in the project

Monday.com

Monday.com is an AI-powered project management platform designed to help teams streamline workflows, manage tasks, and automate routine processes. The platform leverages AI to automate repetitive tasks such as task assignments, notifications, and status updates, significantly reducing the need for manual intervention. Teams can create fully customizable workflows that cater to their unique needs, enabling them to automate complex processes and track project progress in real time. With real-time status updates and AI-driven notifications, team members stay aligned on project milestones and deadlines without the constant need for follow-ups or status meetings.

In addition to its task management and workflow automation capabilities, Monday.com offers progress tracking through customizable dashboards. These dashboards provide comprehensive visibility into project health, enabling stake-holders and project managers to make informed decisions based on up-to-date data. Monday.com integrates seamlessly with popular tools like Slack, Microsoft Teams, Google Workspace, and Trello, allowing teams to connect various platforms into one cohesive workflow. This platform helps teams optimize collaboration, reduce administrative burdens and ensure smooth project execution across different industries and team sizes.

Key features:

>> Automates task assignments and notifications

>> Provides customizable workflows

>> Offers real-time project tracking and reporting

OnePlan

OnePlan is a robust collaborative work management platform that integrates advanced AI capabilities to enhance project planning, resource allocation, and risk management. Built to support teams managing complex projects, OnePlan's AI tools excel at analyzing resource availability, task dependencies, and project timelines. By automating resource allocation, OnePlan ensures tasks are assigned based on team members' skills and availability, preventing both overallocation and underutilization. The platform continuously monitors project data, identifying potential risks and offering proactive recommendations to mitigate them before they escalate into larger issues. This intelligent automation enables project managers to streamline operations and focus on high-priority tasks without being weighed down by manual adjustments.

In addition to optimizing resource allocation, OnePlan's AI-driven features provide real-time insights into project progress, offering a comprehensive view of milestones, deadlines, and overall project health. With a real-time analytics dashboard, project managers can track progress and adjust plans, timelines, or resources dynamically to address emerging challenges. OnePlan's AI also forecasts potential project delays and suggests corrective actions to keep projects on schedule and within scope. By combining powerful AI tools with real-time data, OnePlan allows project managers to proactively manage risks, optimize team performance, and consistently deliver successful outcomes.

Key features:

>> Optimizes resource allocation and risk management

>> Provides real-time project insights and recommendations

>> Supports collaborative project planning and execution

Smartsheet

Smartsheet is an AI-driven platform that seamlessly integrates project management with automated workflows, advanced data analytics, and real-time reporting. The platform is designed to help teams manage a wide array of projects more efficiently by automating routine tasks and streamlining processes. With Smartsheet's AI capabilities, teams can automate repetitive activities like task assignments, status updates, and notifications, which significantly reduces manual effort. The platform's intuitive interface allows users to build custom workflows that cater to their specific project needs, ensuring smooth transitions between tasks and stages. Additionally, Smartsheet integrates with popular tools like Slack, Microsoft Teams, and Google Workspace, allowing teams to connect their existing systems and workflows for a more unified project management experience.

One of Smartsheet's most powerful features is its ability to generate real-time reports and analyze project data to identify trends, risks, and opportunities. Its AI-driven analytics tools provide project managers and stakeholders with actionable insights, helping them make informed decisions based on up-to-date information. The platform's flexibility allows it to accommodate a wide range of project types, from simple task tracking to complex workflows that require real-time collaboration between multiple teams. Whether you're managing a marketing campaign, a construction project, or an IT rollout, Smartsheet offers the tools and scalability needed to handle projects of any size, while providing the data-driven insights necessary to keep everything on track and within scope.

Key features:

>> Automates workflows and repetitive tasks

>> Provides real-time analytics and reporting

>> Supports collaborative project management

Trello with Butler

Trello is a widely used project management tool that leverages visual boards, lists, and cards to help teams organize tasks and manage projects efficiently. Its intuitive interface makes it easy for users to track the progress of tasks, assign responsibilities, and collaborate with team members. Trello's highly customizable structure allows teams to create boards tailored to their unique workflows for everything from agile development to marketing campaigns to content creation. By visually representing tasks and their statuses, Trello provides a clear, at-a-glance overview of project progress, helping teams stay organized and aligned.

A standout feature of Trello is its AI-powered automation tool, Butler, which automates repetitive tasks and workflows to reduce the need for manual intervention. Butler can handle routine activities such as task assignments, due date reminders, and board management. With predefined rules, it can automatically move cards between lists, assign team members based on task criteria, and send notifications when important deadlines are approaching. This allows teams to focus on more critical, strategic tasks while ensuring that essential, repetitive activities are managed consistently and efficiently. Butler's automation capabilities save time, enhance productivity, and ensure that no tasks fall through the cracks, making Trello an even more powerful tool for managing projects.

Key features:

>> Automates task assignments and due date reminders.

>> Customizable automation rules.

>> Streamlines board management.

Wrike

Wrike is a robust project management platform designed to enhance productivity and streamline operations through its powerful AI-driven features. With a user-friendly interface, Wrike enables teams to manage tasks, track project progress, and collaborate seamlessly. One of its standout capabilities is its AI-powered task automation, which allows teams to automate repetitive tasks such as task creation, status updates, and sending notifications. These automated workflows minimize the need for manual intervention, ensuring that routine tasks are handled efficiently, which frees up team members to focus on higher-value activities. For instance, Wrike can automatically generate new tasks based on project milestones, notify stakeholders when key deadlines approach, and update task statuses in real time, creating a more fluid and efficient project workflow.

In addition to task automation, Wrike offers AI-powered predictive analytics that help project managers maintain control over complex projects. By analyzing historical project data and real-time inputs, Wrike's AI can forecast project timelines, identify potential bottlenecks or delays, and recommend adjustments to keep the project on track. For example, if the platform detects that certain tasks are taking longer than expected, it can suggest reallocating resources or extending deadlines to prevent project derailment. These predictive scheduling capabilities are invaluable for teams working on large-scale or fast-moving projects because they provide the foresight needed to address risks before they escalate. By combining task automation with real-time analytics and predictive insights, Wrike helps teams stay organized, anticipate challenges, and deliver projects on time and within budget.

Key features:

>> Automates routine tasks and notifications

>> Provides real-time project analytics

>> Uses predictive scheduling to optimize timelines

Zoho Projects with AI Assistant Zia

Zoho Projects is a comprehensive project management tool designed to enhance team collaboration and efficiency. Its powerful AI assistant, named Zia, leverages AI to provide real-time recommendations, automate repetitive tasks, and offer predictive analytics that empower project managers to make more informed decisions. By automating routine tasks such as task assignments, status updates, and notifications, Zia helps reduce the manual effort required to manage day-to-day project activities. This automation ensures that teams can stay focused on high-priority tasks while the more tedious aspects of project management are handled seamlessly in the background.

In addition to task automation, Zia's AI capabilities provide project managers with valuable insights into potential risks, project timelines, and resource management. Zia analyzes project data to predict possible delays, identify bottlenecks, and suggest corrective actions before issues escalate. These AI-driven insights enable project managers to proactively mitigate risks, adjust resource allocations, and refine project plans as needed. With Zia's predictive analytics and data-driven recommendations, Zoho Projects helps teams stay on schedule, avoid unforeseen issues, and ensure that projects are delivered efficiently and successfully.

Key features:

>> Automates routine tasks with AI assistant Zia

>> Provides predictive analytics and recommendations

>> Offers a user-friendly interface for project management

Index

Workday Adaptive Planning, 87

Wrike, 81, 85

Writesonic, 77

Zapier, 93

Zendesk AI, 230

Zoho Projects, 85

Zoho Zia, 77

Zoom, 69

iterating, based on feedback, 39

J

Jasper AI, 76

Jira, 80, 90, 91, 93, 94, 98, 114, 115, 125, 126, 140, 147, 250, 265–266

Jitterbit, 92

job displacement, 238–239

K

Kantata, 84, 140, 166, 168

Kensho, 86

key performance indicators (KPIs), 36, 46, 131, 183–187

knowledge, in ADKAR model, 234

L

language translation, 123

large language models (LLMs), 12, 16, 70–77

legal experts, in AI oversight committees, 209

Local Interpretable Model-Agnostic Explanations (LIME), 205, 208

long-term gains, 53–54

long-term strategy, building for AI integration, 34–35

M

machine learning (ML), 10–11, 165

Make, 92, 94, 100–101, 102

mapping task dependencies, 141–144

market data feeds, 165

Mavenlink, 98

McAfee, 215

measuring
   AI benefits using qualitative metrics, 50–52
   AI benefits using quantitative metrics, 48–50
   decision quality, 51–52
   impact, 253
   risk reduction, 51
   stakeholder satisfaction, 50–51

Medical Group Management Association (MGMA), 207

meetings
   AI-driven optimization in, 127–128
   generating summaries, 37
   transcribing minutes, 67–70

methods, for measuring AI performance, 55–58

metrics, adapting, 61–62

Microsoft 365, 93, 102

Microsoft Azure Machine Learning, 86

Microsoft Copilot, 76

Microsoft Excel, 98

Microsoft Power Automate, 92, 101

Microsoft Power BI, 91, 93, 94, 98, 103, 110, 116, 156, 160, 165, 179, 180, 184, 185

Microsoft Project, 42, 80, 90, 91, 108, 111, 115, 136, 144, 151, 154–155, 164, 178, 249, 250, 266–267

Microsoft Scheduler, 124

Microsoft Teams, 69, 93, 95, 96, 114, 122, 123, 127, 146, 158, 160, 191, 192, 264, 267, 269

Microsoft Translator, 123

Miro AI, 76

mistakes, avoiding, 255–262

mobile push notifications, 157

Monday.com, 80, 84, 90, 101, 114, 125, 145, 154, 159, 170, 179, 183, 189, 249, 251, 267

Motion, 124, 138

MuleSoft Anypoint Platform, 92

N

n8n, 92

narrow AI, 9–10

natural language processing (NLP), 11–12, 16

Navex, 221

About the Author

Daniel Stanton, also known as Mr. Supply Chain, is an accomplished supply chain project manager with extensive experience across various industries and sectors. Holding a PMP certification, Daniel has managed projects for government organizations, Fortune 500 companies, small and medium businesses, and military operations. His project portfolio spans construction, facility startups and shutdowns, technology infrastructure, systems integration, and software development.

Daniel earned engineering degrees from the South Dakota School of Mines and the Massachusetts Institute of Technology (MIT). He is also a lecturer at the University of Arkansas and a doctoral researcher at Cranfield University. With more than a decade of experience working with AI in project management and supply chains, Daniel is passionate about the advancements in technology and how they can enhance project management practices.

In this book, Daniel shares his insights on how AI can empower project managers, offering both experienced professionals and aspiring project leaders the tools to succeed in an evolving technological landscape. He believes that the most successful project managers combine a strategic view of technology with a global understanding of business, and his mission is to help others unlock these opportunities.

Daniel lives in Charlotte, NC, with his wife and three daughters, along with their 2.5 dogs.

Acknowledgments

Writing a book is never a solo endeavor, and I am deeply grateful to those who supported me throughout this journey.

First, I want to thank my wife, Ruth; our daughters; and our dogs for their patience and understanding while I spent countless hours writing instead of with them. They deserved more of my time, and I appreciate their support more than words can express.

I also want to express my gratitude to my editors — Steven, Charlotte, and Beth — for their invaluable feedback and collaboration. Their keen insights, attention to detail, and guidance helped shape this book, and I am hoping it will be useful for project managers navigating the AI revolution.

A special acknowledgment goes to the innovative companies that are pushing the boundaries of AI and developing cutting-edge applications to enhance project management. As I was writing this book, the technology was evolving rapidly, and I was constantly trying to keep up with the pace of change. I have tried my best to describe your valuable innovations in a way that will help new users find them and inspire project managers looking for better tools to support their teams to adopt them.

Finally, I want to thank the project managers who are reading this book — those who are constantly striving to improve their skills, embrace new technologies, and lead their teams and organizations toward greater success. By learning how to harness AI effectively, you're shaping the future of project management, and I commend your dedication to growth and innovation.

This book is for all of you.

Dedication

This book is dedicated to my mom, Ann Haber Stanton, who loved reading and writing and passed that passion on to me.

Publisher's Acknowledgments

Executive Editor: Steve Hayes
Project Editor: Charlotte Kughen
Technical Editor: Elizabeth Rennie

Production Editor: Tamilmani Varadharaj
Cover Image: © Andrey_Popov/Shutterstock